RICH

LET ME ILLUSTRATE

Stories,
Anecdotes,
Illustrations

DONALD GREY BARNHOUSE

FLEMING H. REVELL COMPANY
WESTWOOD · NEW JERSEY

CONTENTS

FOREWORD

One of the books I intend to write is a book on the whole art and procedure of illustrating the sermon. As an introduction let me tell the story of the time I meditated on the fact that we were chosen in Christ before the foundation of the world. Suddenly I realized that in the plan and thought of God, I was older than the sun, the moon, the stars, the earth, the trees, the garden, and everything else.

"Since God planned me before He planned trees and lakes and mountains, and storms and sunsets," I said, "everything that there is was created in order to illustrate spiritual truth. Everything. I don't care what it is—the way the echo sounds if you clap your hands, the way light gleams off metal, the way paper tears, you name it—you can find a sermon illustration in it. A sermon illustration is in the things right around you."

A tape recorder turning is a wonderful illustration of the fact that all of our thoughts are being recorded, and that some day we shall give an account of every idle word. I was driving with three of my small children. I told them this, and my six-year-old said, "Well, how is the white line down the road an illustration?"

"Oh," I said, "That's easy, 'There is a way that seemeth right unto a man, but the ends thereof are the ways of death.' If I felt that I had a right to go over in the left lane and just stay there, ultimately a truck would come and slam me, and I'd be dead. God says, 'You keep in *my* path, and my path is properly marked.'"

Another child said, "What about the telegraph poles? how are they an illustration?"

I replied, "Well, there's that pole, and somebody in the next town back of us and somebody in the next town in front of us are talking over the wires. Their words are going over the wires in both directions right now. Suppose one of those poles got knocked down, what would happen?"

The child said, "The wires would break, and they couldn't talk."

I said, "Exactly, and exactly the same way we must keep our communication with God because we're talking with God. We say, 'Lord, Lord,' and the whole of our conversation is carried on by the principles that God puts forth in His Word, and we must not allow sin to destroy any of the points of communication, because if sin comes in, then the communication can be destroyed."

Again, one of the children asked, "That bird sitting up on the wire, what can that illustrate?"

I said, "Do you see his little claws holding tight on the wire?"

All three children chorused, "Yes."

I said, "In that wire somebody is talking. Although the words are going right under its feet the bird doesn't know anything about it. Maybe somebody's saying, 'Grandpa died,' or 'Oh, there's been an accident,' or just chatting. These words go through the little bird's feet, but he doesn't know anything about them. In exactly the same way I'm resting in God; it doesn't make any difference what things whirl about me, what messages are bad or evil, I can trust the Lord and know that because I am resting in the Lord, nothing can touch me. None of the bad news that passes through the bird's feet can hurt it. Thus, 'we know that all things work together for good to them that love God.'"

One night a short time later, a friend took us out to get some ice cream. We were talking about the illustrations I had used that evening, and he said, "How on earth do you get such illustrations?"

10

I told him what I had said about illustrations being everywhere. One of the young women pointed to the sugar bowl and said, "Give us an illustration about this sugar bowl."

I said, "This sugar bowl looks as though it costs at least a dollar or two. If, instead of sitting in this modern, good class restaurant, we were in a cheap, dirty restaurant over on the avenue, the sugar would be in a rough, ten-cent mug. This one costs a dollar. If we went over to the Waldorf, we'd probably find fine bone china. Whether you get a crockery mug, or an ordinary one like this, or a very fine one in the Waldorf depends upon how long it has been put in the fire. The Bible says that we are vessels of honor, fit for the Master's use. You must be purged and burned in the fire to take on the proper work. Whether you are going to be an ornament cheap and dirty, or whether you will be a vessel fit for the Master's use depends on how you yield to the Lord for His work in your life."

Donald Grey Barnhouse

LET ME ILLUSTRATE

ACCESS TO GOD

ACCESS TO GOD

THE FRENCH PRIEST

During my student days in France, I was pastor of a little Evangelical Reformed Church in the French Alps. Once a week I went to a neighboring village for an instruction class. Each time I made the trip I passed the local priest, going on a similar errand in the opposite direction. We became good friends and often chatted together for ten minutes or so before we went our separate ways. On one occasion, he asked me why we did not pray to the saints. "Why should we?" I asked. He launched an illustration of the way one might get an interview with the president of the French Republic. One could go to the Ministry of Agriculture, or to the Department of the Interior, etc.; any one of the cabinet members might succeed in opening the door of the president's office so that I might see him. His triumphant smile implied that the simplicity and clarity of the argument were such as to preclude any reply. At that time Raymond Poincaré was President of the Republic; he lived in the Palace of the Elyseé in Paris—the equivalent of the White House. I said to my friend, "But Monsieur le Curé, suppose that I were the son of Monsieur Poincaré? I am living in the Elyseé with him. I get up from the breakfast table and kiss him goodbye as he goes off to his office. Then I go down to the Ministry of the Interior and ask the fourth secretary of the second assistant if it is possible for me to see the minister of the Interior. If I succeed in reaching his office, my request is for an interview with my papa."

My friend was thunderstruck as I added that I was a child of God, heir of God and joint-heir with Christ, and that I had been saved through the death of the Saviour and thus had become a son with immediate access to the Father.

THE FRONT-DOOR KEY

A son, who had gone to military service, wrote to his father: "I am sending you all my keys except the front-door key; some day when I get leave, I may walk in unexpectedly and give you a surprise." When the parents read the letter, they thought, "This is a good son. He has no secrets from us, nothing to hide, no bluebeard chamber that must not be entered, no forgotten corner where old shameful things lie. He knows himself and he trusts us. He gives us the run of all his affairs. He sends us all his keys. He knows us, too. He knows he will always be welcome; that he can always walk in without waiting; that he has full right of entry into his father's house. Our house is open to him, and his heart is open to us."

Give God all your keys, and He will always give you access to Himself and all blessing.

THE GUILTY CLOTHES

An analysis of the dust from the trousers of suspected counterfeiters disclosed that clothes can betray guilt. Particles of certain metals and chemicals used in this irregular way of making money convicted them.

It makes no difference how you are dressed as you approach the Lord God of judgment. Your clothes will betray you; you will be cast forth as was the wedding guest who appeared without the proper wedding garment. The only way to approach the God of all holiness is to be clothed in the righteousness of the Lord Jesus Christ. That will stand the analysis of the light of God. Those thus clad will be seen as "faultless to stand before the throne."

OIL RESERVOIRS

Geologists knew that there were great reservoirs of oil deep down under the ground of west Texas. The ranchers lived in their modest homes and had large flocks of sheep that grazed the vast reaches of the semi-desert plain on the surface. The oil was underneath, but there was no access to it. Then great wells were sunk, and the oil gushed forth and out flowed the black gold. The wealth transformed the lives of those who had entered into its possession. The oil had been there all the time, but access to it determined possession more than a title deed; it made it a present reality.

The believer who is justified through the atoning work of the Saviour, has direct access to the grace of God. We may think of grace as a bountiful store, hidden in the being of our God and Father, but the Lord Jesus Christ has opened up a way—a new and living way—by which we come boldly to the very presence of God (HEBREWS 10:19,20), who is the source of all grace. There we find that with Christ He has given us all things (ROMANS 8:32).

TRIBAL WARFARE

The famous missionary, David Livingstone, spent a year or two with a certain tribe in South Africa. Then, urged on by his desire to spread the name of Christ, he went far into the interior with his wife and child. When he returned to the first tribe he discovered that they were in sore straits. Another tribe had killed many of their soldiers and had taken the chief's own son as a captive. An ambassador in from the victorious tribe asked for friendship and peace. The victors were motivated by the fact that Zulus were about to attack *them;* they wished to protect their rear. The village chief was a good man who desired nothing better than to live at peace with his neighbors. He said to Livingstone, "How can I be at peace with them when they still hold my son a prisoner?"

If this attitude is true in the heart of a savage chief, how much more is it true of God the Father toward those who trample under foot His Son, and who count the blood of the covenant wherewith they were set apart as an unholy thing,

and who continue to despise the Spirit of grace (HEBREWS
10:28,29). Access to God must begin with Jesus Christ. Christ
set it forth in unchallengeable terms: "I am the way, the truth,
and the life; no man cometh unto the Father but by me"
(JOHN 14:6).

ADOPTION

At one time in the Roman Empire it was the custom for men to have a ceremony in which they acknowledged their sons publicly. On the opening pages of *The Robe*, by Lloyd Douglas, Lucia described the ceremony held for her older brother. Her father had bought Demetrius [the Corinthian slave] six years ago and had presented him to Marcellus on his seventeenth birthday. All of their good friends assembled in the forum to see Marcellus—clean shaven for the first time in his life—step forward to receive his white toga. Cornelius Capito and the father made speeches. Then they put the white toga on Marcellus. Lucia had been so proud and happy that her heart pounded and her throat hurt. She was only nine then, but she knew that Marcellus was expected to act like a man now. Marcellus himself described the ceremony in later pages. His induction into manhood was one of the high moments of his life. His father made an address, welcoming him into Roman citizenship. The boy's eyes swam with tears. Then good old Cornelius Capito made a speech, about Rome's right to Marcellus's loyalty, courage and strength. Tough old Capito had a right to talk of such matters, and the boy was proud that he was there. The two beckoned to Marcellus; and he stepped forward. Capito and his father put the white toga on him and life had begun.

Adoption is not just adopting a child into another family; it is the welcoming, as a grown-up man, the child that long since has been born again. We have not received the spirit of bondage to fear, but we have received the spirit of a son come of age, publicly acknowledged by his father in the forum.

19

ADVERSITY

THE MOTH AND THE LION

There is a beautiful picture in one of the Old Testament prophets that shows how God is for us, even in the hard things which He must bring upon us. After speaking of the sin of Israel that took that nation away from Him, God says, "Therefore, will I be unto Ephraim as a moth . . ." (HOSEA 5:12). Some little insect comes into life and nests among the things we value. Suddenly we realize that corruption is there. God means this for a sign that will cause us to turn to Him immediately. If we accept the work of the moth and return to God, He will restore to us all that He has taken away.

But suppose men do not turn to God when He sends His insect-troubles? Two verses later He gives another word which is more terrible: "I will be unto Ephraim as a lion . . ." (5:14). This is the progress of God's love. He will not let us lose ourselves without exhausting all of the resources of His love. The moth may have eaten valuable possessions, but we can turn the rug around, we can put the couch against a wall where the ravages cannot be seen, we can move a lamp so that the light will not shine upon the destruction. Then He is forced to send the lion. With no warning at all, great trouble springs upon us like a beast of prey. Fear grips us. Our blood runs cold. Happy are we, if we realize that this is the Lord of love, who calls us to turn from the path where lions lurk and to run to the path of His will where no enemy can assail us.

Thousands of people, however, have had the moth and the lion and have not been moved by them. God is forced to hide His face from them. They are left, perhaps in unconcern, perhaps in restless and uneasy worry, but in it all, God is being good to them, showing Himself for them by holding the door of salvation open, and calling them to Himself.

NO PAIN

Little Beverly Smith, born in Akron, Ohio, almost never cried. She never cried when she fell down; she never cried when she bumped her head; she didn't even cry when she burned her hand on a hot stove. She cried only when she was hungry or angry.

The doctors soon discovered that she had a defect in the central nervous system for which no cure is known. She could not feel pain. The doctors told the mother she must watch Beverly constantly: the baby might break a bone and continue using it until it could not be set properly; she might develop appendicitis without nature's usual warning of pain. Spanking her to make her more careful about hot stoves and knives would do no good; she wouldn't feel it. Life without pain would be perpetually dangerous.

The spiritual application is simple. The Lord sends troubles into our lives for a purpose. "For whom the Lord loveth he chasteneth and scourgeth every son whom he receiveth. . . . if ye be without chastisement, whereof all are partakers, then are ye bastards, and not sons" (HEBREWS 12:6,8). If we accept the warnings of the little chastisements, we will be kept from the bigger hurts, just as the warnings given us by our nervous systems keep us away from fires and other hurts.

Let every Christian examine himself to see whether he has become insensible to the presence of sin.

TANGLED THREADS

A textile factory with complicated machinery posted instructions: "If your threads get tangled, call the foreman." One of the workers, a diligent and busy woman, got her threads tangled; she tried to disentangle them, but only made them worse;

finally she sent for the foreman. He glanced at the threads and said, "You have been trying to do this yourself." She answered, "Yes." "Why did you not send for me, according to instructions?" he asked. Rather sullenly, she said, "I did my best." He replied, "Remember this: that doing your best is sending for me."

Andrew did. Though he was a sinner like the rest of the twelve disciples, he has no recorded failure. No such failure was recorded because he brought every difficulty to Christ. Our best is to bring our difficulties to Christ.

THROUGH TOMORROW

The night before they were to attack the German lines, a hundred men wrote letters home. The chaplain, whose duty it was to censor the letters, put them in a mail pouch until after the battle. When the battle was over, the men again wrote home, telling of their ordeal. The overburdened chaplain had both sets of letters to censor.

Here is a sample of what he read before the battle: "Dear Mother, we're going to attack in the morning and I've been thinking of home and you, and I vowed to God that if I come through tomorrow, I am going to be a better man." Some even said, "I believe I'm going into the ministry."

But after the battle, in the same handwriting, three days later, to a friend in another regiment: "Dear Joe: Can you get leave? The last time we were in Paris, we had a hot time, didn't we? I've just come through a scorcher up front, and we were near death at every moment. If you can get leave and meet me in Paris, boy, we'll go out on the town!" Before the battle: "Oh, God, if I get through tomorrow!" After the battle: "Well, I got through, God, so I don't need you any more."

For many people God is a very present help in time of trouble; but let the trouble pass, and God moves out of the picture. And there are many people who, when they are sick, cry out, "Oh, God!" but when they get well, "Oh, me!"

ASSURANCE

I KNOW!

I was planning to spend the entire day reading and typing in our motel in Hot Springs, Arkansas. We told the cleaning woman to make the beds but not to touch the books that were spread around. My Bible was by the typewriter, and I said, "Just leave my Bible there." Immediately she seemed interested so I said to her, "Do you know the Lord Jesus Christ?"

"Oh, yes, I know Him. I couldn't have lived without him. My mother died when I was a little girl, and He has been my help through all my life."

"And are you sure that you are trusting Him as your own personal Saviour?"

"Oh, Mister. I don' have t' reckon. I know."

The conversation that followed revealed her clear knowledge of the Saviour, clear insight into spiritual life and clear certainty of full assurance of eternal life.

TRAMPS VS. MULTIMILLIONAIRES

Come with me to an underpass outside of the freight yards of one of our great railroad centers. Here are two or three men—hoboes, vagabonds, tramps. One says, "I hope that I will have a million dollars." Another says, "I hope that I will have two million dollars." A third says, "I hope that I will have ten million dollars." The total assets of the three amount to forty-three cents!

Now go to the paneled board room of one of New York's great banks. Here are several captains of industry. One explains that the expansion of our economy calls for the expenditure of sixty millions of dollars to build a new chemical plant.

ASSURANCE

A Du Pont says that he will put up fifteen million dollars; a Rockefeller agrees to duplicate this sum; a Ford and a Mellon nod their agreement and the matter is settled. But you ask, "Gentlemen! Do you really have money like that?" They nod with assurance and say, "We know that we have it." "You mean that you hope that you will have it?" we question. "No," they reply, "we know that we have it."

The difference between a tramp and a multimillionaire is the difference between a professing Christian who hopes that he will have eternal life and a possessing Christian who knows that he has eternal life.

24

THE BIBLE

THE BIBLE

About a hundred years ago, the King of Prussia had a discussion with his chaplain on the veracity of the Bible. The king said to the chaplain, "Tell me in a word the proof that the Bible is the inspired Word of God." The chaplain replied, "Your Majesty, I can prove to you in one single word that the Bible is the Word of God."

The king looked at him in amazement and said, "What is this magic word that would carry such weight of proof with it?" The chaplain replied, "Your Majesty, that word is *Israel*."

And, of course, he was right. There are other single words that also prove the Bible—sin, salvation, Christ—but the history of the people of Israel is sufficient to show that a divine breath came down upon the men who held the pens that wrote down the Word of God.

THE CARPENTER'S SQUARE

A dozen carpenters sawed boards to make flooring. The foreman measured every board with a carpenter's square, an L-shaped rule that forms an exact right angle. If a man cuts a board at other than a right angle, the fit will be crooked, and the board must be recut to conform to the carpenter's square.

For the Christian, the Bible is the instrument by which every spiritual thought is to be squared. Every idea is to be accepted or rejected according to whether or not it meets the standard of the Word of God as illuminated by the Holy Spirit.

25

THE BIBLE

LEVEL GROUND

In certain spots the contour of hills gives a tremendous illusion that the law of gravity is askew. Near Los Angeles is a hill where thousands of motorists stop their cars, shut off the engines, release the brakes and seemingly roll up hill. But a plumb level placed on the ground where the cars "roll up hill," will be shown immediately that the cars are actually rolling down hill. The eye can be deceived; the level cannot.

God has given us a similar apparatus—the Bible. When my situation in life is placed next to the Word of God, the Holy Spirit immediately establishes the true aspects of the situation and reveals whatever unevenness or distortion there is. It is not safe to form judgments on the basis of our senses or our emotions—we must prove all things, test all things (I THESSALONIANS 5:21).

THE MATCH AND THE POWDER

Let us suppose that there are ten thousand barrels in a field. I am told that dry powder is in some of them; I do not know how many barrels contain the dry powder, and I do not know which ones contain the powder. I am told that it is desirable to light the powder wherever it is found, and I am given an unlimited quantity of matches. These can be struck only upon a certain prepared surface. What shall I do? If I toss unlit matches into barrels, nothing will happen. If I strike the match on the wrong surface and toss it in, it will still be unlighted and ineffective. But if I strike the match on the proper surface and toss it into the right barrel, it will light the powder, if the powder is there, and it will burn out if there is no powder there.

So I am told to take the Word of God with the light of the Holy Spirit and throw it into every life that I see. That Word will fall into lives illuminated by the Spirit; it will set them alight if it falls into the midst of effective, personal faith. "For as the rain cometh down, and the snow from heaven, and returneth not thither, but watereth the earth, and maketh it bring forth and bud, that it may give seed to the sower, and bread to the eater: So shall my word be that goeth forth out of my mouth: it shall not return unto me void, but it shall accomplish that which I please, and it shall prosper in the thing whereto I sent it" (ISAIAH 55:10,11).

THE PLATINUM BAR

In Washington, in the Bureau of Standards, there is a platinum bar that is used as the standard meter for all measurements in the United States. It is approximately 39.37 inches long. This bar is kept in a high vacuum at a constant temperature. An argument about the measurement of any object must be settled, ultimately, by comparison with the standard meter in Washington. If your bar differs from the one in Washington, it is in error. If your bar is exactly the same as that in Washington, you can say that your bar is without error. But it would be wrong to say that the measure in Washington is without error, for that would mean that you are constituting yourself the judge—measuring the Washington meter by some other standard that is above it. We must come to the conclusion simply that the Washington meter *is* and that it cannot be judged.

God has given us His Word; it stands as the only infallible rule of faith and practice. Our lives are tested by its truth. All of our thoughts and philosophies are tested by the Word of God. If we find a human thought that is opposed to what is set forth in the Bible, we say that the human thought is in error. If we find that the human thought is in agreement with what is set forth in the Bible, we say that the human thought is truth. Every little particle of human thought must be judged by the entire revelation of God's truth. But the Bible stands alone as the final court of appeal.

27

THE STUDY OF THE OCEAN

Some time ago we went to Atlantic City to preach in one of the churches there. One of the great hotels had given the church a lovely suite and we enjoyed looking out across the Atlantic in its everchanging moods and enjoyed its beauty to the full.

Let us suppose that a young Iowa friend, who had never had the privilege of journeying to the coast, asked us to write him about the ocean. What would you think if we wrote as follows: "We have a beautiful room and a picture window gives us a sweeping view of the ocean. The window is twelve feet two inches long and four feet eight inches high. It is divided into three sections. We have had a scraping of the glass analyzed and can tell you the chemical formula of the glass. We have had an expert from one of the great glass companies tell us all about the glass; we are giving you herewith a history of the invention and development of glass. The glass is set in steel frames that are painted black; we have had the steel analyzed and the paint analyzed; you can read the analysis in our second and third studies affixed to this letter. We have discovered that the panes of glass are kept in the frames by a putty composition, and we have scraped down some of this putty and are giving you a long addenda on the chemical composition of the putty. Finally, we have inquired and learned from the hotel management their method of keeping the windows clean; you will be delighted to learn from the subjoined study the whole process of window-cleaning and the formulas of the special detergents needed to cope with the salt spray from the ocean. In closing, let us say that we hope you have enjoyed our study of the ocean."

We smile at such a farcical parable, but we must admit that there are people who seem to forget that the Bible exists only to bring us to the Lord Jesus Christ. He is the ocean beyond the window. The young man might decide that seeing the ocean was not worth a trip to the Atlantic Coast; if it were no more than a study of the window through which the ocean might be seen, surely he would be right. Many spend so much time on the Bible itself, that they fail to look through the Bible to see the Lord Jesus Christ.

TREMBLING ON THE ROCK

The old Scotch lady was right when she said, "I often tremble on the Rock, but the Rock never trembles under me."

The Word of God is the guarantee of our salvation and the ground of our assurance. There is nothing evasive about the message; it is direct and sure. This is one reason why so many people find comfort in the Word of God.

WORK CALORIES

According to findings of two German physiologists who studied the relation of food to output in the Ruhr coal mines during the war, it takes three slices of bread for every ton of coal cut by a miner. Each man, they found, required between 155 and 200 calories per ton of coal produced. These represent "work calories," which are required in addition to the 1600 to 1800 calories needed every twenty-four hours just to keep alive. When the proper "work calories" were not supplied, the study revealed that any increased output—stimulated by bonuses and cigarettes—came from the "very substance of the body"; this showed up in the weight lost by the miners. Another study showed that in peacetime work lack of sufficient "work calories" resulted in only about half the performance, so that the job of one man had to be done by two or three.

There are some very important spiritual analogies to be drawn from this. The Word of God is the food of the Christian; every Christian needs a certain minimum of food from the Word of God to live his life day by day. If, in addition, he has special work to do for the Lord, he needs special feeding from the Word. The more his output, the more he must feed upon the Word. The greater his service for the Lord, the greater his need to consume at the table which God has laid. The Word is milk by which we grow (1 PETER 2:2). The Word is strong meat (HEBREWS 5:12,14). The Word is honey (PSALMS 119:103). Those who would advance in God, must, like the prophet, say, "Thy words were found, and I did eat them . . ." (JEREMIAH 15:16a).

BIBLE READING

TRIPPER

Edward Hutton, English author of the finest travel books on Italy, was awarded the highest civilian honor of the Italian government—Commendatore of the Order of Merit of the Republic. In an interview, he described the difference between the Italy of his first studies and the Italy of the present time. Italy then, he said was the land of the traveler. Today it is the land of the tripper, the tourist: "They don't understand what they see." It is so possible for a person with no classical background to look upon the amazing relics of the past and be unaware of their meaning.

Hutton's remark is a perfect illustration of the way in which many Christians read their Bibles. Instead of being travelers, who journey slowly, absorbing the spiritual blessings and plunging into the spiritual depths, they are tourists who rush by at high speed, not knowing what to read. One girl who "traveled" in Italy said she remembered Rome as the place where the shoe polish spilled on her best dress, and Venice as the place where the hairdresser burned her hair with curling irons. Have you really spent time with the Word of God, or are you a tripper?

BODY, SOUL AND SPIRIT

THE THREE STORY BUILDING

We all have seen pictures of the World War II bombings of London, in which the explosion caused the third story of a three-story building to collapse onto the second story. The pictures show large holes gaping in the second-floor walls; we can see the debris of the third floor strewn on the floor below. The first story has withstood some of the shock—it still stands—though there are cracks in the walls and it is ultimately doomed to crash.

Thus it was with Adam. His body was the repository of his soul, and above that was his spirit. When sin came into his life, the spirit fell down into the soul; the debris of the two became hopelessly confused so that, as we consider fallen man today, it is impossible to distinguish between the soul and the spirit.

CALL OF GOD

THE UNEDUCATED MINER

An uneducated miner in Scotland began to preach among his fellow workmen with great power. Soon his witness took him far beyond the confines of the mining towns. Someone asked him how he had received his call to preach. He replied, "Oh, I had such a burden on my soul for those who did not know the gospel, I argued with the Lord that I had no education and no gift. But He said to me, 'Jamie, you know what the sickness is, don't you?' I answered, 'Yes, Lord, the sickness is sin.' 'And you know what the remedy is, don't you, Jamie?' I answered, 'Yes, Lord, the remedy is the Lord Jesus Christ.' And He said to me, 'Jamie, just take the remedy to those who are sick.' That is my call to preach."

This is God's call to every believer.

CHOSEN BY GOD

DEAREST

George Beatty of Cleveland, Ohio, had a wonderful jewelry store, remarkable for its window displays. Over the years, Mr. Beatty had bought a stock of small precious stones that he kept in pint cups. He had a cup of small rubies, a cup of topazes and a cup of diamonds—all sparkling brilliance. Some of them were small stones and chips that were worth very little. Early in the morning, before the customers came, he made pictures by placing the stones on black velvet squares; a magnificent peacock with its tail spread out was on one. He put these portraits in stones in the window, and many people stopped to look.

After one of my meetings, Beatty invited me to come to his basement workshop. Here he worked in wax and made settings for rings and pendants. Into the wax molds, he poured the liquid platinum; after the platinum was molded with an artistic and beautiful scroll design, he set the jewels in it.

A wealthy customer wrote Mr. Beatty that his dearest granddaughter was going to have a birthday; he wanted something distinctive of real beauty. Five times in the letter, the customer spoke of the granddaughter as "dearest." The old man looked at me and said, "I prayed and asked the Lord to give me an idea. I noticed how many times 'dearest' appeared, so I underlined it. When I sent my customer the sketch and told him what I proposed to do, he was greatly pleased and thought my idea was wonderful."

Mr. Beatty sent him a ring with baguettes so beautifully cut that the light scintillated from them. Across the top of the ring,

34

the first stone was a diamond; the next, an emerald, then an amethyst, a ruby, a second emerald, a sapphire, and then a topaz. I looked at it and asked, "But why do you have two emeralds?" He smiled and said, "Because there are two e's in 'dearest.' If you take the initials of those stones, it spells the word 'dearest.'"

Before the Lord God Almighty created the sun, the moon and the stars, He chose us, and—as it were—He put us in a ring to be worn as a signet upon His hand. Spelled out in the heart of God, we are his dearest.

CHRISTIAN GROWTH

THE ARTIST

An artist, visiting a museum where one of his masterpieces was on exhibition, saw one of his early paintings. He turned away from the comparison with sadness. A friend told him he should be pleased because of the progress he had made. The artist smiled sadly and replied that he was grieved because he had realized so little of the promise he had shown in his youth.

Let us, who are Christians, be delighted with the progress that we see in the revelation of the Son of God in others; but let us be grieved that we see so little development in ourselves as we realize how far we fall short of showing a perfect portrait of our Lord Jesus to a world which so sorely needs a sight of Him.

THE BRIDE'S FIRST KISS

In Africa we stopped overnight at the mission house of a young American bride and her Australian husband. The subject of their wedding came up, and they brought out some pictures a friend had taken of the affair. There was some good-natured chaffing on our part, and the young husband said, "I had always said that the last thing I would do is marry an American." We laughed, and he continued, "You know, she never let me kiss her even once until the wedding ceremony." We all laughed again; she blushed and started for the kitchen. He called after her, "But after I got the first one, the rest came easy."

The young bride turned as she went through the door and cast her husband a blushing look; it did not take much perspicacity to know that he had found the way to her heart and that he might come instantly. It may have taken him a year to find the way, but once it was found, it was forever open.

And this is our Lord's way with us. We do not have to repeat the slow processes of Christian growth. The steps, once taken, are taken forever.

BUILDING FACTORIES

An engineer, who was responsible for building great factories, said that all such construction is now planned with the machines that are to be housed in the factory in mind. The walls and floors of the buildings are constructed so that a machine can be built into the very foundation and structure of the building, rather than set in as an afterthought.

This is the way the Lord builds believers into Christ. We are built upon the foundation of the apostles and prophets, Jesus Christ himself being the chief cornerstone, and in Him all the building is fitly framed together, so that it groweth unto an holy temple in the Lord (EPHESIANS 2:20,21). That is surpassing even the modern engineers. They can frame their building and foundation and machines together "fitly," but they cannot make the building "grow." The true believers are fused in Christ and grow in Him together with Him and together with one another.

LEARNING TO FLY

When an eagle wants to teach its little ones to fly from the nest high upon a cliff, hundreds of feet up in the air, it prods one of the little eaglets and with its beak, noses it out of the nest. The eaglet starts to fall, and the great eagle flies underneath, puts its wing out, catches the little one on its back and flies a mile into the air. When you can hardly see the eagle as a point in the sky, it turns sideways, and down falls the little eaglet, goes fluttering maybe a thousand feet. Meanwhile, the eagle circles around the eaglet and underneath it; the eagle catches the eaglet on its wings and carries the eaglet up in the air again. After dishing the eaglet out again and letting it go, the eaglet comes down farther and farther—sometimes within a hundred feet of the ground. Again the great eagle catches the little one on its back and up they go another mile. The little eagle is at perfect rest and learning to fly. Way up there in the sky, the great eagle will bow over again and little by little the eaglet will learn to fly. The eagle knows when the eaglet is tired; it spoons the eaglet into the nest, noses out the next one and starts off again.

God says, "That's the way I take care of you." But you may say, "I don't like to have my nest stirred up. I like everything cozy and tidy, and I just like to stay in my baby ways where I am." But God loves you. That's why He won't let you stay as a baby; He wants you to learn to fly. Sometimes you have to be carried aloft, and you may have a horror of having to go by yourself, but it must come if you are to grow.

CHRISTIAN LIBERTY

THE ARGENTINIAN SPEED RACER

For a time, an Argentinian was the world's champion automobile speed racer. He could drive a car at 150 miles an hour, and he had won all the great road races of Europe. On the public highway he was the most careful and conscientious of drivers; young men drove alongside, gunned their motors, and grinned at him. He could have left them as though they were standing still, but he never used his ability for his own ends. If he saw that someone wanted to pass him so they could brag about it, he would drive under the speed limit. He sacrificed his pride for the sake of his example. If he sought to exercise his ability according to his liberty, he might say, "You slow-pokes! You cannot react as quickly as I can. I can change direction in a tenth of a second, without harm. If you can't do it, crash into that tree and kill yourself!" If he took this attitude, even though driving at a "safe and reasonable" speed, he would be defying the law of humanity.

Each believer stands before God in perfect liberty, but each is bound before God as to how he uses his liberty. And if a believer in Christ uses his liberty for himself alone, he defies not only the law of humanity but the greater law of love.

HINDU VEGETARIANISM

One of the principal tenets of the Hindu religion is that the cow is a sacred animal; its flesh must not be eaten. This belief has led to complete vegetarianism. Suppose we Christians move into an Indian town; whether we are professional missionaries or employees of the United States government, we are ambassadors for Christ. Now, there is no butcher shop, since nobody in town eats meat; but, animated by the love of Christ, the believer will not make an issue out of it. He will abstain for the sake of the weak ones who watch him. If people in the town become Christians, they must be taught the heart of the Christian doctrine of grace; they must learn that vegetarianism is not a requirement of Christianity. The American Christian may travel away from the town and eat meat freely in the hotels and restaurants of the large cities of India, but he will not flaunt his liberty before these babes in Christ. Instead, for the love of Christ, he abstains from eating meat while living among them.

On the other hand, if I were living under such conditions and had been the means of bringing some Hindus to a saving knowledge of Jesus Christ, I would seek to teach them the liberty that is in Christ. When traveling with them to a large city, I would teach them the necessity of eating meat at least once to prove their liberty in Christ, and to aid their spiritual growth. When they returned to their hometown, they would resume the practice of vegetarianism before the weaker brethren and the unconverted; but they would never make it a matter of legalism within the framework of Christianity. In time, all the believers might grow strong enough to include meat in their meals. On a large scale, this would not only bring spiritual liberty to the believers, but would certainly improve economic conditions in India.

WALKING FREELY

In America we are at liberty to walk around as we please; at night we can go out in the garden and enjoy the stars or the cool air of the evening. On the missionary field, no one may walk freely at night; no one can spend too much time looking at the stars. One must keep one's eyes on the ground and a flashlight on the path ahead for the cobras that come out of their hiding places at night and slip among the paths. It would be as much as one's life is worth to plant a foot on the body of a cobra.

Someone might say, "Do I not have the right to walk freely, without carrying a light at night? May I not exercise my right to keep my eyes on the stars?" And the answer is that you really do not have the right to your own way in this matter. To insist on your rights would mean death.

Thus it is in the Christian life. There are many restrictions that we voluntarily place upon ourselves; not because we are not free to do something, but because it is not expedient to do so. The believer who has understood the Christian way will gladly carry the light in his hand; he will gladly accept this limitation of his freedom so that he may see the path that the Lord wishes him to follow, and avoid the cobras the enemy may seek to put in his way.

CHRISTIAN LIFE

A CLEAN KITCHEN

After an evening meeting that followed a dinner in the home of a young minister, a group returned to that home for a time of fellowship. The young wife began to work hard in the kitchen cleaning up after the dinner. She said, "I hate to come down to a dirty kitchen in the morning, so I always clean it up at night before I sleep."

At the end of every day, we must come to the Lord and let Him clean up absolutely everything in our whole life. "If we confess our sins, he is faithful and just to forgive us our sins, and to cleanse us from all unrighteousness" (1 JOHN 1:9). This cleans up the kitchen; this cleans up the bedroom; this cleans up the living room; everything is ready for the next day. We open our eyes in fellowship with Him and smile. There are no hangovers from a previous day to mar the beginning. All is in fellowship, all is clean; God has done it, and the new day lies before us.

THE CONGO

I first saw Africa's great Congo from a plane, flying from Libreville in French Equatorial Africa to Leopoldville (now Kinshara) in the Congo. We swooped down out of the clouds to fly two or three hundred feet above some of the greatest rapids on earth. It was a marvelous sight from the air, and a few days later we set out to see the Congo at closer range.

At and above the city of Leopoldville, the Congo River is as calm and placid as a mill pond. The Stanley pool swells out until it is almost forty miles across. We crossed the river to

Brazzaville, on the lower edge of that pool, and could hardly see a ripple. We had to look closely in order to see the direction of the river's flow. Then we took a car and drove ten miles down the river; we walked a mile or so under the tropical sun, crossed a small swinging bridge high above a tributary, and came, at last, to the rocks on the edge of the rapids. The vast flood of the Stanley pool and the waters of half a continent push down through a narrow place between the rocks, scarcely half a mile wide. The roar of the water is like thunder. The pressure is so tremendous that at times, waves fifty feet high are tossed into the air. The river is chocolate brown from the erosion of more than a million square miles; it flows in a still basin forty miles across, and churns through rapids that are tearing in their torment. Up the river, calm and peace; down the river, rapids.

So is the life of the Christian as it is revealed to us in the Word of God. In the highest heavens, seated with our Lord in the throne of His Father, we have a peace that passeth all understanding. In the lower heavens and on the earth we have a turbulent roaring conflict. Yes, the Christian life is a downright wrestling match, not with human beings our own size and weight, flesh and blood which we might compass, but we wrestle against principalities and powers, against the world rulers of the darkness, against spiritual hosts of wickedness in the Heavens (EPHESIANS 6:12).

THE CORMORANTS

While we were in Japan we went to Cifu. Just after dark, fishing boats sweep down the broad river; fires burn in the cages that hang from the prow of each boat. These fires attract the fish to the surface. Each master-fisherman manages a dozen large birds—cormorants; each bird is tethered by a cord ending in a metal ring, fitted around the neck of the bird. The cormorant thrusts his bill into the water and scoops up a large fish which will go down his long throat only as far as the ring.

43

The master-fisherman then draws the bird back into the boat. The bird disgorges the fish and is fed a smaller one that slips down his throat past the ring. He then dives into the water again to catch another fish. It is amazing to watch the master-fisherman hold the cords of a dozen birds and keep them from tangling. The birds dart about after their fish; sometimes two will struggle for the same fish, but the master-fisherman keeps them all in order, without fouling the lines.

I applied this illustration to myself and the management of my life. I thought of how I have allowed lines to get tangled, and how difficult it is for any of us to keep all our lines of communication from tangling. When we understand that God is running the world, we stop threshing around and become quiet in Him. How wonderful to know that He has all things under control, and that He is working all things after the counsel of His will!

DIKES

Every child learns easily the geography lesson of Holland because of the fact that most of the land lies below the level of the sea and that the power of the water is restrained by great dikes. The Hollanders know from experience what their sea walls have done for their nation in rolling back the encroaching ocean, hungry to swallow up their low-lying land. Any breach in the dike would be repaired immediately. Any attack upon it from men or nature would be ruthlessly resisted.

The Christian should be just as sensitive to any encroachment on the barriers God has put up for our protection. The first day of the week is for our rest, worship and feeding in the Word of God—"Not forsaking the assembling of ourselves together as the fashion of some is . . ." (HEBREWS 10:25). This is one of God's dikes. Time spent every day in the study of the supernatural Book, time spent in prayer, these are God's dikes. The power of the enemy is ceaselessly helpless against them.

The Christian must be most energetic in watching unto their preservation.

THE DISCORDANT CHIME

An old clock that stands in a corner once had a beautiful chime; now it has a harsh metallic sound. A bit of broken spring fell against the chime while it was being repaired, and this little piece of metal is causing all the discord. As soon as this bit is removed, the hour will strike again in a rich, full tone.

Is there discord in your life? It takes but a bit of anything to deaden the note of joy. Whatever it is, great or small, it may be removed by yieldedness to our Lord Jesus Christ. David knew where to go when he cried, "Restore unto me the joy of thy salvation . . ." (PSALMS 51:12).

THE EMPTY GAS TANK

A garage man in Mangum, Oklahoma, answered the distress call of a woman motorist, whose car had stalled. He examined the car and informed her that it was out of gas. "Will it hurt," she asked, "if I drive it home with the gas tank empty?" It would be cheaper to drive cars without gas, and quite pleasant, but anyone who has ever tried it has found out that it just does not work.

The same is true in the Christian life. Those who attempt to go on without power divinely provided by God may find that they are able to coast down hill for awhile—even roll up a little grade for a moment—but soon a time will come when the road will not permit further coasting; then life is stalled. Fortunately, God provides the power for us any time we are willing to have it, if we keep the funnel unclogged with sin and turned toward the supply that comes from His grace.

THE FLOWER SHOW

I turned on the television in our motel room, as the presentation of a great flower show was beginning. Our TV was in black and white. The camera peered around various exhibits, each darker and gloomier than the one before. It was a colossal waste of time. Anyone who had never seen a flower show would get a wrong idea; anyone who had seen a flower show would be disgusted. There was neither color nor perfume, and, in fact, little form.

Thus it is when people try to have religion without Christ. You cannot capture the fragrance of Christ and the unfolding beauties of His presence in test tube or logical argument. He is received by faith, manifested in love, and awaited in hope. We should so live that everyone can see Him in us.

FORESTS

A *New York Times* editorial, "Fingers of the Forest," points out that once there were forests over much of the northeastern part of our country, and that most of our civilization has been planted on clearings in that once great forest. It then points out that wherever man has left a hedgerow between fields, the forest extends its fingers. "A hedgerow is a germ of a woodland. It has all the elements of a great forest and is a unit in itself. Young trees form the frame of the loom; the pattern is woven of alder and sumac, osage, high-bush cranberries, poison ivy and bittersweet. . . . Over the Northeast man has pushed the forest back, but the power of the woodland waits, keeping its fingers extended over man-made clearings."

This is a great illustration of the life of the believer in Christ. Our dwelling place is carved out of territory that was once occupied by the forest of our Adamic nature. We have made clearings, and with the help of the Lord, we keep the fields plowed and planted and cultivated and bearing a good harvest.

THE GARDEN

I saw a garden overrun with weeds. Then cover plants were set at intervals among the weeds. After a year one could see that a battle was going on between the weeds and the cover crop. As time went on, the cover crop outgrew the weeds and, in a few years, it completely crowded the weeds out.

The Christian life somewhat resembles this process. The Christian starts out by being a part of this world and by becoming alive through the new birth. Henceforth, though he is in the world, his roots have been cut and a new planting has taken place. Christ must dominate every part of our lives. This is God's purpose for us and in us.

THE HELMSMAN OF THE LEADING YACHT

When the jumble around the starting line of a certain yacht race cleared, the helmsman of the leading yacht remarked rather uneasily, "I never expected to find myself in the lead." He made the same remark several times, but his crew told him it was nothing to complain about. As they rounded the first mark, well ahead, he said, "I think we'll have to let this boat pass us." "No we'll not," said the crew, "we're doing fine." "The trouble is," said the helmsman, "that I don't know where to go next. I was so sure there would be other boats in front that I didn't take the trouble to study the course."

There are too many Christians who will have a poor place in heaven because they are living their Christian lives like this helmsman. They were meant to be conquerors, but the last shall be first and the first last because they did not study to show themselves approved unto God—workmen that need not be ashamed.

IN DADDY'S FOOTSTEPS

The story is told of a man who had to be very careful of his life because he realized that he was the ideal and example for his son. One Christmas afternoon the father made the rounds of several houses and partook of various brands of cheer; he made a crooked path as he weaved his way across a field on the way home. Finally, he heard the voice of his five-year-old calling out behind him. He turned and faced the lad coming

47

by a very crooked path. The father was sober enough to realize the boy was not walking straight; he realized, as he saw the lad taking giant steps in the snow, that the boy was following his father's trail. With a smile the boy said, "See Daddy, I'm walking right in your footsteps." The father resolved that he would have to mend his ways; he would have to be more careful of the way he walked, if his son were to walk after him.

But when we walk after the steps of our Lord, we need have no fear, for He has furnished the perfect example for the Christian. Only the believer can look to the Lord's life as the example of his walk.

Be ye followers of me.

KILLING THE SOUND WAVES

A gadget has been invented that reaches out to kill sound waves before they hit the ear. Electronically they are able to reduce the air pressure in the vicinity of certain apparatus just enough to cancel out sound waves. The result is a small "quiet zone." For a distance of two feet, it reduces to one-quarter the loudness of deep-toned noise. The effect is like shutting a door against the noise. They expect to build a gadget run on one watt of current that can be hung over the head of a sleeper to protect him from sleep-destroying noises. The gadget will be used in airplanes so the deep roar of the engines will be reduced, while the higher tones of the human voice will not be effected as much.

A spiritual gadget like this has existed for thousands of years. God speaks, and men have accustomed themselves to making a "quiet zone" around their ears for all sounds coming from Him. Any voice that is from the world, the flesh or the devil can get through, but Christ was forced to say, "He that hath ears to hear, let him hear" (MATTHEW 11:15).

THE LOCKED GATE

While taking a walk at sunset in a north India hill station, our host led us on a path that followed the flank of the moun-

48

tain. Here and there private paths led from the main one to the homes that dotted the hillside. At one of these junctions the owner had planted a post on either side of his private path, and between these posts he had placed a gate. The posts were strong, the gate was heavy, a chain held it shut, and a padlock secured the chain. But the posts were not connected to any fence. Within a step of one of these was a well-worn path that led around the gate, and anyone who wished could walk on the path and go his way as readily as if the postholes had never been dug or the gate planted across the path.

Is this not a picture of much of Christian effort toward a life of victory? The forms of religion are well planted; ideas of sanctification may be securely locked into the framework of proper doctrine. But it is not joined up to life and living. Provision has been made for the flesh in direct disobedience to God's command.

NOISE

Scientists report that noise has a definite effect on our working efficiency. Noise increases the pulse, quickens the blood pressure, and upsets the normal rhythm of the heart.

Spiritual noise has just as bad an effect on spiritual life. The man who is occupied with the things that keep him from hearing the voice of God in his heart is spiritually frustrated. It is impossible for those who are spiritually noisy to have true peace of mind, peace of heart, and peace of soul! This is why God has said, "Be still, and know that I am God . . ." (PSALMS 46:10).

OLYMPIC GAMES CONTESTANTS

Before the last Olympic games the contestants who represented our country were chosen according to certain rules. Anyone in the whole nation could have run up and down in the vicinity of the stadium. Before entering the stadium, many visitors might have confused such a person with the real members of the team. But none of these imitators would have been allowed by the judges to compete in the events; and therefore, none of them would have been eligible for the prizes.

It is precisely the same with the race of Christian life. Many people are running around in Christian uniform, drawing the gaze of the casual onlooker who does not know the marks of a true Christian and who does not realize that not all Gentiles are Christians, and that many thousands of church members do not possess the supernatural life of Christ.

THE OLYMPIC TEAMS

Every four years great contests are held in the world of athletics; they are known as the Olympic games. It is considered a great honor to be on the team that represents our country at these events. Not everyone who desires can compete. There are elimination contests and finally the team is chosen. Then the team crosses the ocean and the various contests are held. Our athletes compete against men of other nations and some will be fortunate enough to be prize winners. After the teams have been chosen and the boat has sailed, the status of the athletes is fixed. If, after being chosen, one man does not seem to show the form that had been promised by earlier tests, he is, nevertheless, accepted; he is not dropped from the competition, though he may not be a prize-winner. Another man, who passed the tests with the thought that he might be a mere pacemaker may turn out to be the world's champion when the moment of the test comes. But their eligibility to compete depends entirely upon the fact that they have passed the elimination tests and have become members of the national team.

So it is in the Christian life and judgment. God tells us that the Christian life is a race. All who desire may enroll for the race. That is equivalent to becoming a Christian. The only way to become a Christian is by accepting God's verdict about the sinfulness of your own heart outside of Christ and by accepting

God's verdict about the eternal satisfaction of all of His demands since Christ has perfectly satisfied them by His death upon the cross.

A PIECE OUT OF THE CAKE

The little girl watched her mother put the finishing touches on a newly baked cake. "Mother," she said, "your cake would look like the pictures in the magazines if you would cut a piece out of it."

Your Christian life would look more like that pictured in the Bible, if you would start giving yourself away. What you keep grows stale. What you give becomes nourishment for the whole of the true church. We feed on what the Lord multiplies of Himself through us.

THE POOR MILLIONAIRE

Several years ago, I preached in a church in the southwestern United States. When I went into the pulpit on Sunday morning, the pastor whispered to me, "Notice that woman on the front row who is badly dressed and who wears a broken shoe." I saw a miserable, pitiful figure of a woman, probably in her late sixties; one foot stretched out to reveal a large hole in the sole of the shoe, the edge of which was so worn that the leather stood away from the sole. Her dress was patched and dowdy, and her old hat looked like something out of a rag barrel. A wave of pity came over me, and my first thought was to give her a few dollars to help her in her misery.

Later, the pastor told me that this woman and her husband had been sheep ranchers, pasturing a large herd on ground that was almost desert. Their miserable cabin's toilet facilities were fifty yards away in one direction, a hand-pumped well fifty yards in the other. They drove a jalopy of ancient vintage and lived most simply. Then oil was discovered on their property, and they became very rich. After a time, the husband died, leaving everything to the wife. She was extremely

51

frightened and refused to sign the papers the lawyers brought her. Her royalties began to pile up. Drilling continued until there were a hundred wells on her ranch. Within a few years she was worth several million dollars, but she spent hardly a cent. She still lived in the old cabin, used outdoor facilities, and pumped water by hand. She still drove the old jalopy. Possessing enormous wealth, she lived in abject misery.

I pointed out to my preacher friend that her manner of life exemplified the spiritual life of multitudes of believers. We have been told that we are heirs and joint heirs with Christ, that all things are ours, that we have been blessed with all spiritual blessings in the heavenly places in Christ, and that God has given us all things richly to enjoy. God tells us that we have not because we ask not, and that we ask and do not receive because we ask in a wrong spirit. The riches are there; the supply is unlimited, but many simply do not avail themselves of all that God has promised, or of even a small fraction.

THE RED ROSE

Some years ago, a friend of mine moved into a new home. The house had been unoccupied for a long time; the garden was untended and high with weeds. The first morning my friend looked from an upstairs window into the garden, and among the weeds he saw a beautiful red rose. He went to pick it, but the weeds were so high he could not find it. Returning to his upstairs window he located the rose, noted landmarks near it, and on his second trip to the garden, succeeded in finding it. As he pulled it from the weeds, he discovered that the stem ran nine feet to its root in his neighbor's well-cultivated garden!

That is the Christian life. Rooted in Heaven, it blooms among the weeds of earth.

SEEING THE GOSPEL

A man came to a mission station in Central China and asked to become a Christian. When he was questioned, he replied that he had never heard the gospel preached. He also said that he could not read. When he was asked how he knew about the gospel, he said that he had seen it. Although his village was far removed from any preaching center, he explained, there lived a man who had long been known as a worthless opium addict and a lazy, good-for-nothing. The man had journeyed to a faraway town and had returned absolutely transformed; he uprooted the poppies in his garden, repaired his house, planted and tended his crops, and provided for his family as a decent man should. The former good-for-nothing said that the gospel of Christ had changed his life; his neighbor, hearing about it, came all the way to the mission station to become a Christian.

The gestures of the Christian life explained more simply and more potently than any arguments could have done. May we define our Christian life in this way.

THE SNOW TRACKS

Five boys, playing in the woods one winter day, decided to see who could make the straightest set of tracks in the snow. They were very careful to put one foot directly in front of the other, but when they had crossed the clearing, one track was curved, one was crooked, and two were almost zig-zag. Only one boy had a straight track. When they asked him how he did it, he replied that he had not looked at his feet; he had picked out a tree across the clearing and had walked straight toward it.

If we are to leave a straight track in our daily walk, we must not have our minds centered on ourselves. We must fix our gaze upon the Lord Jesus Christ. We are to "run with patience

53

the race that is set before us, looking unto Jesus . . ." (HEBREWS 12:1,2).

SPENDING

A wife can never be satisfied merely because her husband is a good provider. If he laid everything at her feet that money could buy, there would still be a lack of just exactly everything because he had delved into his purse instead of his heart. But many a happy woman gladly does without the fripperies of luxurious living, if she has not only the large bills, but the small change from the heart of the man she loves.

The analogy may be carried into all the relationships of our life. Never spend money from your purse for that which should be purchased with your very self. The Christian knows that this spending of the heart is the natural—or should we say, the supernatural?—pouring out of the life that is released through the indwelling presence of the Lord Jesus Christ. He Himself said, "He that believeth on me, as the scripture hath said, out of his belly shall flow rivers of living water. But this spake he of the Spirit, which they that believe on him should receive . . ." (JOHN 7:38,39). Even the money that comes from the purse will have the effect of self that pours from the heart, if it is spent in the light and life of the Lordship of Christ.

STILL OR MOVING PICTURES

We went to the steamship office at Kobe to get baggage that had been checked through from Yokohama. An English-speaking Japanese was detailed to take us to the custom house. As soon as we were in the taxi, we began to talk with him about Christ. He had been in contact with Christianity and was under deep conviction. What were his objections to Christianity, I asked him. Many Christians did not live up to their profession, he replied. It was easy to say, "I am a Christian, I am a Christian," but especially for the poor man, it was not so easy to be a Christian. Japanese employers, especially those in the hotel business in which he had spent many years, wanted their employees ready to lie; they did not wish to employ men who might develop a conscience. These are not his exact words, but the thought is conveyed. Then he gave us a real message. He said, "A true Christian should be a moving picture, but many of them are only still pictures, and there is all the difference in the world between the dull flat photograph and the depth and animation of the highly developed cinema."

We are, all of us who name the name of Christ, living epistles, known and read of all men. In modern days, the world has learned to illustrate everything; twentieth-century Christians are living epistles—illustrated editions. The non-Christian is finding that many who call themselves Christians present still pictures to the world—often under-exposed, out of focus. The result is a caricature instead of a reflection of Christ.

SURE-FOOTED

As a young man in Europe, I did considerable mountain climbing in the Swiss Alps and in the more dangerous and difficult French Alps. Roped together with other young men, I scaled many a peak; my snapshot book records moments of difficulty and peril that make me wish to restrain others who might venture into similar places. The first time I went out with a young Frenchman, son of a pastor, and a young Swiss bank clerk; they gave me sound advice, "You have two hands and two feet," they said, "and that makes four. Always be sure that three out of the four are firmly on the rock. It is the only rule of safety."

This advice is also the rule of spiritual safety in our Christian life. In one of the Psalms, David told of slipping feet. He had been looking at men and their circumstances. He saw the righteous suffering and the wicked flourishing, and he could not understand; he was, in fact, dismayed. He had looked at men and their doings instead of looking at God. It is as dangerous to take your eyes from the Lord in spiritual things as it is to take your feet from the rock in mountain climbing.

THE THREE PILLOWS

An old lady was very calm as she approached death. Her minister said, "I have noticed your calmness in so many things." She said, "When I was just a girl, an old preacher told me that each night he slept well because he rested his head upon three pillows—God's grace, God's power, and God's wisdom."

There is no doubt that if you have those three pillows, it is going to make easy sleeping, easy dying and easy living day by day; your attitude toward the Lord will be such that prayer changed the whole attitude in life, because prayer is the linking of your soul to the Lord in absolute trust.

TWO RULERS

Mr. Six-Year-Old came into the study in tears. In his hand were the two pieces of a broken ruler. Mr. Nine-Year-Old had done it, he affirmed. The investigation, however, showed that the older brother had merely set an example by putting his ruler in the inkwell hole and bending it. When the small brother followed the example the ruler snapped because there was a knot in the wood. Actually, the smaller brother had done the breaking, but we took the good ruler and gave it to the younger child while the older brother had to be content with a nicked and stained substitute of inferior quality before it was finally replaced at the end of a month. Another punishment was given to the boy who had done the actual breaking.

There had to be some explanations. The older boy was not quite sure of the justice of the punishment, but ultimately it led to the explanation of the responsiblity of the stronger for the weaker. It is a distinct Christian principle that the strong must help to bear the infirmities of the weak. The life of Christ within our hearts makes any small privation pleasure. He never allows Himself to be in debt to us, and when an honest heart has given up something that might cause no harm to self, the

Lord has a way of filling up the emptiness with "solid joys and lasting pleasures."

WALKING ON ICE

Walking on an icy street in Haddonfield, New Jersey, a little boy reached up, caught hold of his father's finger, and slipped. As he slipped, he let go of his father and went down. The father helped the whimpering boy up and they walked on. The father tried to take hold of the boy's hand, but the boy slapped at his father's hand and finally caught hold of the finger by himself. Once more he slipped; the automatic reflexes opened his hand and down he went. He whimpered again, and this time the father just reached down and caught the little fellow by his fist. The boy still wanted to do the whole thing, but the father wouldn't let him and so they went along. All of a sudden, the boy's feet slipped and the telegraph reflexes from the boy's fist ran through the father's arm to the father's head; before the boy's feet could fly out from under him again, the father lifted him up. The boy kicked in the air for a moment; the father set him down, and they walked on together again.

There are two ways of trying to live the Christian life. If you try to hold on to God's finger, something is going to happen, and you are going to try to let go. But if you say, "Lord God, I can't stay on my own feet, hold me," He'll do it. When you slip, you may kick around in the air for a minute, but He is strong enough to let you kick and then to put you down again very quietly and let you get your footing and start on again. He will keep you this way.

WALKING WITH FATHER

Many of us can remember, perhaps, incidents of our own childhood when we walked before our own parents. I can recall our Sunday morning walks to Sunday school—skipping along the sidewalk, stopping to examine a place in the cement where a group of children had left the prints of their hands and bare feet and another spot where a horseshoe had been imbedded in the walk. At a certain place I used to run far ahead, then wait at the curb for my father so that I might cross with him. There was one yard before which I paused, waiting for my father to come up close, that I might have him near at hand before passing a huge barking dog. Walking before my father was a place of absolute safety. His eye was ever upon me, and his voice could call out, if I strayed from the way he wanted me to go.

Certainly it is so with our Heavenly Father. He has us walk before Him in the path of great security. "He knoweth the way that I take. . . ." (JOB 23:10). We need never fear when our Father, our Heavenly Father, is behind us. He started us on this walk, and put us there in His sight, and He expects to bring us home.

WALKING WITH THE CHILDREN

Each day I watched a father and his children taking their walk, in the midst of the big city. Perils of traffic, and other city dangers were on every hand. Their training went on, day by day: the children walked ahead of their father; they were permitted to run ahead to a certain tree, some fifty yards away. If they ran beyond it, they had to walk just five steps ahead of their father for many sedate minutes while they fretted for their liberty. If they promised that they would observe his limits, they were freed again. I can see them running up to the fixed goal, standing with their toes to a line—little soldiers obeying with absolute precision. When once they learned to stay within their prescribed limit, the distance was lengthened to one hundred yards, and more. Finally, they were released at a certain point and given permission to disappear around the corner, if they stopped at a certain known goal. When that lesson had been learned, they were allowed to cross a quiet street where there was little danger of traffic. Once such a crossing had been successfully negotiated on many successive days, the children were permitted to cross at a busier corner. Time was passing. Where three-year-old steps had been halted at fifty yards, and four-year-old steps had been permitted to go around a corner and out of sight, five-year-old steps were crossing streets.

One day the father sent the boys a block ahead, where they had to cross two streets, gave them money to go into a familiar store, make a purchase, and wait there for him. The distances were lengthened, the sums of money entrusted to them were increased, the importance of the errands grew. Finally, there came a day when a ten dollar bill was given to them and they were told to go to a bank three or four blocks away, get change and bring it home. Faithful in few things, they were made faithful over many.

This is the desire of the father-heart. This is why the heavenly Father tells His children to walk before Him. He desires their growth, their discipline, their training, that they may be strong in the powers He has given them.

THE WELL-DRESSED CHRISTIAN

In a certain city in the western part of the United States, lives a woman who has become famous in Christian circles because of her great testimony for Christ. She has transformed the life of one of the greatest churches in the land, and has led dozens of young people into full-time Christian service. This woman dresses in stylish clothes; her grooming is equal to that of the most worldly people with whom she associates. In a nearby town lives a godly shoemaker who makes good money and lives on the slenderest budget; he supports much Christian work with his gifts. One day, the shoemaker attended a banquet at his church; the city woman was the special speaker—splendidly coiffed, gowned and well-manicured. When the service was over, he asked her why she dressed the way she did. "Why are you wearing a necktie?" she asked. He was taken aback and finally stammered that it was the custom; that if he did not wear a necktie, people would think that he was queer. She then answered that she lived and moved among multitudes of people who dressed well and for whom the custom was to appear much as she appeared at that moment. If she did not dress somewhat as they dressed, she would be conspicuous and they would think her queer; they would not be willing to listen to her presentation of the gospel. He nodded and turned away without further argument.

How important it is for Christians not to judge one another in trivial things. Each one of us must answer to God for the way we dress, the way we walk, the way we talk, the way we act, the way we live, the way we think, the way we manifest the love of the Lord Jesus Christ to those who are around us, dead in trespasses and sins.

WE'VE WON

As Canon Guy King stood waiting for a train to London, a train discharged a football team returning home after a game in another city. It was before the days of radio and telephone, so nobody knew the result of the game. A small boy pushed through the crowd and asked one of the players. Leaping joyfully, he ran outside shouting to the others, "We've won, we've won." He was not a member of the team, nor of the school represented by the team. But he was filled with joy over a victory with which he associated himself.

Thus it is, that we face our daily life. We can live in joy and in triumph. We can shout, "We've won!" over the victory that was accomplished by our Lord Jesus Christ on Calvary nineteen hundred years ago. If we are in the midst of some defeat in our lives, we have the right to know what our Lord won for us, and to enter into the triumph of it.

WILTED ROSES

Back in the days of the depression, a Philadelphia woman of Scotch ancestry, who also had a Scotch name, was called Mrs.

Mac. She and her husband had a lovely home, chauffeur, gardener, hot house and all the rest. Mrs. Mac taught a Sunday-school class of high-school girls. One day her car drove up before the house of one of the girls in her class. The chauffeur hopped out, and gave the girl a big box of roses. When the girl opened the box, she saw that the roses were wilted and faded and that the petals were beginning to fall and turn brown. Why on earth would Mrs. Mac do a thing like that? Had the chauffeur been given them two or three days ago, and forgot to deliver the package?

When she met Mrs. Mac on the street later that day, the girl said, "I want to thank you for the roses you sent me this morning."

Mrs. Mac said, "Oh yes, they were so beautiful, I cut them last Monday, I have had them in my bedroom, and I have been enjoying them to the full. This morning I noticed that some of the petals were dropping and they were beginning to get old and faded, so I thought about you, and I decided to send them to you.

She said, "But Mrs. Mac, I don't understand."

Mrs. Mac said, "Just the other evening Mr. Mac and I stopped in front of the drug store. While Mr. Mac went inside on an errand, I sat in the car in the dark. Some girls came down the street. I heard one of them say about the meetings that we were having over at the church, 'Well of course, I mean to be a Christian sometime, but now while I'm young, I want to have a good time.' "

The girl's head dropped. She said, "I remember I did say that, but I didn't know you were in the car listening."

Mrs. Mac replied, "Don't you see what you're really saying is 'Lord, here's my life. I'm young, I have youth and charm and beauty, and I want to enjoy myself, I want to live for myself. When I begin to get wrinkles and I'm not as popular as I was, when I'm beginning to fade, why Lord, you can have what's left. I'll give you the rest, but while it's young I want it for myself.'"

There are people who, when they were young, lived utterly for themselves. And only when they began to be wrinkled and weren't as popular as they were at eighteen, twenty or twenty-five, they began to turn to the faith and come back toward the Lord.

CHRISTIANS

A GOOD AUTOMOBILE DRIVER

A good automobile driver never thinks about his driving, he merely reacts. If it were necessary to think about putting on the brake, the delay of a fraction of a second could cause many accidents. When someone else is driving, a good driver may frequently "put on the brake," automatically reacting and stamping on the floor boards. His mind is so conditioned by thousands of miles of driving that certain motions become natural in certain situations.

The Christian, through thousands of hours of fellowship with the Lord in prayer and Bible study, over the years acquires a conditioned pattern of thinking that becomes more glorious as time passes. The burden of sin is gone; he knows that he is saved; sensitive to His presence and His holy hatred of sin, he learns to glance at Him when danger threatens; by reason of use he has his senses exercised to discern (HEBREWS 5:14). His thought of death is one of glory, not of fear; life is filled with praise.

THE ASPIC SALAD

A lady makes tomato aspic for a luncheon party. She pours the aspic into individual molds and sets them in the refrigerator. When her guests arrive, she takes the molds out of the refrigerator and turns the aspic out onto salad plates. The firm shape of each aspic bears the imprint of the mold.

We are in the mold of the world, but God Almighty puts us into fire until we melt, then he pours us into the mold of Christ. We meet the temptations of the world by refusing to be

63

conformed to it; we yield ourselves to God so that He may make us like Christ.

THE BATTLESHIP, MISSOURI

A few years ago, the great battleship Missouri was stuck on a sand bar in the harbor of Hampton Roads. *Time,* reporting the incident, said that the Navy's face was red. And well it should have been, for some navigator had defied the evidence of charts of the harbor and had run the ship onto a sand bar.

Many Christians know what it is to be perched on a reef while the tides of life pass them by. They wonder how they got there and how they can get back into the channel. God is willing to refloat any man's life if the man will confess his own inability and ask for the leading of the Lord.

THE BAVARIAN WOOD-CARVER

A Bavarian wood-carver found a piece of wood in the mouth of a sack of grain. The wood was exactly the same color as the grain. The man carved imitation grains of wheat on the wood until he had a small handful of them. He mixed them with real grain and defied his friends to tell them apart. The wood-carver had performed his work so well that he, himself, was not able to tell the natural from the artificial. Ultimately, the only way to tell the two apart was to put them in water for a day or two. The natural grains sprouted. The carved ones remained exactly what they were—dead imitations.

God has created life within the hearts of those who have been born again. It may be possible for men to imitate the life of the Christian by copying some of his ways and echoing some of his words, but in the long run, the difference between the two shall be made manifest by the gaze of God who can tell the difference between the real and the false. In the meantime, we who are Christians must be "careful to maintain good works" (TITUS 3:8).

THE BROKEN TOY

One rainy day, two small children whiled away the hours by playing with a Noah's Ark. They pleaded to float their ark in the bathtub, and permission was reluctantly given. From the next room the mother could hear the conversation of the children; as they decided to pull the plug and let the waters abate on the face of the earth while the ark came to rest upon the Mt. Ararat of a sponge.

"What did they do after that?" asked small sister.

"They offered a sacrifice," replied the brother who knew his Bible stories.

"Well, what shall we sacrifice?" asked the little girl.

There was silence for a moment as the children poured the little wooden animals out on the rug, and then the boy answered, "Here is a camel with a broken leg. We can offer this up in sacrifice."

Thousands of Christians give offerings of the same nature as the children's broken toy. If it be applied to the unsaved, the analogy lies in the fact that the Lord cannot receive the offering of their "good works" which are not good in His sight. If it be applied to believers, the Lord will judge them for their lives after they are saved. "I beseech you therefore, brethren, by the mercies of God, that ye present your bodies a living sacrifice, holy, acceptable unto God, which is your reasonable service" (ROMANS 12:1).

THE BURMA SOLDIER

During the Burma campaign a soldier was forced to live month after month in the rotting jungles. He went from foxhole to foxhole, underwent the torments of the tropics, was blinded by the sweat of his labor. As he slogged his way forward, he dreamed of a white cottage with a garden path running through the flowers and his love standing at the door. When the turn of the battle called forth supreme effort, the etching of his dream was more sharply drawn, and from this source of his life he drew the morale for his daily fight. "If ye then be risen with Christ, seek those things which are above, where Christ sitteth on the right hand of God. Set your affection on things above, not on things on the earth. For ye are dead, and your life is hid with Christ in God" (COLOSSIANS 3:1-3).

DR. ALEXIS CARREL

When he was only a boy, French physician Alexis Carrel, Nobel Prize winner and one-time head of the Rockefeller Institute in New York, determined that he was going to be a surgeon. At a very early age he began to prepare his hands for the flexibility and suppleness necessary to perform delicate operations. One means was to secure the cover of a matchbox, place it over the two smallest fingers of either hand, and with a needle and suture, to stitch the edges of cigarette paper together. Then he tied a fine knot in the suture to finish off the "operation"—all this in the narrow confines of that box top. As a surgeon he later amazed the medical world with his manipulative skill in the narrow recesses of the human body. Dr. Carrel's head was in complete mastery of his fingers.

In the domain of the spiritual life we are frequently awkward because we have not allowed the Head, the Lord Jesus, to control our coordination and to teach us the possibilities of complete domination by our Lord. In the Word He has set before us the possibility of bringing into capitivity every thought to the obedience of Christ. The world will never look at clumsy handlers of the problems of life, but will stop in some awe before the life that has trained itself to a skillful proficiency in the craft of Christian living. Men did not admire Carrel's fingers, they admired his head; men will not admire the man, but the Lord Jesus when they see your good works. Our Lord Himself has said that such living would cause men to glorify the Father which is in Heaven.

THE ELECTRIC LIGHT BULB

An electric light bulb may be screwed into the socket and the current turned on, but if there is no filament in the bulb, there will be no light.

A human being may have the outward form of a Christian, a professing Christian, but only by the miracle of the new birth, the creation within of the new man by the touch of God, can the light of Christ shine in any life. Some obstruction may cause the current to be cut so that there is but a tiny glow on the filament, but it is still capable of lighting up with full power. The presence of the Lord Jesus Christ is what makes a Christian.

FALLING OUT OF BED

A little boy constantly fell out of bed. No matter what his parents did, the boy could not sleep without rolling out of bed. An uncle came to visit, and in the middle of the night the usual thump and cry was heard. In the morning, the uncle teased the boy and asked him why he fell out so frequently. The little boy thought a moment and then replied, "I don't know, Uncle, unless it is that I stay too close to the place where I get in."

Certainly, this is the valid explanation of the fall of many Christians. They have come to the place where they have believed in all sincerity that they are lost sinners and that Jesus Christ took their place on the cross to bear the weight of the wrath that was due on account of their sin. They have been seen of God as being in Christ and so have passed out of death into life. The tragedy is that they seem to remain in that same spiritual condition so that no one can really know whether they have been born again or not.

IN HIS FIRST UNIFORM

The first time a recruit of the United States Marines walks out in his uniform, he pulls himself a little taller. From the Halls of Montezuma to the shores of Tripoli the cloud of witnesses moves before him. The splendor of names fill his memory—Guadalcanal, Saipan, Okinawa; he knows he belongs to a proud first-rate outfit.

When God tells us we are compassed about with a great cloud of witnesses (HEBREWS 12:1), we must not think that our departed loved ones are watching us—conscious of our secrets and our failures—for the next logical idea would be to pray to them. The cloud of witnesses is real, yet invisible. The Christian may be sneered at by little minds and sinful hearts, but he holds himself straight. Abel is whispering in his ear; Enoch is walking before him; his Father Abraham is setting an example of faith; he knows he marches to join that host.

IRRIGATION

Irrigation is necessary in many parts of our country, because ordinary rainfall is either seasonal or insufficient for the needs of the land. If the channels are not kept open the land will revert to its arid condition and the crops will fail. From those great valleys, teeming populations of the past drew their life from the rich soil, but today, the valley, like the Euphrates and the Tigris, are half desert, half lands of low yield. Archaeologists can trace for you the system of canals that carried water to the far fields in ancient times. The dams were allowed to fall into disrepair; the channels became filled with silt; dryness and the death followed the breaking down of the flooding system.

The situation is similar in the hearts of believers. They must lay bare their hearts before the examining gaze of the Holy Spirit, so that He may flush out the debris that has clogged the channels of living and bring the smooth flow of love to its highest level.

THE KING'S SHILLING

For generations recruiters for the armed forces of Great Britain have handed a shilling to the man who joined up. Once he has accepted the King's shilling, the recruit is considered "in": he is subject to military or naval discipline; he is dependent upon the government for support. He has accepted the King's image on the shilling, and he is, henceforth, the king's man. The nation will not hold him guiltless if he takes the king's shilling in vain.

So it is with those who receive the Lord Jesus Christ as their Saviour. They are "renewed in knowledge after the image of him that created [them]" (COLOSSIANS 3:10). Having taken the Lord and been given His invisible image, they belong to the Lord. They may expect Him to care for them in all things and may expect to be subject to His discipline. ". . . the Lord will not hold him guiltless that taketh his name in vain" (EXODUS 20:7).

THE MEXICAN SPIDER

A certain kind of Mexican spider does not spin a web to catch insects as our spiders do, it lives on tiny edibles that grow on the bottom of shallow streams. The spider blows a bubble of air around itself, then goes down under the water and feeds at the bottom of the stream. When he has exhausted the oxygen in his bubble, he lets go of the pebbles, and the air carries him to the surface where the bubble breaks. Another bubble forms, and down he goes once more.

Since he has been born again, the Christian's very breadth of life is of an atmosphere that is not of this world. He must indeed work and live and find his pleasure in the midst of a deep flowing stream that is at odds with the very life principle that is within him. But God has viewed him as being in Christ, and as we move out into the world system that knows not God this is our protection. We are here in the world system because we have been sent here by Christ. This is the sphere of our present activity. This is where He has placed us.

NOISE

Records, kept for a year before and a year after the installation of sound-absorbent walls in the offices of a large insurance company, showed that the decrease in noise resulted in a decrease in errors that amounted to 29 per cent by typists and 52 per cent in the work of calculating machine operators.

Many verses in the Bible call the Christian to quietness and stillness with God. The frenzied rush of life must be stilled if we are to get what God wants us to have. The percentage of errors in life will decrease if we learn to "be still, and know" our God (PSALMS 46:10). ". . . in quietness and in confidence shall be your strength . . ." (ISAIAH 30:15).

THE ORCHESTRA CONDUCTOR

It was long past midnight; my elder son and I had talked for hours. The conversation turned to music, to the Boston Symphony Orchestra, to the role of the artist as distinguished from the role of the composer. I wrote down one paragraph from our conversation, for I saw its immediate importance as a parallel for every Christian life.

My son said, "A man like Koussevitsky must be the servant of his art. He must be nothing but the medium between the composer and the people. He himself must be completely subjected to what the composer wrote into the score of his composition. Any deviation or shortcoming from this subjection is adulteration of the music. The conductor is nothing but a channel."

Apply this to yourself as a professing Christian in any walk of life—minister, banker, lawyer, nurse, soldier, sailor, student, homemaker, whatever you may be. Then say of yourself, "A man like myself must be the servant of my faith. I must be nothing but the medium between the Lord and the people I meet in Christian witness. I must be completely subjected to what the Lord wrote into His revelation; any deviation or shortcoming from this subjection to His Lordship is an adulteration of the Christian life. The Christian is nothing but a channel."

REMINDERS

No matter where he traveled, a sailor from Colorado kept his watch on mountain standard time in order to remember home. When the watch said five A.M. he knew his father was milking the cows; in the evening at seven-thirty he knew the family sat around the table, thanking God for what was on it and asking Him to watch over the absent son.

"It's thinkin' about those things that makes me want to fight when the goin' gets tough. I can find out what time it is where I am easy enough; what I want to know is what time it is in Colorado."

So the Lord, our Father, has surrounded us with innumerable reminders of what is going on in heaven. It's easy enough to see what is going on on earth. A flower can remind us of God's power—a baby of God's holiness, some great need of Christ's intercession for us. Set your affection on things above.

THE SCOTCH SHEPHERD DOG

If a Scotch shepherd dog is left to guard his master's coat, he will not leave it until the master returns. Nothing can draw him from the task to which he was appointed. If a rabbit runs by, almost under his nose, he will not move. A deer may break from a copse and cross the glen, so close that the dog could easily bring him down as prey; the dog will not move. If the dog had the mind of some Christians, he might reason, "Oh, my master was unaware that a rabbit would pass or a very valuable deer. Surely, he expects me to use my intelligence and leave my appointed job to run after the game."

Many Christians run away from the thing to which they have been appointed. The lure of the great and the showy draws them away from the steady devotion to their humble appointed task.

THE STOLEN MONEY

Henry Trotter, a railway worker of Marshalltown, Iowa, reported to police that his life's savings of $14,000 had been stolen. The money, which he had been accumulating for many years had been kept locked in a bureau drawer in an unused bedroom. Imagine the consternation of this worker when he discovered that all the penny-pinching and years of labor had resulted in absolutely nothing.

So it will be with many Christians who build upon one foundation of wood, hay and stubble. Their works shall be burned away and they will be saved so as by fire (I CORINTHIANS 3:11-15). It behooves us to lay up our treasures in heaven.

TOPPLED TREES

One autumn, a great hurricane ripped across the middle Atlantic states and left a swath of toppled trees. A great pine tree, almost a hundred feet tall, blew over on the roof of my kitchen, ripped a hole four by five feet in the roof and brought a stream of water into the house. When the storm subsided, I went out and examined the root structure of the great pine and was amazed to see how shallow it was. Although it had spread out in a large circumference, seeking its food from far surfaces, it had no taproot to anchor it; the storm had bent it over with ease. As I drove through the countryside during the days after the storm, studying the effects of the wind, I saw hundreds of such trees, similarly uprooted. I decided to replace the fallen monarch, not with another pine, but with a tree that would develop a strong taproot. Although I would not live to see it, the years would strengthen and beautify the tree so it would stand and withstand the gales of the future.

People are like trees in many ways. Some are brittle and snap with easy pressure; some bow before the winds of adversity; some stand the severest tempest and live through the ages, like the cedars of Lebanon and the oaks of Mamre. So should the Christian be able to stand. If the dry rot of sin is not infecting the heart, the Christian should be able to withstand any pressures that life may bring.

TWO RUSSIAN FORTUNES

During the Russian Revolution, a certain nobleman had all of his goods seized by the Bolsheviks. An Englishman living in Russia befriended him, took him and his family to his own home, provided all expenses and gave him the necessary money to leave the country. Some time later the Englishman returned to London and found himself a wealthy man. The Russian friend had not only accounted for every penny, he had also invested so wisely that a fortune had amassed in the Englishman's account.

At the same time, another Englishman in Russia refused to deprive himself; he helped no one, but worked hard to gather a fortune in rubles—only to see it valueless as straw. Forced to flee, he arrived in London penniless and so he remained. Both of these men had been diligent: the latter in a selfish cause, the former in an unselfish one.

The Christian must exercise his zeal to provide himself with a fortune in Heaven that cannot be corrupted; he must give of himself instead of acquiring an earthly currency that has no exchange value at heaven's frontier.

CHRISTIANS, CARNAL

THE PERFUME BOTTLE

A man, visiting Paris, bought a bottle of perfume and brought it into the United States under his customs deduction. The perfume was very expensive and in a beautiful bottle. His wife was delighted and used it freely. Even after the perfume was used up she kept the bottle on her boudoir table to impress friends. They came into her room and exclaimed, "Oh, how wonderful—such-and-such a perfume." A function turned up and the woman longed for some of the expensive scent, but the bottle was empty, so she put a handkerchief into the bottle and closed it. Enough of the perfume was left to give a faint fragrance to the handkerchief but after that it was done. Enough odor remained around the bottle however to elicit, "Oh, that was such-and-such," from friends.

Many people in our churches are like that. As far as they are concerned, their bottle is empty. They have no life and fragrance of Christ.

I told the story that way once, and at the close of the meeting, as I walked down the street to my hotel, I overtook three people who had attended the church service. One of them was saying, "I liked the story he told about the perfume bottle because it reminded me of a very expensive perfume that Frank brought me from Paris. It is a beautiful bottle. But I have never broken the seal. It sits right there on my dresser and the light shines through it. It is a beautiful amber."

When I broke into the conversation, they recognized me and laughed that I had overheard them. I said, "Don't you see that the perfume was given to you for use? And what an illustration that is. Too many Christians have been given so much, yet they keep it tightly sealed in themselves. No one passing near would know for a moment that they have the life of God in them, for not the tiniest particle of the essence is allowed to come forth. The wonderful thing about God's perfume is that as fast as we waft it forth He keeps filling the bottle; its fragrance may change and grow, but it is more glorious every time we send it forth. That is God's way." "Now thanks be unto God, which always causeth us to triumph in Christ, and maketh manifest the savour of his knowledge by us in every place" (II CORINTHIANS 2:14).

WORLDLINESS

A young minister, starting off in his first parish, had an elderly woman warn him against a woman in the congregation. He was not to entrust this woman with any spiritual task, because according to the gossip, she was "worldly." The pastor had already been apprised of the true situation and defended the accused woman. His informant persisted: the woman in question danced, drank cocktails, smoked and used too much makeup. The pastor knew his Scripture; he answered, "On the contrary, you have not told me one item that would make me think she is worldly. She is what the Scripture calls 'carnal'; you are the one who is worldly." The aghast woman protested that she did not do this, she did not do that; she abstained from this, she avoided that. The minister replied, "Nevertheless, you are the worldly one. All the things you mentioned against her are in the realm of the flesh. You are worldly because you are the one who wishes power and who loves display. You want to be the head of organizations. You delight in show and position. When the various circles met in different homes, the other women finally returned to the church for the meetings because none of them could keep up with you. When the women went to your house, you made an ostentatious show of your linen, your china, your crystal. As you have no children, you have more income to spend on other things. Your conversation concerned the cloth and napkins you bought in the Azores, the ornaments from Dresden, the antiques from a little shop in England. Your supposed coat of arms is framed in a prominent place on your wall; every time anyone remarked on any of your heirlooms you explained from which ancestor it had come and described, without understatement, his particular honors in life."

For the average Christian there is widespread confusion as to what constitutes worldliness and what constitutes carnality.

WORLD MAPS

You can't put a round world on a flat map. Mercator's projection distorts the polar regions in order to get more accuracy near the equator. Other projections have other distortions; all are faulty in some manner. Most important in modern warfare is the azimuthal projection that shows the shortest lines between two points, it shows the shortest way from New York to China as directly over the North Pole. On all such maps the distortion increases geometrically away from the point of projection (center) until the geographical shapes near the edge of the map become almost unrecognizable.

In spiritual matters the map of life for the unsaved man or the carnal Christian is projected on the center of self; everything away from self is distorted. Only when the constraining love of Christ (II CORINTHIANS 5:14) moves us from the center of self to the new sphere of Christ can we bring all things into relationship with reality. The Greek word of separate in I ROMANS 1 is *aphorizo;* note that our word "horizon" is kin to it. When we are separated unto God, we are moved from the distorted horizon around the center of self to the perfect horizon center of Christ.

CHRISTIAN SERVICE

THE FELLOW WHOM A JOB HAS

Charles F. Kettering of General Motors once said that he didn't want any fellow "who has a job working for me." Kettering wanted a fellow whom a job has. The job must get the fellow, not the fellow get the job. That job should get hold of this young man so hard that no matter where he is the job has got him for keeps. That job should have him in its clutches when he goes to bed at night. In the morning, that same job should be sitting on the foot of his bed telling him it's time to get up and go to work. When a job gets a fellow that way, he'll amount to something.

If the world's industrial leaders desire this kind of service from those who are their lieutenants, what kind of service does our Lord have the right to demand of us? We are to be "instant in season, out of season . . ." (II TIMOTHY 4:2); we are to be "in diligence not slothful, fervent in spirit, serving the Lord" (ROMANS 12:11, RV). When we have done all those things that are commanded, we must say, "We are unprofitable servants: we have done that which was our duty to do" (LUKE 17:10). But we serve the best Master man ever had; living with Him will make our work for Him live.

CITIZENSHIP

THE DRUNKEN DRIVER

Many years ago, parked on the street of a large city on the West Coast, I witnessed an accident just a few yards away. A car wove crazily through traffic and collided head-on with another car. The driver, obviously drunk, was pushed from his seat by a companion who took the wheel, and awaited the arrival of a policeman. The pseudo-driver complained bitterly to the policeman that the driver of the wrecked car was at fault. I spoke up immediately, showed where I had been seated, and told how the exchange of drivers was effected. I identified the drunken man as the actual driver at the time of the accident. There was a growl from the crowd that had gathered: Why should I interfere, they wanted to know. I answered, "There is a matter of right and wrong here. This good driver is being accused of bad driving; actually, the fault is this drunk's. I was not twenty feet away when the other man took his place and removed him from behind the wheel. If this man perjures himself in court, by swearing that he was driving, I will come from Philadelphia to testify against him, and I will identify this drunken driver by the scar on his cheek." The policeman took my card; I gave my name and address to the innocent victim. As I returned to my own car, bystanders cursed me. I don't know why they were against the law. Perhaps they figured that the penalty would be less for the innocent driver than for the drunk; perhaps they knew the latter personally. Whatever caused their attitude, they were violating every principle of righteousness—human or divine—they were failing to hold fast to that which is good. They were willing to

78

be party to perjury, the friend of wrong, willing to see an innocent man condemned. They were not willing to stand for truth, honesty and right.

A Christian must stand up and be counted wherever there is a moral issue. If it is necessary, a Christian must be willing to lose two or three days' pay to go to court to testify on the side of truth. A Christian must be willing to take the sneers of the world of evil, which hates those who stand for righteousness without regard for cost.

COMPASSION

THE DRAB TYPIST

One evening in New York, I said to a group, "You who have any place of leadership, turn your smile on the little underlings who will never have a place of leadership." A few weeks later I was reminded of my words by a young woman who was private secretary to the president of a large commercial firm. A brilliant personality, she had risen to her privileged and highly-paid place by her rare gifts. The day after she heard me speak, she walked through her outer offices and saw a typist, whose sallowness of personality was due to a certain loneliness. The secretary invited her to lunch. The two girls lunched together, and the drab girl thanked the brilliant one at least a score of times for her kindness. During the next few weeks the private secretary greeted the typist, smiled at her, occasionally lunched with her.

The brilliant one said to me, "It is a trifle embarrassing. She looks at me like a dog at his master, and some of the other girls can't understand my interest in her." After a few weeks the drab girl came to the knowledge of Jesus Christ and the secretary said to me, "I don't think I have ever been happier than when she prayed with me and thanked the Lord Jesus for bringing me into her life, and for the salvation of her soul. "And now," she continued, "I try to smile at all the file clerks, and the lesser assistants, and say a cheery word to the porters and elevator operators. Some day I shall be able to follow up my gestures with a word for Christ."

We underestimate the number of lonely hearts that are in every neighborhood. If we have been blessed with robust vigor, we should turn our strength toward the feeble and the weak.

CONSCIENCE

THE SUNDIAL

The conscience may be likened to a sundial that is made for the sun, even as the conscience, rightly directed, reflects God's will. Suppose a sundial is consulted by moonlight—the dial may read ten o'clock, but it may be only two. By a candle or some other light, the dial may be made to tell any hour, at the whim of the one who holds the light.

Conscience, which man took from Satan, can be a safe guide only if it is turned toward God for His illumination. Once a man turns away his conscience from God and lets some other light shine upon it, his conscience is no longer reliable.

CONTENTMENT

THE AFRICAN PORTERS

A missionary told about getting a company of bearers to carry his goods through an African trail. They went along day after day, the missionary forcing them, because he was anxious to get to his destination. They were all at full stop one morning; the missionary impatiently said, "Why don't they get up and start?" The headman replied, "No, massa, they're not moving today. They all say they have to wait a day for their souls to catch up with their bodies."

A great many people in our country need to wait a while to let their souls catch up with their bodies. So many people are in movement, and too often the movement is that of a merry-go-round. It has jingle; it has noise; it has movement, but it never gets anywhere. Now they need to come and rest in the Lord and to know how the Lord is taking care of us.

BEING THE JONESES

I saw a cartoon recently that illustrates American suburbia —perhaps all of America. The cartoon showed one of those household tragedies where one mate was screaming at the other; the caption read, in effect, "You are not content with trying to keep up with the Joneses. You want to be the Joneses with whom everyone else is trying to keep up."

To such attitudes comes the Christian command: ". . . be content with such things as ye have . . ." (HEBREWS 13:5)

FIVE POUNDS

Lord Congleton overheard one of his servants say, "Oh! if I only had five pounds, I would be perfectly content." He thought the matter over and decided that he would like to see someone "perfectly content," so he walked into the kitchen, and handed the woman a five-pound note (then about $25.00). She thanked him profusely. He left the kitchen, but paused outside the door for a moment. As soon as she thought he was out of earshot, the woman complained bitterly, "Why on earth didn't I say ten pounds?"

The human heart can never find contentment in the things of this earth. We are told by God to be content if we have the necessities of life, and to be content with such things as we have. Paul learned to be content, regardless of the state he was in. It is still true that "godliness with contentment is great gain" (I TIMOTHY 6:6).

NO TWO THINGS ALIKE

No two blades of grass are alike. No two grains of sand are alike. The invention of the microscope was able to confirm a fact that had been known in the sphere of the great to be true also in the sphere of the small. God never repeated Himself in his work. A photographer, who succeeded in photographing more than ten thousand snowflakes, found each one of different design and all were mathematically perfect.

God never made any two people alike. Although we have our varying personalities and diverse needs, complete satisfaction in all things is to be found in the heavenly Father. For our infinite needs we have an infinite Lord. Come just as you are; you will find that the One who made the blades of grass and the grains of sand will take you to Himself in a newness of reality that will give you perfect peace and satisfaction.

CONTENTMENT

SHEEP

A shepherd, who had spent many years with flocks on the hills of Scotland, asked me if I had ever seen a sheep eat while lying down. When I confessed that I had not, he told me that no one had ever seen a sheep eat in that position. "If a sheep is lying down," he continued, "there may be a lovely tuft of grass within an inch of her nose, but she will not eat it. She will scramble to her feet, lean over and eat the grass that was in easier reach before."

When the Lord, our Shepherd, makes us lie down in green pastures, we have so much, we just can't take any more; we are beside the still waters, we have slaked our thirst with the contentment that comes alone from Him.

CONVICTIONS

ERIC LIDDELL

In the summer of 1924 the young Scot, Eric Liddell, faced two great moments of his life: As a student of the ministry he was soon to be ordained; as an aspiring sprinter he was favored to bring glory to England by winning the 100-meter dash at the Olympic games in Paris.

When Liddell discovered that this event was scheduled for a Sunday afternoon, it was a crucial moment for him; he believed that it was not to the glory of God for him to compete on Sunday.

The young Scot made one major change in his daily round of study and athletic practice; he dropped his customary nightly discussion with his classmates. After the evening meal he left the dining hall, disappeared, and returned to his room hours later, tired and spent. His friends were perplexed, but he never told them where he went.

The whole world learned his secret, at the Olympics. Eric Liddell, received the Gold Medal as 400-meter champion.

Eric Liddell not only made a record for speed in the 400-meter class; he made a record of God's work in a man's heart, and a testimony to faithfulness. Eric Liddell was faithful in one thing, and the Lord honored him in another.

God needs men and women who are willing thus to be made strong for Him—to go forward without compromise. Even if you do not become a champion and receive the plaudits of the world, the day will come when you may stand on God's winners' platform and hear Him say: ". . . Well done, thou good and faithful servant: thou hast been faithful over a few things, I will make thee ruler over many things: enter thou into the joy of thy lord" (MATTHEW 25:21).

CULTS

THE PRACTICAL JOKE

Many years ago, when I was just in my teens, a group of friends and I decided to play a practical joke on some unthinking passersby. We went to a busy intersection and stared intently up in the air. One of us pointed, another said, loudly enough to be overheard by the passersby, "It is not." A third member argued, "It is so." One or two people stopped and began to look in the same direction we were looking and pointing. As our argument grew more heated, others stopped to gaze fixedly at the point our group discussed. One by one we slipped out of the crowd; we regathered a few yards down the street to watch the result of our strategem. By this time about fifteen people were looking and talking. One man who had left the group said to another, "I think it is a balloon." (Remember this was about 1915 or 1916). The crowd continued to change; as new passersby came along they joined the group, and those who had been staring longest left. Twenty minutes later several people were still looking upward; several had drawn off to the side and were leaning against a building, looking upward for something that was not there and never had been there.

That little incident is a good illustration of all the earth-born religions. People talk about having faith; they tell you to look in a direction where there is absolutely nothing. Some people are so desperately in need of seeing something that they will look till they are almost blind, yet they never catch a glimpse of anything real. Their persistence in looking for something that does not exist reduces their vision to see the truth, which they really do not want to find.

DEATH

THE DYING SHEPHERD

A Scottish story tells of a fearful old man who lay dying. The minister, an understanding man, asked him if he had not been a shepherd. The old man replied that he had watched the sheep many a day. "And," asked the minister, "did you never stand on the hillside and watch the wind drive a cloud across the valley?" "Many a time," said the old man. "And when the shadow of that cloud came racing along the heather, coming toward you and your flock, were you afraid?" The old man drew himself up on his elbow and cried, "Afraid of a shadow? Jamie has covenanter's blood in his veins, and he has never been afraid of anything." And then the wonder of the passage broke upon him as the minister read, "Yea, though I walk through the valley of the *shadow* of death, I will fear no evil."

It is only the shadow of death that can touch the believer. The grim reality of death laid hold upon our Shepherd, as it must one day lay hold upon those who are not His sheep, but the shadow of death is all that can ever touch the one to whom He has given life eternal.

HOME FROM THE ARMED FORCES

An aged mother talks constantly about the return of her son who is in the armed forces. "When John comes, he will take me riding." "When John comes, he will dig the garden." "When John comes, he will fix that shelf." "When John comes, he. . . ." "When John comes, he . . ." One day there is a step on the stair; the door opens and the delighted mother cries out, "John, you. . . ." Why does she change the pronoun? The answer, of course, is that John has come in; and she is no longer speaking of an absent one; he is one who is there in her presence.

With this in mind let us read the twenty-third Psalm. "The Lord is my shepherd, I shall not want; He maketh me to lie down in green pastures: he leadeth me beside the still waters. He restoreth my soul: he leadeth me in the paths of righteousness for his name's sake." "*He . . . he . . . he. . . .*"

But let death approach us and see the marvelous change. "Yea, though I walk through the valley of the shadow of death, I will fear no evil: for thou art with me; thy rod and thy staff they comfort me." "*Thou . . . thy . . . thy. . . .*"

It is not alone that He is with me, or that His rod and staff shall comfort me in that hour. That would indeed be comfort, but the comfort of an absent Lord is somewhat like the comfort given by the photograph of a loved one in comparison with the warm embrace of one that is loved. So it is when death comes, there shall be no more parting. Then shall we speak no more of the Lord as distant on the throne of Heaven. Then the door of Heaven has swung open. Then He has moved to the bedside of the dying one.

THE MURALS OF PUVIS DE CHAVANNES

In Boston for a few hours, I went to the public library to look once again at the wonderful mural paintings there. Some of Puvis de Chavannes' most wonderful work is there. One of his paintings typifies modern invention and intercommunication; wires are stretched through his picture, indicating the telegraph; two beautiful figures painted with the thrill of speed vivifying them, hasten with their messages. One is all in white, bearing an olive branch—message of good tidings. The other is in black; the hand that is not guided by the wire covers the face of the angel messenger of death.

Unhappy the home this Resurrection Day that does not have the Lord Jesus there to take the hand away from the face of death and let us see that it is no longer a grim and dread messenger. He has destroyed its power forever. He lives who once was dead.

DISCIPLINE OF CHILDREN

THE HOLE IN THE FENCE

A father told his son the story of the lost sheep: it found the hole in the fence and crawled through—how glad it was to get away—it wandered so far it couldn't find its way back. Then he told the boy about the wolf that chased the sheep, and of the shepherd who came and found the sheep and carried it back home. The little boy had only one question: "Did they fix the hole in the fence?"

Preventive care for a child is far more important than work among juvenile delinquents. The only proper way to fix the hole in the fence is to lead the child to a knowledge of his own sinfulness and his need of the Lord Jesus Christ.

THE MISSING PENNY

One day we took a street car out to the Cleveland, Ohio, airport. Two girls, of four and five, got on at a kindergarten and got off again near their home. The fare for school children was a penny. One little girl put her penny in the conductor's box; the other, standing on tiptoe, made a movement as though she were putting the penny in. The fingers opened, but there was no rattle. The hand was empty. The conductor asked her where her penny was. First she said that she lost it; then that her mother had not given her one. He scolded her severely, and, of course, let her off; she ran away with a gesture of contempt. When the car had started once more, the conductor said, "Some mothers are terrible. Every day we have children who are taught to lie, and mothers are surprised that they grow up wrong."

We agree that too much attention cannot be paid to little things, but Christian parents should certainly be meticulous in teaching their children what we might call the pagan virtues—virtues which even the unsaved expect to have.

OBEYING A FIVE-YEAR-OLD

In a large hotel, I heard a mother ask her five-year-old child if she might leave the table in order to go and see someone across the room. She explained that she would be back in a moment. The child answered with a blatant, "No." The mother asked pleadingly two or three times more, and the child said, "No, if you go, I'll not eat my meal at all today." The mother sat there helpless; by her own lack of discipline she had created a monster who now ruled her.

Prayerful discipline of children in a biblically stern fashion is one of the most important Christian doctrines. It is included in the commandment, "Honor thy father and thy mother." Any parent who fails to enforce this commandment by disciplining his children is guilty of definite sin against God. Christian parents should see to it that the wills of their children are brought into subjection to the parents' will on all matters where it is right to have such discipline. The wills should be guided to self-choice of the right wherever possible, but if the child will not accept the right with his own will, he should be forced to accept it prayerfully, and if necessary with the utmost chastisement. "He that spareth his rod, hateth his son . . ." (PROVERBS 13:24). This is the definite Word of God, and its application by parents is an act of believing faith.

THE SCREAMING CHILD

An item in the *New York Times* reported a court case of a mother who brought a nine-year-old son into Juvenile Court; the boy screamed, stamped on the floor and pounded with his fists. The court psychiatrist said, "It is sheer blackmail. He screams to blackmail his mother. When he gets his own way, he stops screaming. He has been heard to tell his younger brother to scream for what he wants. Now the younger boy has become a kind of deputy screamer." The boy was perfectly normal at school and only screamed for his mother. The psychiatrist said, "This is an extreme case of individualism, and the symptoms are a pathological manifestation."

These are long words for what the Bible would call an outburst of the "old Adam." If the child had been spanked when he was a baby and refused his own way, he would not have grown up to blackmail his mother. If the first time the child had ever screamed, he had had a sound application of the "board of education to the seat of knowledge" the screaming would not have been repeated. The Bible says, "Train up a child in the way he should go: and when he is old, he will not depart from it" (PROVERBS 22:6).

DISCIPLINE OF GOD

DISCIPLINE OF GOD

THE ARM AMPUTATION

One of my dearest friends, a man of my own age, lost his left arm at the shoulder when he was only seven years old. Until he was twelve, he cried himself to sleep every night. It was hard to regard this amputation as the good, well-pleasing and perfect will of God. Then he began to conquer his handicap. By tucking a longhandled hoe under his armpit, he learned to hoe as many rows as his brothers; and he didn't get as tired as they did hoeing, for in using two arms they overworked their wrists. Later, he sold life insurance and was a success. He learned to play handball, soon beat all comers, and held the national championship for many years. One day he learned that a thirteen-year-old boy had just gone through the same amputation. The boy had no will to live, and his condition was rapidly worsening. My friend took his scrapbook and went to the hospital to see the boy. Nothing was said about the arm, but the boy looked at the various newspaper clippings that recounted the one-armed champion's prowess at golf, hunting and fishing. Finally, he asked if it were really true. My friend removed his shirt and showed his armless shoulder. The boy sighed deeply and soon fell asleep. Three days later he was on the mend, and soon after left the hospital. My friend has spent his life with insurance, athletics and Christian work among young people, in that ascending order of importance; he has testified many times to his satisfaction with life and with the will of God for him. It was not well-pleasing at first, to be the town cripple, but the compensations were so great that he soon learned that God's way was the best way for him, and he would not have it any other way.

Whenever we recognize the rights of God and trust in the Lord Jesus Christ as Saviour, He takes up this work of discipline in order to give us His best.

DISCRIMINATION BETWEEN GOOD AND EVIL

POISON AND CLEAR WATER

There are poisons that look like crystal spring water. A glass of such poison, placed next to a glass of clear water will fool the eye; the two look exactly alike. But one has death in it, the other life. You have to discover by other means than drinking the true nature of the two liquids.

In the same way there are many things in life that are deadly, but have the seeming appearance of goodness. This is why, when you must make a choice about some pleasure, amusement, or action, you must not come to your decision on the basis of appearances.

POUTING BABY

In a hotel, I watched a mother tell her child to come inside. The child, about two or three years old, rebelled with no uncertain terms and gestures. The mother said nothing and started toward the stairs. The child came inside and stamped her feet. The mother continued on upstairs and out of sight. The crying child went to the foot of the stairs, and started slowly up, stopping occasionally to stamp and cry louder. The mother was nowhere to be seen. I followed the child; eventually she reached the top of the stairs, turned down the hall and entered a room.

The scene comes back to me again and again as an illustration of how so many of God's children act with Him. He gives His commands, and the Holy Spirit has told us that they are not grievous. Yet we stamp our petulant way, step by step, drawing back from what is certainly better than our own choice, and ultimately we make a little progress.

READING THE NEWSPAPER

I know a man who spends considerable time each day reading the newspaper. He can tell you the doings of all the comic-strip characters and the standing of all the great baseball teams. Ask him about the tension between China and Russia, or what is being done to help the emerging peoples of Africa, and you will draw an absolute blank. He is simply not interested. He is wise to that which is ephemeral, but ignorant of any of the great issues that will affect his life and the life of his children.

It is the desire of God that we grow in our knowledge of all that is good, and that we remain naïve concerning that which is evil. We must develop a Christian life that excludes the worthless and builds the worthwhile.

ETERNAL LIFE

DEAD LEAVES

Shortly after the Armistice of World War I, I visited the battlefields of Belgium. In the first year of the war the area around the city of Mons was the scene of the great British retreat; in the last year of the war it was the scene of the greater German retreat. For miles to the west of the city the roads were lined with artillery, tanks, trucks and other material of war which the Germans had abandoned in their hasty flight.

It was a lovely day in spring; the sun was shining; not a breath of wind was blowing. As I walked along examining the German war material, I noticed that leaves were falling from the great trees that arched above the road. I brushed at a leaf that had blown against my breast; it became caught in the belt of my uniform. As I picked it out I pressed it in my fingers, and it disintegrated. I looked up curiously and saw several other leaves falling from the trees. It was not autumn. There was no wind to blow them off. These were the leaves that had outlived the winds of autumn and the frosts of winter.

Now they were falling, seemingly without cause. Then I realized that the most potent force of all was causing them to fall. It was spring; the sap was beginning to run; the buds were beginning to push from within. From down beneath the dark earth, the roots were taking life and sending it along trunk, branch and twig, until that life expelled every bit of deadness that remained from the previous year. It was, as a great Scottish preacher termed it, "the expulsive power of a new affection."

In the measure that we allow the new life of God to fill our

97

being, that life will naturally care for the question of what we do and how we act as Christians.

THE INSURANCE SALESMAN

An insurance salesman once told me that he had schooled himself to think constantly in terms of selling life insurance. When he met a man for the first time, he was alert for an opportunity to sell insurance. Even at a social function, a church service, a funeral or a wedding, he sought to form acquaintances in order to get new customers. He joined a lodge and took up golf, in order to meet men and approach them about life insurance. He spoke to the attendant at the gas station, to the clerk in the grocery store, to shoe salesmen, and to the tailor who made his suits. Consequently, he sold a lot of life insurance.

Paul had this same type of mind, but he pleaded with the lost to take eternal life insurance; and for those who knew Christ, his desire was that they might grow.

LIVE SOLDIERS

Imagine a battlefield with troops advancing under heavy fire. They flatten themselves to the ground and hold their prone position until the enemy artillery is silenced. Imagine further that all of the soldiers are either dead, or alive and unwounded. He that gets up and walks has life. Does that mean that life is given to the soldiers who get up and walk or that the soldiers who possess life manifest it by getting up and walking? It is obvious that the latter can be the only meaning.

This meaning is illustrated in the passage in the fourth gospel: "He that heareth my word, and believeth on him that sent me, hath everlasting life . . ." (JOHN 5:24). The hearing and believing are the marks of the existence of the new life of God implanted within the individual.

THE LOVERS

Think of a couple in love; it is autumn and they know they cannot be married until the end of the school year. Before long the young man says, "Darling, think! we will be married in just two hundred and fifty days!" The two delight in counting off the days: the two hundred and thirties, the two hundred and twenties; one hundred and ninety-nine days is a landmark. The numbers decrease, but slowly, oh! so slowly; it is the one hundred day mark. Ninety days, sixty days, thirty days, ten days, tomorrow! All true lovers know this loving groaning toward their day of hope, the consummation of their joy. This was the purpose of their falling in love, that they might be together, that they might be one.

When God planted eternal life within us, it was nothing less than the life of eternity that is to be lived in time, and we groan while we wait for its fulfillment.

ETERNAL SECURITY

BELONGINGNESS

A young pastor attending summer sessions at a State University heard a visiting lecturer of psychology speak of the importance of security in the normal development of a child. The professor said, "Security is that feeling of 'belongingness' which is based not on what one is, but on who one is." The child may be naughty, yet still enjoy the security of the parental home simply because he is a child of the parents.

How well that sentence illustrates our security in the heavenly family! We are saved because of what Jesus Christ is; we know it because of what He says. The fact that we feel secure is, of course, based not on what we are, but on who we are. The whole denial of the security of the believer by those who teach that a person may be lost after he is truly born again is based on self-works. Those who believe in the security of the believer are giving glory to the Lord. We are saved, and boasting is excluded. Is it not wonderful to know that "the peace that passeth all understanding" is based not on what we are, but on who we are? "We are the sons of God, therefore the world knoweth us not," but we can say, "Behold, what manner of love the Father hath bestowed upon us . . ." because He has made us the children of God (1 JOHN 3:1).

DUPLICATE BILLS

A cleaner and dier had to take his accounts home one night because his bookkeeper was ill. By mistake he sent out several hundred statements to people who had already received similar statements some weeks before. Some of his customers wrote or called, questioning their bills; they showed receipts that proved them paid. The cleaner apologized and explained his error. But to his amazement about one-third of the accounts were paid a second time. People were careless about their own bookkeeping and relied upon his honesty; they sent in their check a second time. The cleaner set up a system: he sent bills promptly on the first of each month, but the bills overlapped— each included work done over a period of about thirty-five days. If anyone complained his name was removed from the special list and correct bills were sent thereafter. But his list of those who paid double was a profitable one for him.

One day, however, four men came into the clubhouse after playing golf. One of them pulled an envelope out of his pocket and said, "I think so-and-so has a very poor bookkeeper. I think I paid that cleaning bill last month." Another man said, "I had exactly the same experience with him." A third man said, "So did I." The fourth man said, "I have been paying my bills as they came in, but I thought them rather steep." They all agreed that it looked rather crooked, and when more men came into the locker room and joined the conversation, they decided to turn the matter over to the Better Business Bureau. It was not long before an investigation brought up the indisputable evidence of the systematic practice of collecting accounts twice, and the man was sent to prison.

The man who holds that a believer may get out of the body of Christ, may undo the baptism of the Holy Spirit, and leave the identification with Christ on the cross, is, in reality, making out that God is a chiseler. Having collected the account in full from the Saviour, God now seeks to collect a second time on an account that He Himself once receipted in full by the resurrection of His Son from the dead. What God does is well done, and eternally done. The Christian has been identified with the death of Christ in the complete removal of his guilt and his consequent justification in the sight of God.

GIVING AWAY A SOUL

Martin Luther had a servant named Elizabeth, who, in a fit of displeasure, left without giving any notice. She subsequently became dangerously ill and asked Luther to visit her. He said, "Well, Elizabeth, what is the matter?" "I have given away my soul to Satan," she replied. "Elizabeth, listen to me," rejoined the man of God. "Suppose, while you lived in my house, you had sold and transferred all my children to a stranger. Would the sale and transfer have been lawful and binding?" "Oh, no, for I had no right to do that." "Very well, you had still less right to give your soul to the archenemy; it no more belongs to you than my children do. It is the exclusive property of the Lord Jesus Christ; He made it, and when lost, He redeemed it; it is His."

Anyone who believes that one who has been truly born of God can get out of relationship with God and be finally lost is blind to great sections of truth in the Word of God. They look at some experiences in life instead of at the Word of God; they judge the Word by what they see in life, rather than judging life by what they see in the Word.

SEALS

In modern times the use of the official seal is diminishing, but official documents are still marked with a seal. On a United States passport, the seal of the nation is crushed into the fabric of the paper so that it would be impossible to eradicate or alter it. Corporations still have seals, and these are affixed to legal documents. A notary has a seal that confirms the oath of an affidavit with that seal. In ancient times each man had his own seal and carried it with him at all times. Most people could not write, so the seal was affixed as a mark of the individual's responsibility. Today we know that the signature of an individual cannot be duplicated without chancing detection as forgery. The signature takes the place of the seal. If you add together everything that is confirmed by an official seal and a personal signature, you get the idea of the biblical meaning of the seal. ". . . grieve not the Holy Spirit of God, whereby ye are sealed unto the day of redemption" (EPHESIANS 4:30).

Salvation is not dependent upon the whim of an individual Christian, but upon the justifying work of God. The Holy Spirit is implanted once and for all; when the believer is placed in Christ by the Holy Spirit, the same lord—the blessed third person of the Godhead—puts the seal of certainty upon us and shuts us into Christ. We are not only saved, we are safe.

THE SPRING FRESHET

During the spring freshet an express train rode confidently through a flooded area even though the tracks were covered with water. The steel rails underneath accounted for the confidence of the engineer and the safety of the train.

No matter what flood covers the path of the believer, he can go forward with true courage. God has traced his way for him.

ETERNITY

MEMORY

As we grow older the years seem to pass much more quickly than in the days of our youth. A chemist offers an interesting formula to explain this. A child of eight remembers about four years back—one year, or 25 percent of the total. By the time the child is twelve he remembers eight years, and one year is only 12½ percent of the total. All through life the ratio continues to dwindle, in old age a single year represents only a small fraction of man's remembered time—it vanishes into the past at a rapid speed.

But with the child of God, who has entered the path of the justified ones, which shineth more and more unto the perfect day (PROVERBS 4:18), there is a reversal of the process. God has put eternity into the heart of the believer (ECCLESIASTES 3:11, RSV); time becomes relatively unimportant, its passage leaves no regrets, brings delight that the fullness of eternity approaches at such a rapid pace. But that swiftly passing time is to be redeemed (EPHESIANS 5:16), for the days are evil, and the Lord has entrusted us with time for His purposes.

FAITH

THE BROKEN BRIDGE

Faith is worthless in itself. If faith is not properly founded, it can lead to nothing other than disaster. One night cars sped along the main highway between Jackson and Vicksburg, Mississippi. The drivers had faith in their cars and in the bridges over the streams. They passed over some bridges at fifty or sixty miles per hour. Everything was lovely, the concrete spans stood firm over the rivers and bayous, and the cars went on their way. Suddenly, the twin taillights in front of a truck melted into the road and disappeared. The driver of the truck caught only a glimpse of a black gap in the concrete before he too plunged into the stream below. Breaking glass, he succeeded in freeing himself. He swam ashore, but before he could reach the highway, other cars zoomed smoothly up to the gap and vanished. Frantically, he tried to flag three others. Their drivers ignored the dripping, scarecrow figure and sped on into the void. Each time there was a single booming splash, sometimes followed by a few hoarse shouts and screams.

All the drivers had faith in a bridge that was out. There is only one bridge across the gulf of death. Christ has said, "No man cometh unto the Father, but by me" (JOHN 14:6). Woe to the man who attempts any other highway. His faith will carry him to a Christian eternity and not to heaven. Faith must have a proper foundation—Christ.

CAPTAIN OF THE GUARDS

It is said that Napoleon, while looking at some papers, let slip the bridle of his horse, which reared so that the Emperor

105

was in danger. A corporal of the grenadiers leaped forward and caught the bridle, bringing the horse under control. Napoleon saluted the corporal and said, "Thank you, Captain." "Of what company, Sire?" asked the corporal. "Of my guards," replied Napoleon. The young corporal picked up his musket, hurled it aside and walked across the field toward the Emperor's staff, tearing off his corporal's stripes as he went. When he took his place among the officers, they asked him what he was doing. He replied that he was a captain of the guards. "By whose order?" queried one of them. "The Emperor's order," he replied.

The incident may never have taken place, but the truth involved is supreme. God is ready to do a great deal for you, if you are ready to take Him at His word. A man of less faith might have picked up his musket, stepped back into the ranks and boasted for the rest of his life that Napoleon had called him captain. This describes the difference between the Christian of little faith who has a head knowledge of the position and titles which the Lord Jehovah has given each believer in Christ, and the Christian of applied faith, who takes God at His word and enters into the blessing.

HYSSOP

Botanists have not been able to agree on the identification of the plant, hyssop, that is mentioned in the Scriptures. It certainly has no relationship to the plant of the same name that has been domesticated in parts of our country. But a verse in Kings speaks of the wisdom of Solomon, who studied many things: "the hyssop that springeth out of the wall" (1 KINGS 4:33). I saw a plant that fulfills this description in Palestine, under interesting conditions. The first time I was in Jerusalem I was taken into the palace of the Grand Mufti and then into the Hall of the Sanhedrin, where few tourists ever penetrate. In this room is a window that looks down upon the wailing wall. At the foot of the wall, beating their heads slowly against it, were groups of Jewish rabbis, mostly from central Europe, and as they bowed forward they wailed—reciting the book of Lamentations over and over again.

Above their heads was the high expanse of wall, and from it grew the long trailing plant that was identified as the hyssop of the Bible. The remarkable thing about this particular plant is that it has a very short root—sometimes not over half an inch long. It can cling to the surface of the rock, drawing its sustenance from the air, from the wind, from the rain when there is any, from bits of dirt that fall from above or are borne on the wind to the meager roots, or from particles of nourishment in the rock itself. From that tiny root the plant flourishes, sometimes twelve to fourteen feet long. What a great plant to grow from such a slender root. Is it any wonder the plant can be such a symbol of faith?

Faith, in itself, is worthless, just as a root is worthless if it is unattached. If one grasps the branch and pulls the root away from the rock, the branch will soon die. Faith to be of any value, must cling to the rock. Faith, nothing in itself, becomes everything when it clings to the Lord Jesus Christ, the Rock of Ages.

"IF"

We constantly use the word "if" to express disbelief and to express belief. A young man might tell his parents that he was leaving the house to go to the drugstore, and his sister might look after him and say, "If you're going to the drugstore, I'm Joan of Arc." Later the mother of the household might start to leave the house, saying that she was going to the drug store, and the daughter might say, "Oh, if you're going to the drug store, bring me some tooth paste." In the one sentence she expresses doubt and disbelief; in the other sentence she expresses confidence and trust. The "if" in the text, "Now if we be dead with Christ, we believe that we shall also live with him" (ROMANS 6:8) is of the latter variety. Because we died with Christ, we believe that we shall also live with Him.

We possess that life, that new man, in and around and

overshadowing all of our thoughts and actions and being. That new man not only resembles Christ, but that new man within us is Christ Himself; for we are made partakers of the divine nature, and it is Christ in us which is our hope of glory.

PLOWING THE FIELD

When I first learned to plow, I got on the seat of the tractor, pulled the lever that dropped the plow into the ground, and started across the center of the field. After I had gone a few feet, I turned around to look at the furrow and was entranced by the rushing flow of topsoil along the plowshare—rich and black, the soil turned over. Then I turned back to look where I was going. When I had turned around the first time, I had unconsciously carried the wheel of the tractor with my movement and gotten away from the straight line. I pulled the tractor back into line and looked back at the furrow once more. Behind me, wavering across the field, the undulating line of my furrow revealed, as though etched in the earth, the wandering vision that I had had.

I soon learned that there was only one way to plow a straight furrow. When you are about to accelerate the tractor and pull the lever that sinks the plow into the ground, you must sight across the field at a distant point and keep the nose of the tractor squarely on the sighting point. You must not turn around to see how the furrow is coming; if you do, give only a hasty glance to see that all is well. Make certain that the fixed point is straight ahead, and bring the eye back to it. Now I can plow across a field and leave a furrow black and straight a quarter of a mile long; because I have learned that when the guide furrow is being laid in the field, the plowman must keep his eye on a fixed point, be it a tree, a barn, a distant hill, or some other point. Woe unto the man who plows his furrow looking aside, or looking behind, or looking at a crow that may fly across his line of vision.

If we are not to waver, we must have our eyes fixed steadfastly upon the Lord Jesus Christ.

"SUKIYAKI"

We received a telephone call from a Japanese girl, who had promised to cook up her native *sukiyaki*. One member of the household copied down a list of things to be bought—beef cut in a certain way, rice of a certain grade, and special vegetables —and told someone else to buy them. The Japanese girl would bring other ingredients which we could not purchase. Now this incident was an exercise in faith. The person who answered the phone believed the Japanese girl, and the other person believed her report of the conversation, so they acted on the information received. They spent money and brought home provisions, all on the basis of a few sentences in a telephone conversation.

This is exactly how we must believe God. He has given us promises, and how many and how wonderful they are! He tells us to commit ourselves to Him and believe Him, and He will work in our behalf. If you can believe what a voice says to you on the telephone, you can believe the Holy Spirit's pleading for control of your heart, where He wishes to spread a feast for you.

THROUGH THE WALL

True faith does not look at the obstacles, but rather at God. A dear old woman had a very beautiful faith; she was obedient, and obedience is the only beauty of faith. Some one said to her, "I believe that if you thought the Lord told you to jump through a stone wall, you would jump."

The old lady replied, "If the Lord told me to jump through a wall, it would be my business to jump, an' it would be His business to make the hole."

It would be impossible to define more simply the exact relationship between obedience and faith. Here is the essence of true faith. Although we do not understand every step of the way by which we must walk, we are fully persuaded that whatsoever God has promised, He is able to perform (ROMANS

109

4:21), and we leave all of the matters that are not comprehended to the mind and heart of the God whom we know to be the loving heavenly Father, through Jesus Christ, our Lord.

TRADING STAMPS

One member of our household was collecting trading stamps. For months we gave her all we got in trade, and various friends saved stamps for her. One day she exclaimed that she had 8,400 stamps, sufficient to get an electric blanket. She believed the announcement and the promise made in the premium book. She telephoned the trading-stamp company and was told that the redemption store was twenty miles from our house. She believed them, got into her car and drove the twenty miles, taking the stamps with her. Two hours later she returned, proudly bearing a large package; she opened it with great glee and triumphantly displayed the electric blanket. At every step of the transaction, she exercised faith.

The faith exercised in these household transactions is exactly the same kind of faith that we need to exercise in the Christian life. If you can believe what you read in a book of instructions about trading stamps, you can believe what you read in the Bible. If we take the trading stamps of faith to the place of redemption, we shall enter into the joy of the daily premium of full contentment.

FAITH AND WORKS

FIRE AND SMOKE

On an early May morning a man walked down the street. He was about two blocks from his house when he saw a large puff of smoke arise from his chimney. As well as though he had been standing in his living room he knew what had happened: the furnace had been allowed to die down several days before, and now a chilly spell had caused someone to light a fire in the fireplace. He was in a position to get a good view of both scenes; his physical eyes saw the smoke, his imagination saw the scene in the living room.

This is the exact difference between the epistles of Paul and James. In Paul's epistles, God tells how He looks upon the heart and justifies men by the true faith in Christ. James tells how an outward observer can see the effect of the inward faith. With Paul it is justification by faith; in James it is works by the justified which demonstrate faith. The one is a divine view, the other is human.

ROWING

You cannot row a boat properly without two oars. If you use only one, the boat will turn around and around and make no progress forward.

We must have both faith and works in the Christian life. Belief alone is not sufficient, for faith without works is dead. Works without faith will disturb the surface of the pond, but will not take the boat forward. The two must go together. Paul emphasizes faith in Romans for he is describing salvation from God's viewpoint. James emphasizes works in his epistle for he is describing salvation as men see it.

111

THE FALL

A SLIDING SCALE OF PENALTIES

We have adopted a sliding scale of penalties for what we consider a sliding scale of aggravation. We send a man to prison for ten days for stealing a dollar. He will get a sentence of ninety days for stealing ten dollars, a sentence of two years if he enters an open house and steals a moderate amount of jewelry. He will get five years if he pries open a window or a door, ten to twenty years if he steals ten thousand dollars worth of loot; if he has a blackjack or a revolver on his person at the time he commits his burglary, he may get a fifty-year sentence. No human court in the world would consider the death penalty against a man who stole some fruit from an orchard, not even if he had come with a truck and stolen all the fruit from all the trees in the orchard.

After one single act of disobedience on the part of Adam, God passed the death penalty against him, and against all of Adam's posterity to the remotest generation; not only was the sentence of condemnation passed, it was executed against every member of the human race.

RUNNING AWAY

The pathetic little figure carrying the valise down the front steps of his home could not have been more than five. Around the block he trudged, and around again. He kept going around and round until it got dark. A policeman stopped him. "What's the idea?" the officer asked. "Runnin' away," explained the boy, sadly. "Look," said the officer, "I've had my eye on you and you've been doing nothing but walk around the block. Do you call that running away?" "Well, what do you want me to do?" cried the boy tearfully, "I ain't allowed to cross the street alone."

Ever since Adam fell, mankind has been running away—but God has arranged it so that man cannot run away from his fears; man cannot run away from his frustrations; man cannot run away from sin and its fruits; man cannot run away from death; man cannot run away from himself. There is only one refuge—go back into the house to God, who awaits on the other side of the cross. That is the way in and the way to peace.

FALSE MOTIVES

THE OFFICE BET ON THE BABY

A young fellow who works in an investment house was impressed and very appreciative at the interest his business associates took in the news that his wife was going to have a baby. Every day one or more of them would drop around to his desk to inquire: "How's the wife doing?" "What does the doc say?" "Any news, old man?" "Many more days?" He did not know that every man in the office had a bet upon when the baby would arrive. The interest in his affairs really concerned a greedy desire to win the office bet.

It is possible for Christians to have false motives. This is why the Holy Spirit says, "Let love be without dissimulation" (ROMANS 12:9). The Greek says, "Let love be nonhypocritical."

FATHERHOOD OF GOD

"JUNIOR" THE IMPOSTOR

Police court annals tell the story of a young man who registered at one of the leading hotels in New York shortly after the turn of the century. He wrote down one of the most famous names in the United States, and the hotel clerk was very deferential to him. He had an air of being to the manner born. When packages began to arrive from several large furnishing houses and a jewelry store, the hotel received them and paid the accounts. After a few days the time for settling came; the young man brushed them off with excuses, which aroused the suspicion of the hotel management. They notified the police and a quiet investigation revealed the startling fact that the famous man whose name the young man had written on the register with "Junior" after it, did not have a son. The young man, confronted by the authorities, put on an air of bravado; he blustered that there was some mistake. Finally, it became necessary to take him down to Wall Street, to the office of a well-known millionaire. The latter walked into the room and looked at the culprit. He said simply, "I never laid eyes on this young man before in all my life." That sealed the doom of the impostor.

Multitudes of people who claim that God is their Father are just as guilty as was this young man. In order to address the Creator of the universe as Father, an individual must have accepted the truths which make this relationship possible.

FEAR

THE BOATMAN AND THE RAPIDS

Back in the middle thirties, before the railroad was finished between Changsha and Canton, in the south of China, I went overland through hundreds of miles of the most primitive country imaginable. At one place we had to take a boat in order to travel down a river treacherous with boiling rapids. Although I had been told that the passage would be dangerous, I also knew that Chinese traders went down river in their own boats, so I assumed that the stories were exaggerated. My doubts started as we neared the rapids. Two or three miles before we plunged into the swift current, the boatman took a chicken, a knife and a bowl to the prow of the boat. He placed the bowl beneath the prow, and we moved over to the shore to a place where stairs were built into the stones of a high cliff. We made fast and followed the boatman and his helpers; they climbed several hundred steps to an altar where they placed the sacrifice and burned joss sticks on the altar. From the little temple, we could look down the gorge at the turbulent waters, and I could understand the fear of the boatmen. Only after such preparation, would they commit themselves to the swirling waters below. We, of course, were trusting in the living God who had made the waters and who controls all things. Although it was impossible for me to communicate with these men, I was able to read, written large, their sense of the supernatural—their belief in powers outside themselves and greater than themselves; it was evident that they had great fear of death and of that which might follow death.

Even paganism is shot through with the sense of sin, and the consequent sense of the fear of death and the necessity of going out to face God.

THE BRIDE'S FIRST MEAL

Several years ago I married a young couple who were, and still are, very much in love with one another. They had met when they were thirteen and fourteen, had never looked at anyone else, and wouldn't today after all these years. They went away on their honeymoon and after a few weeks came home again. I saw them in church the next Sunday and greeted them with a little pleasantry. I asked the groom if his bride had burned the roast for the first dinner. They laughed, and she said, "Oh, I was afraid that I was going to. I had read so much about the bride being unable to cook that I decided that John was going to have the very best meal a bride could prepare for her husband. So I began about three o'clock. I got everything out and started to work. When I finally put things on to cook, I wanted everthing to turn out well, and I was afraid they wouldn't, and, of course, he had to be a little late, and I was so afraid things would be spoiled." I interrupted her and said, "You have said three times that you were afraid. Did you think that he was going to beat you?" She pouted and said, "Of course not." She looked at him with all the love of her heart in her eyes. "But," I persisted, "you said that you were afraid." She broke in, "You know what I mean." And of course I knew what she meant. Her fear was not fright; her fear was a great desire to serve the one to whom she had given herself entirely. In this case the fear of John was the beginning of good cooking.

Perhaps that will enable you to understand how the fear of the Lord is the beginning of wisdom. Some Christians do not understand the difference between fear of the Lord and fright of the Lord. If you have bowed before God and accepted the gift of His love and mercy through the Lord Jesus Christ, you need have no fright. Fear in the Bible sense is a godly thing, a wonderful thing, a lovely thing.

117

FELLOWSHIP IN CHRIST

BROKEN FELLOWSHIP

One evening I was the dinner guest of a young Canadian minister in Toronto, Ontario. Seldom have I seen a child brighter or better disciplined than his beautiful little daughter, Jean, aged three, who sat at the table in her high chair. During the meal, she did some childish thing that caused her father to admonish her. "Jean," he began in a firm tone. The child looked up and raised her hand, just as a policeman might lift a hand to halt traffic. "Don't speak, Daddy," the child said, as though she were in command of the situation, and then repeated it, "Don't speak." Thus quickly had her sense of guilt been aroused. Thus quickly she felt that she had offended against love. Thus quickly did her hand arise to ward off the separation of fellowship that might come even for a moment.

The child of God who has his sense of guilt aroused, who knows that he has offended against a holy God and a loving Father, who feels the chill that comes from broken fellowship, is in a situation quite different. We need not raise our hand to say to God, "Do not speak." For God has spoken and God has acted. His words of grace and His act are the act of the cross. If for a moment I am tempted to lift my hand as though to ward off some blow from Him, I hear Him say, "Put down your hand, child. Fear not. I did not spare My Son: I delivered Him up for you. You have all things in Him."

THE FALL ON THE DECK

A man, walking along the deck of a ship, might fall. His fall might hurt him, but it would not be the same as falling off the ship.

118

The believer, when he sins, has "fallen on the deck," but he certainly has not gone overboard. When a man is born again, he cannot be unborn. He may get out of fellowship, but he cannot get out of relationship. God has made provision for restoring him to fellowship. Christ will see to it that no wave—death, left, angels, principalities, powers, things present, things to come, height, depth—shall ever sweep us off the deck.

THE LOST WATCH

A man who operated an icehouse lost a good watch in the sawdust. He offered a reward, and men went through the sawdust with rakes, but they were not able to find the watch. When the searchers left the building for lunch, a small boy went into the icehouse; a few minutes later he came out with the watch. They asked him how he had found it, and he replied, "I just lay down in the sawdust and listened. Finally I heard the watch ticking."

Some of you have lost more than a watch. If you will be very still and listen quietly, the Lord will speak to you and show you just where you lost the power and the victory which you so sorely miss. Then you will find it again—through the Lord Jesus Christ—as He shows you how sin came and interfered, and how you can get back into fellowship and peace.

THE WAYWARD SHEEP

A Scotch shepherd had a sheep that ate from his hand and followed him everywhere. When he was asked to explain the close relationship, the shepherd smiled and said that the sheep had been the most wayward in the flock. In its first year of life, the sheep had wandered away many a time; it had cost the shepherd many dreary hours of search. Finally, the shepherd took the sheep and broke its leg. He then bound the leg in a splint and carried the sheep with him to the hills; he fed it by hand and brought it water for its needs. Day by day he took care of it, and when the sheep was fully healed, it never went

119

astray again; it followed the shepherd more closely than a dog would follow his master.

The shepherd leads us to the still waters from the eternal springs. Then the wandering sheep feels the need of restoration, for we have within us the seeds of sin, and they send forth a tangled growth that must be cut back day by day. But when we have wandered away, "He restoreth my soul."

FORGIVENESS

FORGIVENESS

An elderly woman, Mrs. X, has a daughter whose close friend is Miss Y; Miss X and Miss Y are mature Christian women. Many years ago, in a letter to Miss X, Miss Y made an indiscreet statement concerning the mother; the letter was read by Mrs. X, and from that time, she has never permitted Miss Y to enter her home. Miss X, is the major support of that home, she respected her mother's wish, and the two Christian friends, met outside the home.

Only a few days ago we pointed out to Mrs. X, the necessity of Christian forgiveness; we suggested that she show the Christian spirit and invite Miss Y to her home for dinner. We were horrified to hear her reply, "Oh, I forgave her long ago but she can stay in her own place."

Forgiveness without forgetting is like vultures feeding on a dead carcass—even the breath of prayer smells of the putrid thing. You will find that a double blessing of God comes to you when you ask that He bless those who may truly have offended you.

121

FRUITFULNESS

THE BANYAN

The banyan is one of the most beautiful trees of the tropics. Its height and spread and the thickness of its trunk make it a glory of shade and beauty. Its branches reach out and down to the ground. Wherever the tip of a branch touches earth, it takes root and a new tree springs up. This is one of the reasons why tropical forests are so impenetrable.

The Christian, if he is living up to the last command of his Lord, is putting out branches that bear "fruit," "more fruit," "much fruit" (JOHN 15). This is because of the power given by Christ through the Holy Spirit (ACTS 1:8). But the quality most needed on the part of Christians today is that spiritual virility which will enable them to beget a spiritual posterity that in turn will produce fruit unto eternal life. It is what Christ speaks of "your fruit that should remain" (JOHN 15:16). It is by this fruit ye shall know believers.

THE WIRED PLANT

Once I had a small flowering tree in my garden. A wooden tag was attached to one of its branches by a tiny wire. As the branch grew, the wire began to cut into it. I saw that the leaves were not flourishing like those on other branches, so I removed the wire. In a few days life was flowing to such an extent that the branch began flowering. Soon the marks of the wire disappeared.

Some of you may be in danger of withering because of the constrictions of sin. If you will return to the abiding place which is Christ, you will discover that He will begin to work through you; once more you will demonstrate that abiding in Christ is the sure condition of fruitfulness.

FULLNESS OF GOD

A PINT OF SEAWATER

Preaching on the Pacific Coast gives one an opportunity to look out over the broad expanse of the largest ocean on this planet. The glorious stretches of shore, sky, and sea are wonderful. Imagination quickens and thrills as our littleness is placed alongside that of the unending expanse. Suppose I were to take a pint jar to the edge of the water, lean down and allow the ocean to run into the jar? It will take just one gesture to fill that jar with the Pacific Ocean. But how could I fill that jar unto all the fullness of the Pacific Ocean? If I carry my bottle back to Kansas, to someone who has never looked upon the ocean, and tell him that he can now understand the ocean because I have it in my bottle, he will not see what the ocean really is. All he will see is a pint of seawater. There will be none of the mighty sweep of distance, none of the power of the waves, none of the swelling of the ocean surfaces, and none of the wonders of its depths. I cannot put into a bottle the combing breakers or the vast reaches of the sea.

Such a sampling might be the comprehension of the verse, "filled *with* all the fullness of God" if it were to be rendered, merely, that God proposes to fill us with His fullness. But if it were possible for me to put the whole of the ocean into the bottle, then we could understand what God proposes to do with those He has redeemed.

He does not purpose to make us little samples of the Deity. He does not look upon us as little beings who shall display pints of His power. He purposes to increase and enlarge our capacities forever and ever. We are to be filled *unto* all the fullness of God.

FULLNESS OF GOD

QUEEN MARY

In 1935, I reached Jerusalem from India just at the time of
the jubilee celebrating the twenty-fifth anniversary of the
coronation of George V. There was celebration in all of the
British Empire. On the actual day of thanksgiving, an announcer, broadcasting from the steps of the National Gallery
in Trafalgar Square, told us that he could see the royal carriage emerging from Whitehall. The roar of the crowd grew
greater as the carriage approached. The announcer described
King George and Queen Mary as they answered the plaudits
of the multitude. He then turned us over to another announcer
in Charing Cross and the progress of the carriage moved from
announcer to announcer as the cavalcade accompanying the
royal carriage swept on into Fleet Street. Finally, from St.
Paul's Cathedral, we heard the great organ sweep into the "Te
Deum" of praise to God for His grace. All of the announcers
had described Queen Mary, fully. Yet who was she? Was she of
queenly birth? Was she a queen by inheritance? She was not.
She had been Princess Mary of Teck. There were a hundred
princesses of equal rank among the noble families of Germany.
But he who was to become a king set his love upon her, and
immediately she became the fulness of him that filleth all in
all in the British Commonwealth. Without his love she would
have been unknown. With his love she became queen. There
she sat in regal splendor, her every action casting praise and
glory upon her husband-king.

If we can understand this on the level of the throne of the
British Commonwealth, we may be able to catch a faint
glimpse of what it will be for us, who have been chosen to be
the bride of Christ, the fullness of Him that filleth all in all in
God's universe.

124

GENEROSITY

THE BRAZILIAN TAXI DRIVER

One morning in Brazil, I stepped into a rather rickety taxi; the driver was very poorly dressed. I gave him a certain number on Buenos Aires Street, and he responded, "That is the Bible House! Are you an evangelical?" I answered that I had come to preach on the occasion of the one-hundredth anniversary of Protestantism in Brazil. When I asked if he were truly saved, he gave a heartwarming testimony. I asked about his family; he said that he had never married because he had taken in first one, then two, then three small street orphans; he fed and clothed them and took them every morning to school; on Sundays he took them to Sunday school and church. At the Bible House I asked the driver to wait while I went to the fifth floor to meet a friend. The friend said he would drive me back to the hotel, so I went down to pay the taxi driver. In American money, the fare would have been under two dollars; in *cruzieros* it was twice that amount, but the driver would not accept my money. He said it was such a joy to drive the North American pastor that he wanted to do it free, in the name of the Lord Jesus. He had never had an opportunity to exercise hospitality as the New Testament said believers should do, and he wanted to do this for the Lord.

How wonderful to look into the eyes of a simple man, to see the love that Christ has planted within, and to realize that he is seeking to live for Christ and to do everything in His name.

CHRISTIAN LEPERS

In Formosa two Christian lepers took a third leper into their hut at the government leprosarium, because there was no official

125

opening for him. Although the two were already existing on little more than starvation rations, they willingly stretched the rice they received for two, and made it do for three.

They knew the Lord Jesus Christ, and in receiving Him, they received the gift of giving liberally. They were giving their very life. This is the exercise of a divine gift.

PRESENTS FOR MOTHER

After the first world war, I traveled extensively in Europe, and I often sent gifts to my mother—a bit of lace from Brussels, a marble vase from Rome, and so on. Suppose I had written to her, "I am sending you these gifts so that you will love me." My Irish mother would have answered sharply that she loved me before I was born, that her love for me did not increase or diminish by the gifts I sent. But I did tell her that I sent her the gifts because I loved her. This heightened her joy and increased my own.

This is true Christian giving. We give because we have received all things from Christ, and we are moved by the love of Christ to do for others as He has done for us.

THE VICTORIA CROSS HOAX

In London, the Queen gave a garden party for some 300 holders of the Victoria Cross—Britain's highest award for bravery. A parking lot attendant crashed the gate by wearing an imitation ribbon and pretending to limp. He was placed in a wheelchair and greeted by the Queen. Authorities fumed when they learned of the hoax. The Queen had spoken to him very kindly and sympathetically.

There need be no regrets in such a case. It is better to do good to ten impostors, than to abstain from helping the truly needy because some fakes might benefit. We work in the name of the Lord Jesus Christ, and He will find His purposes fulfilled by our loving in His name. ". . . let us be not weary in well doing: for in due season we shall reap, if we faint not (GALATIANS 6:9).

THE WOULD-BE SUICIDE

In England I knew an officer in the Cold Stream Guards. When he came to this country for a visit, I met him at the New York airport. For a couple of hours I showed him New York City. Down on Wall Street the traffic was congested, and we had to wait for a place to park. Ultimately, we drove into a service station, and I asked, "Can I have the car greased and the oil changed?" As we got out of the car, one of the most miserable human beings that I have ever seen came up to us. The man looked as though he had slept in a coal bin for weeks. Filth, dirt, and coal grime were in the pores of his skin; his hair was matted. He was one of the most formidable looking creatures of despair. He put out his hand and said, "Will you help me?" The Englishman had no American money, but he put his hand in his pocket and said, "Oh, I don't have anything." I drew some money from my own pocket, and said, "We give you this in the name of the Lord Jesus Christ." The man began to cry; the tears ran down his face. He said, "I know, I was brought up in this." I spoke to him about his soul, and he replied, "You know, I have gone down to the docks at least ten times and said, 'O God, I'm going to throw myself in and drown myself,' but always there's something that keeps me." We talked for probably fifteen or twenty minutes; and after telling him not to use the money for drink, we gave him the name of a mission where he could be taken care of. The man said, "Oh, thank you, thank you." We said, "You know we give you this in Jesus' name." And he replied, "God bless you."

Now, I don't know that man, but when I think of Christ on the earth, I think of that man. For Christ said, ". . . Inasmuch as you have done it unto one of the least of these my brethren, ye have done it unto me" (MATTHEW 25:40). "He that hath pity upon the poor, lendeth unto the Lord . . ." (PROVERBS 19:17).

GIFTS

CAPACITIES

Let us think of each man in terms of capacity. The great and gifted leaders who may be described in terms of thousand-gallon capacity are few and far between. There are more who have hundred-gallon capacity; still more with ten-and five-gallon capacity; multitudes with the one-gallon capacity, and vast multitudes that must be measured in terms of quart, pint, even gill-capacity. Judged by worldly standards, those with great capacities seem to have all the breaks. Honor comes their way. They are seen, known, praised, and rewarded. They own the larger portion of this world's goods. A thousand-gallon tank that is half-full appears infinitely superior to the half-pint jar that is overflowing.

But, as God sees them, they may have great lacks. If the Bible teaches anything, it is that God is more delighted by the overflowing half-pint than He is by the thousand-gallon tank, half-full of its own doings. When any person becomes enamored of his own capacity, he becomes useless to God. He forgets the foundation principle of our gifts differing according to the grace that is given to us.

THE CHINESE LAUNDRYMAN

When Charles Evans Hughes was appointed Chief Justice of the Supreme Court of the United States, he moved to Washington and transferred his letter to a Baptist church there. His father had been a Baptist minister, and Hughes had been a lifelong witness to his faith in Christ. It was the custom in that Baptist church to have all new members come forward during the morning service and be introduced to the congregation. On this particular day, the first to be called was a Chinese laundryman, who had moved to Washington from San Francisco. Ah Sing, who kept a laundry near the church, stood at the far side of the pulpit. As others were called they took positions at the opposite side. After a dozen people had been called, Ah Sing still stood alone. Chief Justice Hughes was called; he took his place beside the laundryman. When the minister had welcomed the group into the church fellowship, he said, "I do not want this congregation to miss the remarkable illustration of the fact that at the cross of Jesus Christ the ground is level." Mr. Hughes behaved like a true Christian. He took his place beside the laundryman, and by his act he prevented embarrassment to the humble Chinese; he showed, too, the love of Christ—he had this gift of standing by.

So often people hate Christianity because they do not want to stand on a level with others. Spiritual pride takes a terrible toll among those who are vindictive in their hatred of true Christianity; it is because they have no respect of persons, race, family, wealth, culture, social position, character or morals. Men stand level in their lost condition before God, and God stands ready to meet the universal need. Let everyone of us who has named the name of Jesus Christ understand that we are to take our places quietly beside those in need.

THE CUBE AND THE SPHERE

One day I went into the nursery and watched our two-and-a-half-year-old son; he was occupied with a lesson from his mother. A blindfold was placed over his eyes; I placed little wooden objects in his hands and asked him to identify them by their shapes. He answered correctly as his little fingers felt the cube, the sphere, the cylinder. In order to make it one step more difficult, I placed in his hand the cube and the sphere and asked him to hand me the cube. I would not have confused the little mind by asking him to give me something that

129

he did not have in his hand. First I gave to him, then I asked him to give back to me.

This is precisely God's way of dealing with His children. The Word of God establishes the principle that God never asks anything of his child that He has not already provided as a gift. He asks us for perfection, but only because His grace has provided it for us freely at Calvary. After we are born again He asks many things of us, but only because He has already provided these things for us in Christ.

DIFFERENT ARMY DUTIES

In an army, many men perform many different duties. The man who carries the rifle must be backed by the interworking of the whole army. In order for one GI to land on the Normandy beachhead in World War II, he had to be supported by artillery, naval and air units. These, in turn, were supported by those who supplied food, ammunition and fuel. The man below decks in the engine room of the tanker knew that he was helping to keep the tanker moving so that the oil and gasoline on board might be delivered ashore. There the truckers would deliver it to a forward position; and there, the planes that landed on the first airstrips could be fueled and go up to blaze the path for the infantry.

We forget, at times, that this is how the church of Jesus Christ interlocks. Each believer is given some gift by God; each is put into a particular place to perform a particular task for Christ; each is empowered by the Holy Spirit.

"HERRPS"

We were sitting in the study, talking to Leland Wang, the Chinese evangelist. Wang thanked us for the help our office had provided in arranging meetings, forwarding correspondence, writing scores of letters introducing him, smoothing out schedules for him, and doing other odd jobs that are difficult for a stranger in a strange land.

We said that one of our chief delights was playing office boy for those who were in the work of the Lord. He looked out of his Oriental eyes and said, "Herrps." We did not understand, and knew that somewhere there was an English word corresponding to that sound, but we had not yet arrived at the meaning.

"Herrps," he repeated, and then continued, "It is in I Corinthians 12:28. The Lord speaks of the gift of 'herrps.'"

We had to look it up before we compassed the Chinese difficulty in pronouncing the letter "l"; we found that which we had often read and never taken in fully: the Lord has given to some the gift of "helps." And how needed this gift is.

THE SKATER

One winter day, passing through Rockefeller Center in New York, I watched the skaters whirling about on the ice. A girl in her teens was getting instruction from a brilliant skater. She moved around the large orbit of the rink; the man skated in a smaller orbit, nearer the center, but close to her. One could see that she was not sure of herself; once her hands went up, and it was evident that she was going to fall. Swiftly her teacher came to her side and steadied her with a touch. She went on a little more surely; he executed classical figures, but kept his eye on her every moment. Again she became unsteady; in a flash he was by her side, his hand on her elbow helping her to maintain her balance.

It was a perfect picture of the life to which the Lord Jesus has called us. God has given to many of us the gift of helping those who are younger in the Christian life or those who are in need. We live our own life, but our eyes must always be open to the needs of those around us. We must be ready with the helping hand, but we must extend that hand without show. The unsteady one will know that he has been helped, and that the touch at the right moment kept him from falling. The world will not notice that we have helped him, but he will know and the Lord will know. This gift each of us may have.

GOD

BEAUTIFUL FLOWERS

I have a friend who is a great florist; sometimes I have seen thousands of plants at his hothouses. He never had time—no one ever could have time—to go all through those great greenhouses and say, "Oh, look how beautiful this flower is. Now look how beautiful this flower is!" You cannot, when there are a hundred thousand of them.

But God saw every one of them. He saw every petal. If you should take a magnifying glass and put it to one of those petals, you would say, "Oh, how exquisitely beautiful!" Well, God does not need a magnifying glass. The invisible things are clearly seen by the things that are made. So the creation is God's poem.

THE "BIG-GODDER"

I learned the idea of a great God and a little god from my old professor of Hebrew, Robert Dick Wilson. Wilson was one of the intellectual glories of Princeton Theological Seminary in the days of Warfield, Davis, Machen, and others. After I had been away from the Seminary for about twelve years, I was invited back to preach to the students. Old Dr. Wilson came into Miller Chapel and sat down near the front, while I set forth the Word of God. At the close of the meeting, the old gentleman came up to me, cocked his head on one side in his characteristic way, extended his hand, and said, "If you come back again, I will not come to hear you preach. I only come once. I am glad that you are a big-godder. When my boys come back, I come to see if they are big-godders or little-godders, and then I know what their ministry will be." I asked him to explain, and he replied, "Well, some men have a little god and they are always in trouble with him. He can't do any miracles. He can't take care of the inspiration and transmission of the Scripture to us. He doesn't intervene on behalf of His people. They have a little god and I call them little-godders. Then there are those who have a great God. He speaks and it is done. He commands and it stands fast. He knows how to show Himself strong on behalf of them that fear Him. You have a great God; and He will bless your ministry. He paused a moment, smiled, said, "God bless you," and walked out.

Men are always in difficulty with their faith because their God is too small. If they once see the true God, and get the perspective that sees Him as filling all in all, then the difficulties of life will rapidly diminish to their proper proportions. God knows all, is all-powerful, unchanging, eternal, never-failing. He has never made a mistake; He has never been surprised by anything that happened, for He has always known and decreed all things.

FATHER AND SON

If a man begets a son, in consequence of that act, he is always, the father of that son. There have been men who have been fathers of sons who have never been fathers *to* their sons. But many a man who begets a child, gives himself to that child. He is with the mother in the training of the child. The boy is with the father in his free moments. The father enters into the boy's studies; he participates in the boy's games. He makes the boy's hobbies his own hobbies. No question of the boy is beyond the patience of the father. He explains things to the child in great detail whenever the child shows interest in an answer. He trains the boy, leads him on, truly educates him. It can be said in the highest degree that this man is not only father *of* the boy, he is father *to* the boy.

This is the picture that our God wants us to have of Him.

133

More than any earthly father could be a father to his son, so God is a God to us.

GLASS

Here is a simple illustration that expresses a great spiritual truth: If we look through a piece of red glass, everything is red; through blue glass, everything is blue; through yellow glass, everything is yellow, and so on.

The glorious truth is that when we believe in the Lord Jesus Christ as our Saviour, God looks at us through the Lord Jesus Christ. He sees us in all the white holiness of His Son. That is the great New Testament doctrine of the imputation of our sin to the account of Christ and His righteousness to our account.

THE HAND LOOM

The first time I saw a hand loom was in a little village in Belgium. It stood in a corner of the large kitchen; an unfinished white bedspread upon it. I was very eager to see how this weaving was done, so my host showed me how the threads were placed, first on the frame and then in the shuttle. He operated the loom to show me how the shuttle moved back and forth over the threads, creating the even, firm texture of the material and developing the pattern that existed in the mind of the weaver. Little by little, the small threads that fell from the busily moving shuttle became the tissue and pattern of the material.

The principle which I saw demonstrated in that loom was in the mind of the Holy Spirit, when He inspired some of the sacred writers to express the idea of thoughts. "For my thoughts are not your thoughts, neither are your ways my ways, saith the Lord" (ISAIAH 55:8). The word which is here translated "thoughts," means literally "weavings." "My weavings are not your weavings," we might paraphrase it. Everywhere in Scripture we are face to face with the absolute

difference between God and man in all of God's ways of
thinking and doing.

ORIENTAL SILVERSMITHS

In the great bazaars of Istanbul, Damascus, or Cairo, you
will see men sitting at their places in the section of the silver-
smiths. Beside them you will generally find piles of United
States twenty-five, fifty, and ten-cent pieces. Thousands of
travelers give American coins as tips, and all of those monies
are melted back into silver and poured into little silver charms
that are sold back to the tourists. This is done in the most old-
fashioned way. I have watched a silversmith drop a coin
into the molten silver; in a little while the coin is melted down
under the hot fire. Every once in a while the man gets up, lifts
himself over the little bowl of silver, and goes back to sawing
on some little pin that he is making, a silver clasp or ornament.
Again he will get up and look in the bowl; he will take a sieve
and scrape off the scoria that is on the top. He takes away the
dross, and if you should ask him, "What are you waiting to
see," he would say, "I keep it on the fire until there is no more
scum; when I lean over it, I can see myself reflected there as in
the best mirror."

That is what it means in Malachi when it says that God shall
sit as a refiner of silver. God says, "I am going to keep you in
the fire until I see My face in you; this is what I'm working for.
I want to purge away the dross. I want to make you like the
Lord Jesus Christ. I want you to understand the particularity
of love that I've bestowed upon you, that I have called you my
sons; and whom I love, I chasten and scourge every son whom
I receive."

THE PET DOG

A small boy has a pet dog which he loves very dearly. He
plays with that dog every day, and the dog sleeps beside him at
night. One day the boy opens the door of the family garage just

135

in time to see his father killing the dog. The fatal shot rings out; the boy screams and rushes toward the dog. The father catches the boy who kicks at him and screams: "You killed my dog. You killed my dog. I hate you. I hate you." The father carries the boy into the house and says, "My son, I will tell you why I had to kill him." But the boy runs from his father, screaming, "I hate you. I hate you. You killed my dog."

In order to make our parable fit the spiritual facts we are trying to explain, we will continue in a somewhat absurd way. For men who act in an absurd way toward God may not see their own absurdity in the parallel. This boy, we will say, continues to live in his father's house, eating the meals that are provided by his father, wearing the clothes that are provided by his father, yet constantly saying that he hates his father because his father killed his dog. The boy grows up and begins to have some understanding of disease and pathology; he is given clippings that tell of an epidemic of rabies in his neighborhood, and that a mad dog had bitten several children—some of them had died. He even finds a clipping that states that the mad dog bit several other dogs in the neighborhood and that it was necessary for the owners to destroy those pets. From his maturity the boy can look back on his own childhood and see how warped were his opinions of his own father. He had carried hatred of his father through the years because his father had crossed his childish will. Now he sees evidence that his father was acting in wisdom and love, that his pet dog might have bitten him and caused his own death.

We should understand that God has reasons which are unknown to us. It should be sufficient that we have God's Word for it.

THE POTTER

Years ago, when I was living in France, I knew a potter who made various types of vessels for all sorts of uses. Often I went in to watch him turning the wheel and molding the various vessels according to his desire. At times he let me work a lump of clay, although I worked awkwardly at the craft that he did so beautifully. I had been reading the great passages in Isaiah and Jeremiah that have to do with the prophet's visit to the house of a potter, and the illustrations that grew out of that craft. One day I asked the potter what determined his choice as to what he should make. I saw him make tableware, then kitchenware, even spittoons. He said that he got the feel of it as he began to work. When he was rested he made beautiful things; when he was tired, he would slap the clay on the wheel and turn out ordinary vessels that sold in the market for menial uses. He put clay on his wheel; I asked him to make a menial vessel, and he tossed one off in a moment. I then asked him to make a vase, and with great care and love he made a vessel of beauty. I asked him if he ever switched from one object to another while he was in the midst of the work. He began again and speedily there arose before my eyes a vase. While the clay was still wet and whirling, he struck it from above with a heavy sweep of his hand and crushed it to a lump and speedily ran up the form of another vessel. Moment after moment I watched various forms succeed each other, all according to his desire, and all from the same lump of clay. A deft touch and a bowl appeared—a plate, a cup, a dish. He was absolute master of his clay.

God sets before us that He is the absolute Master of His creation. He does not work by whim, nor is He ever so tired that He should shift to another pattern. He has His purposes that are right according to all that He is in His inward nature, and it is this that He wants us to recognize, that our hope and trust may be in Him alone.

THE ZEISS COLLECTION

When the United States Army took all of the material in the optical museum of the Zeiss optical plant in Germany, it secured the greatest collection of its kind in the world and gained possession of samples of every lens known to German scientists. One lens was so powerful that pictures could be taken of buildings twenty-five miles away; fortifications across the English Channel, for example, showed as plainly as an ordinary photograph. Most extraordinary was a lens that had a 210-degree angle, that could take a picture even of a portion of the scene behind the camera.

Hagar learned to call the Lord "Thou God seest me" (GENESIS 16:13). And we can be sure that our Lord looks upon us at all times, and that nothing is hid from his sight. His look can be a look of conviction as when the Lord looked on Peter (LUKE 22:61); His look can be a look of compassion as when He gazed upon the rich young ruler (MARK 10:21), but above all His is a gaze which sees to the very heart: ". . . for the Lord seeth not as man seeth; for man looketh on the outward appearance, but the Lord looketh on the heart" (I SAMUEL 16:7).

GOD'S POWER

BREEDER REACTOR

In announcing the success of the breeder reactor at Arco, Idaho, Atomic Energy Commission Chairman, Gordon Dean asked his audience to imagine that the world has only one hundred gallons of gasoline; when the gasoline is burned in the presence of water it turns some of the water into new gasoline. If the amount produced is less than the original stock, the world would soon run out of gasoline. If the amount is greater, the gasoline stock could grow bigger and bigger until all the world's water had been turned into fuel.

Breeding atomic fuel works in somewhat the same way. Natural uranium contains only .7% of fissionable U-235. Nearly all the rest of it is nonfissionable U-238. But when U-235 fissions (splits in two) and produces heat, it also yields free neutrons. Some of these are needed to keep the reaction going; they make other U-235 atoms split. Some neutrons escape or are absorbed by structural materials in the reactor. The rest of the neutrons enter the nuclei of U-238 atoms and make them turn into plutonium, which is just as fissionable as U-235 and can be used as atomic fuel.

The importance of this development can only be realized if we consider that one pound of uranium has been the equivalent of about 18,200 lbs. of coal; under the new process the same pound of uranium would be equivalent to 2,600,000 lbs. of coal.

Believers should understand that here, indeed, is a great illustration of the principle of the increase of power from God. The Lord has organized the Christian life on the principle of

139

the breeder reactor. He gives us the knowledge of His power in our lives in a small way and puts before us a small test. As soon as we use His power to overcome the difficulty that is involved in that test, we discover that we have a larger knowledge of His power. With that knowledge comes a larger test, then a larger deliverance and still larger knowledge. As the spiral goes upward, it is expanding at all times. Thus God will never give us a test beyond our present knowledge of power, and we will ever grow into His infinite self.

THE RIVER BASIN

If we look at a map of the central United States, we can see the courses of rivers from many sources, all debouching into the Gulf of Mexico. Waters from Pennsylvania flow into the Ohio River; from Montana and Wyoming they flow into the Missouri River; from Tennessee and Alabama they flow into the Tennessee. All these join the Mississippi, which rises far to the north in Minnesota. If we read this map in reverse and follow the mighty rivers back to creeks, from creeks to brooks, from brooks to rivulets, we have the picture of the source and flow of power. From one spring, all power flows.

All power comes from God, and the powers that be are ordained by God. Power exercised by any creature, even the power of a cat to kill a mouse, or of one insect to kill another, derives originally from God. How much more is this true of human affairs, where God is working out His great plan!

SPLITTING THE TOMB

A "believe-it-or-not" picture showed a tomb with a fig tree growing out of the middle of it; the tree split the great slab of stone that formed the top of the sarcophagus into three great pieces, and pushed out the side walls with the force of its growth. The tomb, it is said, is in the grounds of the parish church of Watford, England, and is that of a naval officer, Ben Wangford, whose dying request was that he might be buried with a fig in his hand. The life of that fig took hold of the death of that hand and the power of the life split the tomb.

If physical life is a powerful thing, eternal life is even more powerful. It is rooted in the wounded hand of the Lord Jesus Christ and out of that hand grows the life of the resurrection which God communicates unto us. Here is a power that enables us to be delivered from sin.

THE UNSEEN KITE

A boy, flying a kite, was so successful that the kite went out of sight. He stood on the green with a cord in his hand that bent upwards into the sky and was lost. Someone asked him how he knew the kite was there, and he let them put their hand on the string; they could feel the pull of the unseen kite.

The world may not recognize the existence of God, but those who know Him in Christ can feel the drawing of the invisible power that they recognize in every phase of spiritual life. And the unbelieving bystander will be forced to recognize that the true believer possesses "something" which he does not have.

GOSPELS

WORKS ON NAPOLEON

The great libraries of France house thousands of volumes printed about the life and work of Napoleon. A quarterly review devoted to studies of the Corsican has been published for over fifty years. If a scholar wants to work on some phase of Napoleon's life it is not necessary for him to include these mountains of accumulated material. He need not even be chronological. If he is writing on Napoleon, the man, the codes or Austerlitz may not be mentioned, but Josephine certainly will. If he writes on Napoleon the strategist, he may never mention Marengo, Iena, Waterloo, and Moscow. Remember, however that he may, for his purpose, mention Waterloo before Austerlitz and may weave events of various epochs of the life of his hero into the same paragraph. I have read a volume on Napoleon that mentioned none of his battles, except incidentally, and never spoke of Josephine or of the empress. It was a book on Napoleon as a codifier of laws.

In the same way the Holy Spirit has used Matthew, Mark, Luke and John to present four different phases of the person and work of the Lord Jesus Christ. Matthew writes to the Jews. His purpose is to show that Jesus was the Jewish Messiah. Mark presents Jesus as a servant. There is no genealogy at all. Mark is writing about a servant, and a servant works from beginning to end. Luke, however, presents Jesus Christ as a man. John presents Jesus Christ as the Eternal God incarnate.

GRACE OF GOD

BATAAN AND GUADALCANAL

When the Japanese launched their attack against the Phillippines, several thousand United States' troops were on those islands, totally unprepared. How bravely they fought on Bataan, slowing down the enemy and making him pay heavy losses for each foot of gain! The men fought on, hoping against hope that reinforcements would soon be available. But our fleet had been severely wounded and there were no reinforcements available. A year or so later, however, we were ready to launch the great offensive in the Solomon Islands. The papers that bore the news of the great battles raging on Guadalcanal, also published an assurance from our Secretary of War. He said, "There is twice as much food as the soldiers can eat; there is twice as much ammunition as the soldiers can fire; there are twice as many nurses and doctors as would ordinarily be needed in any military engagement; there are twice as many medical supplies as could be needed. There are twice as many airplanes as are possessed by the enemy. We are prepared for every contingency."

Most certainly we can say that the method in which the Lord provides for all our needs is like Guadalcanal. God never had a Bataan in all of His dealing with the sons of men. All of God's gifts to us are in abundance.

A BETTER PITCHER

Years ago a minister named Harry Morehouse was walking in a poorer section of the city, and he watched as a boy of five or six came out of a store carrying a pitcher of milk. The little

143

fellow made his way carefully along the street; he slipped and fell; the pitcher broke, and the milk ran all over the sidewalk. The boy let out a wail, and Morehouse rushed to see if he was hurt. There was no physical damage, but the youngster would not be consoled; he kept crying over and over, "My mama'll whip me! My mama'll whip me!"

Mr. Morehouse said to him, "Maybe the pitcher is not broken in too many pieces; let us see if we can put it together again." The boy stopped crying at once; he watched Mr. Morehouse place the base of the pitcher on the sidewalk and start building up the pieces. There were one or two failures and each time the boy started crying again but was silenced by the big preacher. Finally the whole pitcher was complete except for the handle. Mr. Morehouse handed the piece to the little fellow; he poked it toward the place it belonged, and knocked the whole thing apart once more. This time there was no stopping his tears, so Mr. Morehouse gathered the boy in his arms and walked down the street to a nearby crockery store. He bought a new pitcher; then he and the boy returned to the milk store and had the pitcher washed and filled with milk. He carried the boy on one arm and balanced the pitcher of milk in the other hand until they arrived at the boy's home. Very gently he deposited the lad on his front steps, put the pitcher carefully into his hands and asked, "Now will your mama whip you?" A smile broke on the streaked face. "Aw, no sir! 'cause it's a lot better pitcher 'an we had before."

Whether you accept the fact or not, the pitcher of your life and its milk were once spilled beyond regathering. You may have spent much time trying to patch the pieces together again, but God assured you that you were broken beyond repair. When we were thus, broken and hopeless, in the despair of our lost soul and our crashed hopes the Lord Jesus intervened to save us. He may have watched our efforts at patching for a while, until we came to the place where we believed beyond question that it was impossible for us to repair our lives in a way that would ever satisfy the holiness of the Heavenly Father. It was then that He carried us in His arms and purchased for us an entirely new nature, a new life, which He imparted to us on the basis of His loving kindness and tender mercies. It was not because there was good in us, but because there was grace in Him.

CHEMISTRY EXAMPLES

We have many examples in chemistry that show how the introduction of a second element will completely debase or transform a product. If you put a dime in a bottle of hydrogen peroxide, the silver will react so rapidly that a moment later nothing will be left in the bottle but liquid. If you put even the smallest spark of fire into a barrel of gunpowder, you will explode the whole barrel. Terrible oil refinery fires have been caused by a single drop of perchloric acid coming in contact with some heated organic liquid—gasoline, kerosene, or aniline.

If salvation is by grace then it is not of works, for as soon as there is a mixture of even the smallest percentage of works, grace is debased and is transformed into something that is horrible to consider. The whole idea of works is that man can provide a basis that will force God to give him some blessing as a just reward for the works. The whole idea of grace is that God acts toward man according to that which is to be found within His own divine nature of love. The two ideas are mutually exclusive and destroy each other when placed together.

FACING THE WALL

Sir Edward C. Burne-Jones, the prominent nineteenth-century English artist, went to tea at the home of his daughter. As a special treat his little granddaughter was allowed to come to the table; she misbehaved, and her mother made her stand in

145

the corner with her face to the wall. Sir Edward, a well-trained grandfather, did not interfere with his grandchild's training, but next morning he arrived at his daughter's home with paints and palette. He went to the wall where the little girl had been forced to stand, and there he painted pictures—a kitten chasing its tail; lambs in a field; goldfish swimming. He decorated the wall on both sides of that corner with paintings for his grand-daughter's delight. If she had to stand in the corner again, at least she would have something to look at.

When a Christian commits sin and is put into a corner, God does not send him to hell. When a child of God sins, he does not fall from grace. Wonderful though it is, instead he falls into grace. If your particular sin has been confessed, God has restored you; when God put you into the corner, He went to you there and painted a picture of His forgiveness and love.

THE RESERVOIR

If you poured a single test tube of disease germs into a reservoir of pure water—the entire water supply—even that for an entire city—would be contaminated.

This illustration cannot speak strongly enough to show forth the degree of contamination that is to be found where God's free grace is diluted by even a small part of human works.

THE TEXAS OIL OWNER

Suppose that a great depression brings many men to the point of bankruptcy. They wish, of course, to keep themselves above the flood and to bring themselves out by their own efforts. Their natural pride wishes to keep them from confessing their failure and acknowledging the desperation of their circumstances. For the sake of our illustration, let us imagine a small town in Texas that is dominated by a man fortunate enough to have discovered oil on his property; he has also bought all the oil leases in his neighborhood so his fortune runs into scores of millions of dollars. He announces that he will bring all of the business men of that small town out of bankruptcy, if they will write a letter acknowledging the certainty of their failure. He will then pay their debts and supply them with a new capital to start their business afresh. If there are men in the town who are proud to the point of insanity, they may refuse to bow before this offer from a kind benefactor. In that case, they remain insolvent and are forced to pay the penalty of their pride. But there are others who recognize that the man who makes the offer is a man who has known them for years, and that he recognizes that his success is a matter that involves certain obligations and responsibilities; they realize that he holds certain values in trust. He wishes to help them because of the generosity of his nature. They, therefore, determine to write to him and set before him the true nature of their plight and avail themselves of the offer made them in free grace. Immediately, the local bank is instructed to take care of their needs, to pay off their debts, and to grant them the credit they need for the maintenance of their affairs. Someone might say to them, "And because this friend has come to your aid, in spite of the fact that you are absolutely bankrupt, your situation is one of brilliant hope because of the grace that pays your debt and provides the capital which you need."

We are brought day by day to acknowledge freely before God our utter bankruptcy. We can do nothing for ourselves. If then, we are to have any blessing, it must come to us moment by moment from the flowing stream of grace which begins at Calvary and comes to us because of the love of God, and in the power of the Holy Spirit.

GRATITUDE

THANKING GOD

A minister who was visiting an insane asylum, was accosted by one of the inmates, "Sir," asked the patient, "have you ever thanked God for your reason?" The preacher had never done so, but he vowed that he would be unthankful no longer.

There are thousands of things besides your reason for which you might well bow your head right now and give a heartfelt prayer of thanksgiving to the Father.

THE HOPE COLLEGE JANITOR

While I was preaching at Hope College in Holland, Michigan, the janitor, who was an elder in the church, came up to me and said, "I would like to ask you a question. I can understand 'God bless me,' but how can I bless God? 'Bless the Lord, O my soul.' How can I bless Him?"

I said, "Do you have any children?"

He replied, "Yes, I do."

"How old are they?"

"Well," he said, "I have a child who is five and one who is seven."

"At Christmastime do they ever give you a Christmas present?" I asked.

"Yes, they do."

"Do you know what they are going to give you?"

"No, I don't."

"Who picks it out?"

"They do, with their mother."

"Who pays for it?"

148

"I do."

"That's exactly it," I said, "You pay for the Christmas presents which your babies give you. You're so glad that they talk about it and have secrets with mother. I can remember when my own children were growing up, how wonderfully excited they were that they were going to surprise Daddy. They came and said, 'Daddy, here is a blessing for you.' It came from me, but it was a blessing because it had come as the boomerang of love."

So it is when we cry blessing and glory and wisdom and thanksgiving. We bless Thee, O Lord. What with? With the blessing that He puts in our lives. Everything that we have and are comes from Him. How delighted we are to offer it back to Him and to acknowledge before all the world that there is nothing that we have or could be that does not come from Him.

THE YELLOW CUR

One Saturday evening several years ago, on my way to Pensacola, Florida, I had a flat tire and had to pull over to the side of the road. I was tired; I had driven over three hundred miles that day and preached twelve times that week. As I eyed the tire, a jeep came down the road. I flagged it and a young man got out; I told him I would give him a dollar to do the work for me. He agreed with alacrity and came over to my car, followed by a little yellow cur. In order to get to the spare tire, we had to unload about two hundred books piled in the trunk of the car. The young man opened one of the books, and, seeing that the matter concerned salvation, said that his wife would be interested in something like that because she was active in the little Baptist church down the road. When I asked him about his own faith, he expressed total indifference.

As he worked his dog stayed close beside him, nuzzling him when he stooped, putting his head between the man and his task, coming back when he was pushed aside. I remarked that he and the dog seemed to be very fond of each other. He stopped, looked at me with a level gaze, and said earnestly, "That dog saved my life once." I asked him to tell me about it and the story came quickly. The reason he was not in the army—it was at the height of the war against Germany and Japan—was that he had more than a dozen broken bones. He was a rodeo rider and had often been thrown by bulls and horses. He worked as a cowboy, he told me, and once had nearly been trapped in quicksand. He had jumped from tuft to tuft of the marshy ground and had suddenly lost his footing. He threw himself on his back at once, to spread his weight, but he was caught almost to his knees, and he knew that there was no deliverance from any quarter. There was not a human being within a couple of miles. Out of nowhere, the dog had appeared. He came to the man, allowed him to put his arms around his haunches. The man was able to straighten himself, and with the dog pulling, he released first one leg, and then the other and finally reached safety.

The young man said, with a wry smile, "That dog is always with me. He can have anything I have. He eats with me, and though my wife doesn't like it, he sleeps with us." I said to him. "What would you do if, down there at the store where you are going, one of the men deliberately kicked that dog hard?" With a look of unabashed ferocity, the young man said, "Mister, I believe I'd kill him." I put my hand out and touched him on the arm, saying, "Isn't it strange that you take such good care of a dog who saved your life at no cost to himself, yet you treat so indifferently the Saviour, the Lord Jesus, who saved you at such great cost to Himself? For Christ didn't pull you out of the quickstand of sin by a mere effort of strength on your behalf! He actually died for you to save you from hell."

A look of wonderment came into the man's face and he said, "You know, Mister, that's right. We don't take much account of Him. And I reckon it's because we can't see Him, and we can't feel hell like I sometimes feel that quicksand on my legs."

When he finished changing the tire, he rather shyly asked if he could have one of my books instead of the dollar. I gave him both and he shook my hand earnestly. He said, "You know my wife is going to be surprised and glad when I tell her I am going to church with her tomorrow, and when I start reading the Bible. But you know, Mister, that really got me—to think that I could treat a cur better than Jesus Christ who died for me."

Is it not strange that there are men who would treat a yellow cur better than they would treat the Lord Jesus from Heaven? But it is true, and the reason can be found in the depths of sin within our Adamic nature. Mass indifference characterizes the nation and the race of mankind. What David said of the unregenerate can be said even of a man who frequently sits in a church pew: "God is not in all his thoughts" (Psalm 10:4).

GUIDANCE

BABY'S FIRST STEPS

In the evening, the young father came home from work. His wife greeted him with the excited announcement that she was sure the baby was about to take his first step. The baby was all clean and dressed in his best. The father got the motion-picture camera and pointed it toward the child. The mother held the baby by his armpits, his little feet on the ground. She began relaxing her grip so that the child carried all his weight on his own two feet. He sensed the excitement that was in the air. He balanced precariously as he stood all by himself. He lifted one foot, took a tiny step, and held his balance while the camera whirred. There were exclamations of delight from his parents. Did the thought occur to the baby: "Evidently that is just what I was supposed to do—lift up my right foot and and put it forward"? So he lifts the same right foot and puts it forward, loses his balance, and down he goes. Does the father rush at him to spank him? Nonsense. Does the mother scold him? Ridiculous. The mother picks him up with shining eyes, and says, "There's my little man. He took a step. He'll soon take two." And he will, too!

The Heavenly Father is far more eager to lead us out into a developed Christian life than any young father and mother were to see their child take his first step. When we fall, God does not strike us down. He is leading us as one leads a child of tender age.

THE FEATHER FAN

On a country road in Formosa, we saw a farmer driving a large flock of ducks. There must have been a hundred of them, so tightly packed together that some of their heads could not be seen. The only guidance they had came from the breeze of a large feather fan waved behind them by the driver. If a duck strayed from the group, a breeze was fanned at it, and it returned to the body of the flock.

Thus the Lord leads believers. If they will be led by the wind of the Spirit, He will blow His steady guidance. He never takes stern measures to the believer who accepts the soft caress of His breeze.

FLATHEAD LAKE

One summer we had a cabin on the edge of Flathead Lake in Montana. Every day we went into the lake. Father took his small boy just turning five, out beyond his depth. The boy cried and cried, even though he was just as safe as if he had been on shore. Only when he was convinced of that fact could he rest quietly on the water, supported by father's arm.

Oh, Christian! Realize that the Father wants to teach you— He is leading you out beyond your depth with full purpose in His heart and mind. It is the power of the risen Lord Jesus Christ, personally appropriated moment by moment, that gives us our victory and our peace that passeth all understanding.

TRAINING SOLDIERS

We commit the young men of our nation to the authority of our armed forces, and these men surrender themselves to the orders of their superiors in perfect confidence. They do not argue, although they may complain among themselves. They must do what they are told to do. It is galling to the flesh to go through strenuous drill routine; muscles that are unaccustomed to certain exercises cry out on long route marches with sixty pounds of gear on the back. But the soldiers who do any thinking soon realize that they are being turned from boys into men. They must become aware that their flabbiness is giving way to hardness, that they will face their foes in the hour of danger as conditioned warriors and not as awkward fledglings.

If we would only learn from the leadings of our God that He is preparing us for Himself in much the same way that a soldier must be conditioned by all his training.

HEAVEN

GOING HOME

A refugee from Hitler says that so many tales were told about America that his whole family felt they knew this country well. So settled was this knowledge and love of the land he had not yet seen, that as he departed for America his mother said to him, "You are going home, and I am staying in a foreign land."

The Christian who realizes the tyranny of life in this world is glad to escape to the land that is fairer than day. When our loved ones go before us, we are forced to say, with tears for ourselves, "You are going Home and I am staying in a foreign land."

HOLINESS

THE BLIND OFFICER

A young officer who was blinded during the war, met and later married one of the nurses who took care of him in an army hospital. One day he overheard someone speaking about himself and his wife; and they said, "It was lucky for her that he was blind since he never would have married such a homely woman if he had had eyes."

He rose to his feet and walked toward the voices, saying, "I overheard what you said, and I thank God from the depths of my heart for blindness of eyes that might have kept me from seeing the marvelous worth of the soul of this woman who is my wife. She is the most noble character I have ever known; if the conformation of her features is such that it might have masked her inward beauty to my soul then I am the great gainer by having lost my sight."

The Bible says that God seeth not as man seeth "for man looketh on the outward appearance, but the Lord looketh on the heart" (1 SAMUEL 16:7b). The Bible also says that God prefers holiness to glamor (1 PETER 3:4). If a man or woman possesses physical beauty, they may be thankful for it, but they should realize what a temptation it can be to them and must ever surrender it to the Lord.

GENIUS

If we should give you a copy of Shakespeare's dramas, and ask you to produce an equal, you would be forced to reply that you could not do it; you lack the genius. If we should place before you paintings of Velasquez, or Rembrandt, or of any of

156

the other great masters and ask you to create new master-pieces, again you would be forced to reply that you could not do it; you lack the genius. Your answer would be the same, if we offered you great works of music, architecture, or the arts or sciences. Genius must be innate in the true master of an art.

The same is true of the life of Christ. Myriads have looked at Jesus Christ and have known that they were sinners, but no man in this world has ever become holy by looking at the example of Jesus Christ. A Christian is a man or woman in whom God has worked a miracle by planting a new life within. This is the genius of holiness, and it becomes possible for a man to let this indwelling life of Christ be manifested to those about him.

HOLY SPIRIT

THE AFRICAN BREEZE

On landing in Africa, one of the first lessons we learned was to find out on which side of the house the wind was blowing. Coming out the front door to sit on a porch, we walked first to one end, and then to the other. Generally, a breeze would be in one place or the other, and there we placed our chairs. When there was a calm, we stifled; when the breeze blew fresh and strong, we sighed with joy. The movement of air made life livable.

Thus we must seek the motions of the Spirit. When we realize that the Holy Spirit moves as He desires, then we know a revival cannot be pumped up by human effort, but must come from God. At times the wind blows a tempest, at times there is a gentle breeze, at times there is a dead calm of the doldrums. At times He has been pleased to blow us a Luther, a Calvin or a Wesley, great tempests of spiritual movements; at times the church has been in a hot suffocating calm, where the true believers almost gasped for life.

INITIATION

When I was a boy, a group of fellows who lived in our part of town formed the Pastime Athletic Club. It was a big name but it did not mean much. The four or five who started the Club decided to initiate other fellows who were going to join. The boys wanted the initiation to be held in our house because we had plenty of room. The initiation rites were such that my parents would not let me remain a member of the club, but I learned something about initiations that night. An initiation is a work or rite performed by a person who is already a member of a society, upon someone who is becoming a member.

All this will help us to understand the baptism of the Holy Spirit, for it is the baptism of the Holy Spirit that is the initiation of an individual into the greatest of all societies, the church which is the Body of Christ. No one can become a member of the Body of Christ without being baptized by the Holy Spirit, and everyone who is baptized by the Spirit so becomes a member of the body of Christ. This is an invisible society seen by God alone, so this work of the spirit is also invisible.

THE ISOLATED COLONISTS

During the latter part of the eighteenth century many colonists left Virginia and started through the mountains to settle the valleys that lay far to the West. Fear of Indians, the death of a horse or the breaking down of a wagon forced many to stay in the mountains. For over twenty years, these settlers saw no white men at all, until a group of travelers straggled into the neighborhood. Naturally, there was much conversation about the outside world. The travelers asked the mountaineers what they thought of the republic and the policies of the Continental Congress. The isolated ones answered, "We have not so much as heard of a Continental Congress or a republic." They thought of themselves as loyal subjects of the British King, and had not even heard of George Washington or the Revolutionary War. It took them awhile to comprehend their new status, but once they did they became American citizens by knowledge and volition, just as they had been for some time by fact.

In the same manner, many of the children of Israel had traveled down to Jerusalem in the days of John the Baptist; they had heard him, followed him and been baptized by him. Then they returned to their remote homes; since they were

159

isolated they knew nothing of the happenings of the intervening years—that Jesus Christ had been manifested, had died and been raised from the dead, had ascended into Heaven and sent forth the Holy Spirit. But as soon as they were told by Paul, they realized their new status, and they identified with the infant Church and became members of that body by the work of the Holy Spirit.

ORSON WELLES' PICTURE

One day, when Orson Welles was making a picture a cameraman said to him, "You had better wipe that sweat off." Welles replied, "Horses sweat; men perspire, and (looking at the actress who was working with him) she glows." He meant that she had a glowing personality and great physical attractiveness.

Less known, because it's more rare, is the personality that is so filled with the Holy Spirit that it radiates the presence of Jesus Christ. The man or woman who is filled with the Holy Spirit is aglow with His presence; and, like the rulers of Israel, people will recognize "that they had been with Jesus" (ACTS 4:13). The glow of the Spirit is the warmth of the soul touched by the love of Christ.

PAINTING THE BIRD

Several centuries ago, the Emperor of Japan comissioned a Japanese artist to paint a bird. Months passed, then years. Finally, the Emperor went to the artist's studio to ask for an explanation. The artist set a blank canvas on the easel and in fifteen minutes completed the painting of a bird that became a masterpiece. The Emperor asked why there had been such a long delay. The artist then went from cabinet to cabinet; he produced armloads of drawings of feathers, tendons, wings, feet, claws, eyes and beaks of birds; these he placed one by one before the Emperor.

The Holy Spirit operates in the life of the believer, so that

160

we may be conformed to the image of God's Son (ROMANS 8:29). This is not done in the moment of our new birth. That moment is no more than the declaration of the divine purpose; It is just the beginning of the long work. The whole process is a detailed and painstaking progress "until Christ be formed in you" (GALATIANS 4:19). Then the day shall come when the Emperor of emperors will come for us, and the completed work will flash forth in a moment. "It does not yet appear what we shall be, but we know that when he appears we shall be like him, for we shall see him as he is" (I JOHN 3:2).

THE TRUCK AND THE PUDDLE

One rainy day as we drove at more than sixty miles an hour on a highway in the southwest, a great truck approached us; it hit a puddle and flung gallons of muddy water in front of us. As I cautiously applied the brakes, the wiper and the fresh rain worked together to clear the windshield and to restore visibility. At no moment were we endangered by the muddy bath.

Spiritual onslaughts are wiped away by the power of the Holy Spirit who maintains us in the heavenly places in Christ. I have learned to enter into the secret place where "no weapon that is fashioned against you shall prosper, and you shall confute every tongue that rises against you in judgment. This is the heritage of the servants of the Lord and their vindication from me, says the Lord." (ISAIAH 54:17).

HONESTY

WEIGHING HIS THUMB

A butcher, asked what difference it made to him when Christ entered his life, replied, "I stopped weighing my thumb." He then told that before becoming a Christian, he put the meat on the scales in such a way that his thumb trailed down, affecting the weight by as much as an ounce. He had included that thumb in the weight of beef, pork lard, and every other item of his merchandise. But after Christ came into his heart, he stood away from the scales and gave a full sixteen ounces of meat. And when he served customers whom he had formerly cheated, he added an ounce to make up for past peculations.

Christians, especially those who believe in the doctrine of the security of the believer, must be eternally vigilant, yielding to the presence of the Holy Spirit to warn them from deviating from high standards of honesty and integrity. Too many Christians weigh their thumbs when they deal with others. Thus through all the gamut of sins, Christians will permit themselves a thumb's weight on their account.

HOPE, REJOICING IN

THE AFRICAN TWINS

When I was in of Africa, I took a picture of two young women; smiling and beautiful they wore flowers in their hair. They were brought before me for special attention because they were twins—the first twins ever permitted to grow up in that part of Africa. To Africans the idea of twins was horrible. Even today in many of Africa's tribes, twins are killed at birth. Their superstitious religion had a great fear connected with the birth of twins, but in this instance the gospel of Jesus Christ had come to the tribe some thirty years earlier. Shortly after the parents were saved, the Lord gave them these twin daughters. Their newfound faith was strong enough to resist the public outcry against the children, and they were allowed to live. When they reached womanhood, they married two fine young men of the tribe, also Christians. The twins stood before me, living proof of the hope that is in Christ, and I rejoiced in this hope that so transforms individuals and even tribes and nations.

THE JAPANESE BUDDHIST

In the lobby of the Imperial Hotel in Tokyo, Japan, the girl at one of the airline desks spoke Chinese, Japanese and English; she was obviously from a cultured background. I asked her if she was a Christian. She replied that she was a Buddhist. Further questions elicited the information that she had heard of Christ and knew that there was a sacred book, the Bible; but she had never read it and knew nothing of Christian truth. I then asked her, "Do you love Buddha?" She was startled and said, "Love? I never thought about love in connection with religion." I said to her, "Do you know that in the whole world no God is truly loved except the Lord Jesus Christ? Other gods are hated and feared. You have statues of fierce monsters to guard the gates of your temples, and the people stand at a distance and try to awaken their gods by clapping their hands. They burn incense and offer sacrifices to them as though they were gods who had to be appeased. But Jesus Christ loves us; He came to die for us, and those of us who truly know Him have learned to love Him in return. 'We love him because he first loved us' (1 JOHN 4:19). Mohammedans do not love Allah; Hindus do not love their gods, and neither do you love Buddha. But we love the Lord Jesus because He died for us." Before leaving Japan, I arranged for a missionary to take a Bible to this girl and to show her how she might know the Christ of God and enter into His love.

When you meet the sadness of a pagan Japanese who fears her god, you enter into the meaning of the text, "Rejoice in your hope."

THE NIGERIAN PASTOR

At a mission station in Nigeria, I met a pastor who was faithfully ministering to his flock. His skin was very black, his features were sharp-cut and there was nobility about his head. His eyes—those windows of the soul—impressed me especially by their gentleness. He accompanied the missionary and me on a visit to his brother, chief of the tribe. When we arrived at the compound he explained the layout to me. The houses for the various wives of the chief were grouped about the threshing floor; the storehouses for grain were in another part of the compound. Finally we were taken to the large area where the chief lived. Like his brother he had a commanding physique. I asked them to stand together while I took motion pictures. I have looked at those pictures many times since that day, and they speak to me of the darkness of Africa without Christ, and the light and joy of the heart that knows Christ. The difference between these brothers lies not in the gaily colored garments of the chief, and the white robe of the pastor, but in their faces, especially in their eyes. For the eyes of the chief show great cruelty; his features are hard and pitiless. One would never seek mercy from a man with such a formidable look of wanton savagery. The face of the pagan chief was even more revealing as he stood next to his pastor brother, whose face showed calm nobility and gentle goodness. The faces of those two men revealed their inner natures.

The life of Christ made the difference. Once the child of cruelty, the pastor had become a child of hope.

THE SKIDDING CAR

One year shortly after Christmas, my wife and I drove from Philadelphia to San Francisco. We encountered about one hundred miles of ice from western Pennsylvania to the Ohio line, another one hundred miles of icy roads in central Colorado, and a similar stretch in central Nevada. Once we passed the scene of an accident and shortly afterward heard on the car radio the statistics of road deaths over the New Year weekend. We had a heavy car, good tires and were experienced at driving on snow and ice. We had committed ourselves to the Lord and were driving below the legal speed because of road conditions. Suddenly, we felt the car skid. A truck, going much too fast, passed us just as we skidded and covered the windshield with spray. A moment later the car righted itself and we were safe, our vision once more clear. One of us chuckled, and the other said, "I had the same thought." Then we laughed, for we had both been thinking, "Lord, if you want to take us to heaven from the wreck of a car on a highway across the Rockies, that is all right with us." We were sure the Lord had led us by this route. We were in His will and on His business, and we had not a trace of fear. No wonder we laughed! We continued in prayer, often interlarded with general conversation—prayer—bits of humor—prayer—comments on scenery—prayer—discussion—prayer—driving directions. In our car, we were not two but three, for we knew that He was with us so there was constant rejoicing.

We have been delivered from the fear of death and consequently are delivered from the bondage which chains those who do not have our hope. We rejoice in hope.

HUMAN HEART

GENERAL LIU

A news magazine described the Chinese Communist General Liu as taciturn, cold, uncommunicative; a mechanical man who came close to fulfilling his own dictum: "A party member is required to sacrifice his interests to the party unconditionally." General Liu revealed so little about himself that newsmen could get almost no personal data; but, when he spoke, he revealed the true state of his heart. A small child cut its hands tending potato vines in a commune, and the General said, "Don't be scared by a little blood." An educated man remarked to Liu that it was living hell to work in a boiler room, and the Communist leader replied, "We need more such hells."

Here is an illustration of the truth of the Bible—out of the abundance of the heart the mouth speaks. By contrast, out of the abundance of His heart God has spoken for our blessing. In Jesus Christ He has revealed that He is love and holiness, goodness and kindness; that He hates sin and desire men to be saved, that He longs for their highest good.

THE ICE AND THE CLAY

When we were living in the suburbs of Philadelphia in a twin-house, the people who lived in the other half of the house went to the seashore one day and forgot to tell the iceman not to bring ice. He put a great chunk of ice on the back porch in the warm sun. About the same time our little girl went out onto our back porch with a lump of modeling clay in her hands. Another little girl called her to play, and the clay was laid down on our porch, just a few feet away from the ice.

167

What happened, as both lay there in the sun? Did the ice get hard and did the clay melt? Why, of course not. The ice melted and the clay got hard. What was the matter with the old sun? There was nothing the matter with the sun; the matter was with the ice and the clay. It is the nature of ice to melt in the sun and it is the nature of clay to harden.

People's hearts are like that. Some will not receive the gospel, and some will. It shines on all. There is nothing the matter with the gospel; the matter is with the hearts of men which are evil, full of guile and deceit.

SOIL MAPS

One of the most humiliating failures in a government project in modern times is that of the British groundnut (peanut) adventure in Africa. Launched with great expectations, millions of acres of wild land were to be converted to peanut growing in order to produce edible oils for Britain's fat-hungry citizens. But the land turned out to be so full of quartz sand that plows and other implements rapidly wore out. The soil's consistency was like cement; unless ample rains softened it at just the right time, the ground became so hard that the sprouts couldn't push though it. Four years after the project was launched, $100,000,000 had been spent; not enough peanuts had been produced to equal the amount used for seed, and the project had to be abandoned. Lack of good soil maps had doomed the project.

There is no lack of good soil maps for the human heart. The Lord tells us that we must receive the seed into good ground not rocky, shallow, or thorny ground. Then we will have a harvest that is thirty, sixty, or a hundredfold. It is all charted for us in the Word of God.

HUMAN RACE

WEIGHTED DOLLS

Some dolls have a half-sphere of lead in their base so that they will always swing upright, no matter how they are placed. Stand them on their head, and they will almost leap to turn over; lay them down flat, and they will come upright immediately. One of these dolls, fashioned like a clown, has a large head filled with lead; the clown always winds up standing on his head. Place him upright on his pointed feet, and he will immediately turn over and stand on his head.

This is the true picture of the human race since sin entered the heart of mankind. Man looks at everything in his universe from a distorted position. Man's whole world is upside down. When a man is born again, transformed by the power and grace of God through the Lord Jesus Christ, a change takes place in him. It is as definite as removing the lead from the head of the clown and putting it in his feet so that he can stand upright.

INCARNATION

THE JUDGE'S SON

Several years ago, while crossing the Atlantic Ocean, I preached at the Sunday service. After the service a group of college students came to tea; they gathered around me for a discussion of faith and the atonement. One girl became so eager that she sat on the table in front of me, surrounded by her friends. I used the illustration of a judge who saw his son come before him, accused of reckless driving. The charge was abundantly proven, and the judge fined the young man the full amount permitted under the law. Then the judge adjourned court, stepped down from the bench, and paid his son's fine. The girl, who was spokesman for the group, interjected, "But God cannot get down off the bench." I replied, "You have given me one of the best illustrations of the incarnation that I will ever have. For Jesus Christ was no more or less than God, come down off the bench to pay the fine which He had imposed upon us."

INFLUENCE

THE FINGER AND THE MOLTEN METAL

The brother of a friend of mine worked in the steel mills of Gary, Indiana. He was a reckless fellow and a gambler. One day as molten iron was being poured from a furnace, he gathered a group of men and bet each one of them five dollars that he could take his naked finger and whip it rapidly through the inch-thick stream of fiery iron. They all covered his bet. He stooped to the floor, took up a handful of the powdery dust all around the furnace and used it to dry all the body oil from his finger. Coating his finger with this hot, dry dust, he thrust it at the liquid iron and caused the sparks to fly in many directions. Another workman watched the incident, went down to another place in the mill where a similar stream of iron was flowing and bet a group of men that he could whip his finger through the molten metal. They, likewise, covered his bet, and he whipped his finger through the stream of metal. But he did not know the secret of wiping the body oil from the finger with the parched dust. They took him to the first-aid station where a surgeon removed his entire finger. This man's ignorance caused the loss of his finger.

The man who knew the secret might be jocular about it and say that he could keep on at the practice any time that he found anyone foolish enough to wager him on the matter. But the man who has even a semblance of common decency and regard to the weakness of others would say, "I will never use my position of knowledge in a way that would cause another man to lose his finger."

INFLUENCE

There are some things which the believer will abandon because they might have a bad influence upon others. The believer must consider every act of his life in light of how it affects his life and his testimony.

INHERITANCE, OUR

THE DOWN PAYMENT

After World War I, I lived in a home in the Quartier Louise in Brussels, Belgium. Each day I spent eighty minutes on the streetcar going to and from my office. There were some nice residential streets near my office so one day I rang the bell at a house that exhibited a room-for-rent sign. It was just what I wanted—size, location and price. I told the landlady that I would take the room and asked if I might move in in about ten days, as my rent was already paid in the house where I was then living. She consented and then asked me a question hesitantly. The conversation was all in French, and there was one word she used that I did not understand. She said, *"Est-ce que Monsieur voudrait verser des arrhes?"* I showed my incomprehension and repeated the line questioningly, *"Verser des arrhes?"* She replied, in French, that she was sure that I was honest and that I intended to return in ten days, but that if she took the sign out of the window and I did not return after the ten days she would lose ten days of advertising. But if I would be willing to pay something down on account. . . . I comprehended immediately and gave her enough francs to satisfy her. I went back to my office and said to one of my fellow-workers, "What does it mean . . . *verser des arrhes?*" He replied, "It is in the first chapter of Ephesians."

I looked it up and discovered that God tells us that when He saved us, He gave us the Holy Spirit, sealing us into Christ by Him, as the earnest, the pledge, the down payment of our inheritance.

173

THE INHERITANCE

Suppose that you are sitting in your home some night and the door bell rings. A man is there, and he says, "I'm an attorney with such and such a firm, and we're trying to find a relative of a missing person. Your name is so and so. Did your mother come to this country from Scotland fifty years ago, and did she have a brother who went to Australia? You say, "We have the family Bible here. It's all written down. There's my mother. She was born in Edinburgh on such a date. She had a brother and he went to Australia, and we never heard from him since. "Well," says the lawyer, "This is wonderful for this is the last link in the evidence. He went to Australia and had a son to whom he left his fortune; that son died and left no heir. The lawyers in Australia have traced it back to Scotland; the Scotch people traced it over here, and we have come to you for we believe that you are next of kin." You say, "Yes, undoubtedly." "Well," says the lawyer, "I'm very happy to inform you that you have a very large inheritance." You say, "I can get that new Chevy I've been looking for." He says, "It's a very large inheritance." You say, "Buick." "In fact, your uncle had coal mines." You say, "Cadillac convertible." The lawyer says, "Now, of course, it's in the courts and you can't get anything very soon except the down payment. Your uncle owned hundreds of thousands of acres of sheep ranches; oil and gold have been discovered there. It's going to be three or four years before you can get it all, but they have a little down payment that's ready for you now." "Well, what is this little down payment?" "This little down payment is only fourteen million dollars." "If that's the little down payment, what's the whole thing going to be?"

Not all the certified public accountants in the world could ever add up the glories of the inheritance reserved for us. It would be impossible for a team of bankers, accountants and lawyers to get together and tell us what the total is. All they can do is to tell us a little bit about the interest on the interest. That is about as close as anyone can get to understanding our inheritance, because the down payment is God the Holy Spirit. This inheritance is nothing short of the fact that we inherit God Himself.

JESUS CHRIST

THE AMERICAN CITIZEN

Years ago, in the midst of a Latin American revolution, an American citizen was sentenced to death by the authorities who had seized power. As the victim was about to face the firing squad, an American officer took a large American flag and draped it around his compatriot. "If you shoot this man," he cried out, "you will fire through the American flag and incur the wrath of a whole nation." In those days America "spoke softly, but carried a big stick," and the revolutionary in charge knew the force with which he had collided. The prisoner was released and went on his way with the officer who had come to his rescue.

If we are surrounded with the Lord Jesus Christ, then nothing can touch us unless it passes through Him. If Satan is to reach us with one of his fiery darts, he must first of all pierce the Lord Jesus Christ who protects us. Nothing in the world can ever touch us until it has passed through our Lord. As we reckon ourselves to be in Christ, and therefore immune from defeat as long as we have hold of Him, joined to Him in His death, so do we learn to reckon ourselves to be alive unto God.

CAUGHT IN THE CLOTHES CLOSET

When his bed caught fire, Edward Sweeny, of New York City, awakened, ran to the door, opened it, went through it, and slammed it behind him only to discover that he was in a clothes closet and could not get out. Meanwhile other tenants smelled smoke and sounded the alarm. The firemen extinguished the blaze and released Mr. Sweeney from the closet when they heard him pounding on the door.

How like human beings! Caught in the sleep of death, they race to any door and rush through only to be trapped in their false hope. Is it any wonder that the Lord cries through the prophet, "Turn you to the strong hold, ye prisoners of hope . . ." (ZECHARIAH 9:12). Christ is the stronghold and the only door. Any man who attempts to find safety by any other door will find himself trapped forever.

THE DAMAGED OAK

Of several oak trees I planted near my house, all but one grew more than twenty feet high. That one was damaged; it died at the soil line, but the root system remained intact and a shoot came forth—spindly and weak. I was about to tear it out to make room for a new tree, when a horticulturist told me that this shoot would catch up with the other trees. Although I could hardly believe it, I let it alone; after two years it was six feet high; after four years, more than twelve feet. It had a fine branch system, all fed from a root system equal to that of the other trees.

God slices through the gentile forest like a hurricane, lopping boughs with terrifying power, hewing down the tallest trees with His axe of judgment. Then, from the most unlikely stump, comes forth a new tree. Jesse, the father of King David, was in the royal line from Abraham to the Messiah. Who would expect that a ruler of little Israel would surpass the Caesars? God's forestry is not like man's. When He speaks, a dead stump brings forth life: Christ comes to deliver His people.

ELDER KIM

Several years before the second world war, I spent a month in Korea ministering to groups of missionaries. At Sorai Beach, scores of missionary families were spending the summer, and

177

there were many opportunities for social fellowship. One evening a group of us were seated on the sand under a magnificient moon. I said to them, "Now I have been teaching you twice a day for several days, and I want my pay. Tell me your best missionary stories." After a moment of silence, one man said to another, "Tell him about Elder Kim." Here is the story:

Kim, a Korean layman of wealth and prominence, was elected elder of one of the Presbyterian churches in Pyongyang, the chief city of northern Korea. Because of his outstanding character and reputation, he was asked to address the annual meeting of the General Assembly of the church. He began modestly, reminding his hearers that he was a simple layman, not trained in a seminary or Bible institute. He was not going to preach or attempt to teach, but he wished to put before them a great problem and to ask their advice for its solution.

"A year or two ago," he began, "I received a letter from a friend of mine in Seoul. A young dentist, he wanted to establish himself in Pyongyang, and he asked me to find a place that would be suitable for his home and office combined. Although there is a great housing shortage, I did all I could to help him. I seached the town for three days, found a place and wrote to him about it. I told him that the house was in bad condition: the wall surrounding the property was in disrepair; there was a hole in the house wall; the roof leaked very badly; the house was in a very bad neighborhood; next door was a house inhabited by 'singing girls.' Furthermore, the price was exorbitant. In spite of this adverse report, my friend telegraphed me to buy the house. A day or so later I received a check for several thousand yen for the down payment, so I signed the papers to purchase the house. The down payment was made, and the final payments were to be made in three days, at which time the owner agreed to vacate the house. The payments were made, but the owner asked for a day or two more in order to find another house. I granted him this period of grace, but after a week he was still there. Two weeks, three weeks, a month, three months, six months have passed. The man who sold the house has bought new clothing for his family, and they are eating polished rice instead of the cheaper grains. He knows that I am a Christian and that in Korea we Christians never go to court against other Christians, and we try not to go to court against unbelievers. He laughs at me when I come.

"Now, Fathers and Brethren," Elder Kim continued, "my friend is greatly embarrassed because his capital is tied up in this house, and he is in a very difficult position. What am I to do?"

Several of the members of the General Assembly responded. One pointed out that Elder Kim was not acting in his own behalf, but as an agent. Another pointed out that he was evidently dealing with a man who was a thief at heart. All agreed that Kim had the right to go to the authorities and ask for an eviction order. Kim asked for a show of hands, and all voted that he had the right to proceed legally.

Elder Kim concluded: "Thank you, Fathers and Brethren, for the way you have considered my problem. Before I sit down I wish to draw one conclusion. Nineteen hundred years ago the Lord Jesus Christ came down from Heaven to purchase for Himself a dwelling place." Then striking his hand upon his breast, he continued, "He bought this old shack rundown, in a bad neighborhood. He bought me because He wanted to take possession and dwell in my heart. He gave Himself for me, and He gave me the Holy Spirit as a down payment on my inheritance, bringing me innumerable blessings with His redemption. But I cling to my tenement and leave Him outside. Now if you say that I have the right to seek the help of the authorities to evict the man who is occupying my friend's house, what shall you and I say of ourselves when we deny the Lord Jesus the full possession of that for which He gave His own life?"

Christ died and rose again that He might be our Lord. Let us, then, recognize Him as Lord and commit ourselves to Him in obedience. He wants to rule our lives. The Lordship of

Christ in our lives is to be evidenced by our recognition of the fact that since He is Lord of all who trust in Him, no believer can judge another. He is to draw us to Himself. He is to be Lord over all the life of each believer.

THE HOME

When I first met the man I knew little about him. Then I met his wife; she was cultured, charming and spiritual, and my opinion of the man went up, for I saw that he had chosen his wife with the highest part of his nature and had not been looking for the standard equipment of the glamor-girl type. He had chosen character and Christian life, with all the component gifts and graces that go with them. After I had talked to this couple for a while, their charming sixteen-year-old daughter entered the room. The girl had intelligence, charm and manners; she was looking forward to giving her life to the Lord's service. Meeting her made me know her parents better. A few minutes later two boys came into the room, one about fourteen, the other about twelve. Their deportment, bearing and manner gave me further insight into the character and attributes of the father. I could see a home, well-run, well-managed, and with a proper system of priorities—putting the Lord first, and developing all the gifts and graces with which He had endowed the children.

If it is possible to know a man better because I have seen his wife and watched his children through the course of an evening's meal and a social hour of family conversation, how much more will it be possible to exhibit the wonder of His being and the marvels of His grace through all of the infinite company of the saints who have been redeemed by His blood and saved through His grace!

THE IRISH KING

There is a legend of an Irish king who disguised himself and went into the banquet hall of one of his barons. He was escorted to a lowly place among the throng who sat at the feast. The brilliance of his conversation and the nobility of his manner soon attracted the attention of someone with sufficient authority to escort him to a higher table. The same thing occurred once more, and soon he was seated among the nobles of the realm. After a display of great wisdom, one of the lords spoke out and said, "In truth, Sir, you speak like a king. If you are not a king, you deserve to be." Then the king removed his disguise and took his rightful place among his subjects.

When our Lord Jesus came from heaven's glory, His subjects were so blinded by their own darkness of heart that they were not willing to stoop before Him. The King of Kings and Lord of Lords was there, but they received Him not, even though He stated over and over again that He was the eternal God come down to redeem them.

KOREAN PRISONERS OF WAR

Almost a quarter of a century ago, the Reverend Harold Voekel went to Korea as a missionary. When the Korean war began, he entered the United States Army as a chaplain, and was assigned to prisoner of war camps. Tens of thousands of North Koreans were imprisoned in great compounds. The Communists had infiltrated the camps with their agents, and there were riots and rebellion. Chaplain Voekel came with the truth of God. He entered the first pen of several hundred men and began to talk to them in their own tongue; their resistance faded, and they crowded around him and waited for his message. He told them he wanted to teach them a song. It was a rude Korean translation of the child's hymn, "Jesus loves me, this I know." He kept them about an hour and told them he would be back the next day. He then went into the next pen and began all over again. Day after day he entered a dozen or more pens, teaching them to sing "Jesus loves me." Weeks passed and then months. By this time several thousand North Koreans were professing their faith in

Christ as their personal Saviour. The discipline became easier in the camps. The Communists could not find easy followers as they had at first. When the question of repatriation came up, these men insisted that they did not want to go home. They wanted to live in the free world. The commanding officer, General Harrison, testified of the wonderful results that came from the preaching of the love of Christ to these men. When the time came for these prisoners of war to vote for their future, they turned their backs on communism by the thousands and gave the whole world a great example of the desire of men to remain free from red slavery. The message of the love of Jesus Christ transformed these men; it gave them vision not only of the world to come, but of free life here on earth.

The message that was preached to these prisoners was the same simple message that has challenged the hearts of millions through the ages; it is just as effective today as it was when the disciple John leaned on the bosom of Christ.

OLD PHOTOGRAPHS

I once spent some time in a hotel in Florida that was patronized almost entirely by older people taking the winter sun. One day, in the lobby, a group began talking about their grandchildren. Some carried portfolios of photographs while others had snapshots of their loved ones. "Look at that boy," said one old man. "He is the spit and image of me. When I was that age, they took an old tintype of me, and it is just like that." The man's eyes were alight, his face radiant. Other men and women were likewise filled with loving pride at the thought of their children's children.

I can draw no conclusion other than that Christ had a similar joy and a proper pride in all of His redeemed when He ascended into Heaven. He had gone to the cross and died in order to buy you and me. He was proud of us—sinners though we are. For God the Father, Son and Holy Spirit does not see

182

as we see—in the sight of the Godhead we were not only redeemed, but we were already glorified.

STREET-SWEEPERS' WAGES

We might think it strange if the President of the United States met with the Prime Minister of Britain and the heads of other states and spent a good deal of time discussing a common standard of wage payment for street-sweepers in the various capitols of the world. There would be many who would think that these men in positions of great power should spend their time on more important things—things that affect the peace of the world and the flow of history.

In like manner, it might be thought strange that the Lord Jesus Christ should be on the throne of heaven considering the matters that are now before Him. Yet the Bible shows us that He is not now concerning Himself with the great plans of governments and the movements of nations. These things have been planned before the foundation of the world and written down in their permanent form. Nothing can change the course of events that God has determined for this earth. Christ has all the time in the world and in heaven to be occupied with the flood of His love toward those whom He redeemed with the price of His blood. He is seated upon the throne of God, occupied with nothing other than your best interests.

VISITING THE MINT

Years ago when I visited the Philadelphia mint with my children, gold pieces were still being manufactured. We watched men take sheets of gold and sheets of silver—roughly 16 x 20 inches—and feed them into a great hydraulic press. The machine caught the edges of these flat pieces of metal and took them into the middle of the press. Then we heard "clump," and fifty or a hundred coins came out into a basket on the side. The man who was showing us around said to the children, "Pick some up"; the children picked them up, but dropped them very fast, because the tremendous pressure of two hundred tons hitting, knocking a coin out and making it hard, left a great frictional heat. We watched as they poured out twenty-five cent pieces to be weighed, and again the man picked one up. In one place coins were examined through magnifying glasses; a man could tell by looking at a coin what was happening to the die inside the press. By magnifying it tremendously, he could tell from which die a coin came; as soon as any particular die showed any type of wearing, it was taken out and another die put in its place. We could not see the dies inside the machine, we saw only the twenty-five cent pieces but each coin was the express image of the invisible die.

God says that the Lord Jesus Christ was the Lord God Almighty, the express image of His invisible person. God the father is invisible, Jesus was visible.

JOY

THE ATLANTIC STORM

There has never been a storm on the Atlantic, whose roots went deeper than the surface, even if the waves were so great that they combed over the bridge of a battleship. A submarine always finds the water fifty feet down as calm as a pond on a clear June day.

If a believer is not joyful, it is almost certain that he does not possess the peace of God; one may even doubt whether he has righteousness. Joy must not be confused with mirth; the latter is effervescent, but joy is the steady tenor of our being. When all is chaos on the surface, deep down there is joy.

CRACKERS-AND-CHEESE CHRISTIANS

Years ago, a Scotchman arrived in Liverpool where he was to embark for his journey to America. He fingered the few shillings that made up his total earthly capital, and decided that he would economize on food during the trip in order to have more money on hand when he reached New York. He went to a small store and laid in a supply of crackers and cheese to get him through the days at sea. But as the voyage progressed the sea air made him very hungry. To make matters worse the dampness in the air made his crackers soft and his cheese hard. He was almost desperate with hunger. To cap the climax he caught the fragrant whiff of food on a tray a steward was carrying to another passenger. The hungry man made up his mind that he would have one good, square meal, even though it might take several of his shillings. He awaited the return of the steward and asked him how much it would cost

185

to go to the dining room and get a dinner. The steward asked the Scotchman if he had a ticket for the steamship passage. The man showed his ticket, and the steward told him that all meals were included in the price of the ticket. The poor man could have saved the money he spent on crackers and cheese; he could have gone to the dining room and eaten as much as he liked every meal time.

This is a humble picture of the position of many people who have believed in Christ as Saviour. Because of that faith, they are saved, but they go on their miserable way without appropriating any of the blessings that God has for them in Christ. How terrible is the responsibility of these crackers-and-cheese Christians, who show no joy to those who are looking for the reality of joy in life! Such Christians cannot show it because they do not have it. Yet it was all provided for them in Christ. "He that spared not his own Son, but delivered him up for us all, how shall he not with him also freely give us all things?" (ROMANS 8:32).

THE FRACTURED LEG

Imagine a man who has been in an automobile accident. His leg is twisted out of its socket, and the bone is broken. He tells the doctor, "Give me a sedative quickly so that I can be at peace and rest. I want to sleep. Just give me a drug and go away and leave me." What a fool he would be! No man in his right mind would say such a thing, and yet millions are seeking for some opiate of peace without righteousness. The doctor must set the fracture and put the leg back in its socket. Then nature will take its course, and he will know healing and peace.

It is certainly thus in the sequence of God's dealing with man. God simply will not allow any man to know true peace until that man first possesses divine righteousness. One reason for the terrible frustration of mankind is that peace and joy are sought without righteousness. But without the righteousness of

God there can be no peace, and without the peace of God there can be no joy.

THE ROYAL STANDARD

In London, Buckingham Palace flies the royal standard to show that the sovereign is in residence. Day or night the flag can be seen, and the people know that their queen is not away, but at home.

Thus joy flies as the flag over our lives to show that Christ our king is in residence.

TROUBLES OF MY OWN

A layman wished to perform some kind of Christian service, so his pastor suggested that he go to a rescue mission and help. The man duly presented himself to the superintendent of the mission shortly before a service for the down-and-outers who walked along Skid Row. The superintendent told the man to stand out on the sidewalk and invite passing men to come into the meeting. The man accosted the passersby and, in a mournful tone, asked them to enter the mission. Each man to whom he spoke glanced at him and went on. He learned his lesson, however, when one man responded to his doleful invitation, "Brother, wouldn't you like to come in to the meeting?" Cynically, the man looked at his solemn face and said, "No, thanks; I've troubles enough of my own."

We are certainly not good recommendations for the Lord Jesus Christ if we have not learned the great truth that joy is one of the prime requisites of the Christian life.

JUDGMENT OF GOD

AN ANCIENT PALIMPSEST

Exhibited in one of the cases in the library of the Vatican is an ancient palimpsest. Centuries ago, men had written line after line on sheets of papyrus until their work filled an entire volume. Many years later, when paper was difficult to secure, someone found the old volume and wrote a new work across the original manuscript, in lines perpendicular to the first. Today the blacker ink of the second writing is more legible, but the text underneath is still clear enough to read with ease; scholars frequently take more delight in reading the older than they do the more recent writing.

Such is the heart and conscience of man. Across the fresh page in the youth of the race, God wrote the eternal truths of His being, His holiness, His justice, and the certainty of His wrath against sin. Men turned the page sidewise and wrote with blacker ink the history of their doings until, in some places, the earlier writing is almost effaced. But the day will come when the acid of God's judgment will eat away the writings of man, and the strong X ray of the light of God will bring to the surface the original writing by which man will be judged.

THE COAT BUTTON

"Button, button, who's got the button?" may be more than child's play. A woman bought a coat in a shop in Brooklyn for ninety dollars and soon lost a button from it. The shop did not have an extra button, so the woman wrote to the factory. The factory recognized the button as one that matched that from a stolen coat. The woman led detectives to the shop, and the owner was jailed as a fence for receiving stolen goods from shoplifters. From button to coat, from theft to thief—the chain led to judgment.

With man it takes detective work, but to God all things are naked and open. All missing buttons will be located in that day—every wrong will be brought home to the doer unless he has let the Saviour settle out of court for him.

CHURCH BARRIERS

Listen to people crossing from Canada to the United States, talking about how to cheat the customs: "Oh, just say you have been in Canada more than forty-eight hours," one woman may tell another. "You can bring in up to a hundred dollars' worth if you have been here forty-eight hours." "But I only came yesterday," the other answers. "Oh, they will never check up on you." A dozen similar conversations go on.

One day we must all pass the customs barriers at the bar of God. No good works may be imported by the one who has not received Christ as Saviour. Such souls will be naked and speechless before the great Searcher of hearts (ROMANS 3:19). Even those who are believers may enter nothing that has not been done for the glory of the Lord. There can be no deception. "Neither is there any creature that is not manifest in his sight: but all things are naked and opened unto the eyes of him with whom we have to do" (HEBREW 4:13).

THE FALLEN PLANE

We have all read about expeditions to the antarctic and of the possible establishment of an airbase in the south polar region. Let us suppose that a plane comes down in these waters, south of New Zealand. The pilots know that there is no other plane, no ship and no land within a thousand miles of them. Three men are cast into the water: One is able to swim only a few hundred feet; the second can manage to stay afloat an hour or two; the third is the world champion long-distance swimmer. Is it sensible for the champion to show the first man his best swimming strokes? Will the champion say, "Take me as an example?" These men do not need an example, they need a saviour. One will drown in twenty minutes, a second will drown in two hours, and the third will drown in fifteen hours.

Thus it is with men; they do not need an example, they need a Saviour. The convict is like the man who can swim only a few strokes, the average man is like the man who can swim for a while; the very, very good man is like the man who can swim for fifteen hours. But all three are doomed to die under the circumstances I have set forth.

So it is with men before the judgment of God. The very best that a man can do in deeds of kindness and charity does not change the unalterable fact that his character and his works are cursed by God. The only thing that will satisfy a holy God is that man shall take sides with Him, accept the shedding of His blood for the remission of sins, cross the chasm through Christ and stand with God in all His estimates, judgments and verdict.

THE HUNTING ACCIDENT

A hunter experiences a terrible accident. His gun goes off as he climbs over a fence; the bullet enters the back of his friend, killing him instantly. There are some doubts that the death was accidental because the survivor stands to gain financially by the death of his friend, and a coroner's inquest is held. The district attorney wishes to intervene. He thinks the hunter should be brought to trial so that all evidence may be brought forth in court. The lawyers argue over the wording of the indictment. If the district attorney brings in an indictment of murder in the first degree, a conviction will carry a mandatory death sentence. If the indictment is for manslaughter, the accused will be tried, but the penalty will not be death. Or the bill may charge him only with criminal negligence: he may be sued for damages that may take away his property. The wording of the indictment will make all the difference in the outcome of his trial, and in the sentence that will be imposed if he is found guilty.

The sinner is guilty before God. Christ Jesus has carried the penalty of the sinner's guilt. The one who believes in Christ can never, therefore, appear in a judgment where he could be condemned to the second death. That judgment has been removed from him forever. It would be as impossible for God to bring me to a judgment that might end in sending me to hell as it would be for God to send Christ to earth to die again.

MURDER OR MANSLAUGHTER

The cases of two men awaiting trial have been bound over by the grand jury. One of them, the evidence shows, has planned and plotted the death of a friend. He schemed for months, bought his instrument, planned the time and committed the murder. There is every evidence of the sanity of the killer, and there is every evidence of premeditation. The charge against him is murder in the first degree. The second man is also on trial because a man lies dead, but the evidence is quite different. He was driving his automobile on slippery pavement. Evidence shows that he leaned out of the car window and waved to a friend, calling out a message. He had carelessly taken one hand off the wheel and was going faster than the conditions warranted. Suddenly the car skidded and ran up on the sidewalk and killed a man. There is every evidence of carelessness and negligence, so he is bound over for trial; the charge is manslaughter. What will be the difference in attitude as the two men go to trial? The first man has every right to be apprehensive that he will go to the electric chair. Will the second man fear the death penalty? Certainly not. He knows that the extreme penalty for such a charge is but twenty years in prison; he has hope that his known character and ability to pay all the damage claims arising from the accident will probably cause the jury to recommend leniency, and that a suspended sentence may be his lot.

191

In precisely the same manner we may interpret the question of future judgments. The unbeliever has every reason to fear. The penalty that lies before him is that of the eternal separation from God. But that penalty has been removed forever from the believer.

UNPOLISHED SHOES

A soldier found it difficult to get out of bed one morning; he appeared on parade with shoes that were far from polished. The inspecting officer barked at him and asked why the shoes were in that state. Without blinking an eye the soldier replied, "I tried two kinds of shoe polish, sir, and they neutralized one another." The nonplussed officer passed on down the line.

Multitudes of Christians will appear at the judgment seat of Christ with no luster in their life because they have been doubleminded in all their ways (JAMES 1:8)—unstable, neutralizing the power of the Spirit by the drag of the flesh.

UNPREPARED

The Pearl Harbor Report demonstrated that not only were an admiral and a general unprepared, the authorities were unprepared and the whole nation was in a lethargy of self-satisfaction. In spite of all the evidence that an attack would come, people were amazed when it did.

Thus is the approaching judgment of God going to come upon the world; the Bible informs us that judgment is coming. Men are warned to flee from the wrath of God. They are warned that sudden destruction will come upon them, that it will come suddenly as a stroke of lightning from the east and the west and as unexpectedly as a thief in the night. In spite of all these warnings the world sinks in its lethargy of self-satisfaction. It will be awakened by a blow far more rude than Pearl Harbor, for just as the gifts and calling of God are without repentance, so are His judgments.

JUSTICE OF GOD

SCULPTURED JUSTICE

One evening a friend introduced me to a lawyer who practices in Philadelphia. We discussed certain questions connected with the crime situation and the dispensing of justice. I contended that there should be a much more drastic use of the law, and pointed to the traditional conception of justice. When an architect gives a contract to a sculptor for a decorative piece for a courthouse, the result has usually been the figure of a woman—to represent chastity, she is blindfolded, to indicate that justice is no respecter of persons; she holds a balance in which evidence is to be weighed minutely, and a sword without a scabbard, ready to strike wherever there is guilt. The lawyer listened to my description and then added with a smile, "And is to be found only in statuary."

As far as earthly justice is concerned this is probably true. In meting out justice perfection is not to be found in earthly courts. Fearing a mistake and knowing that we are all guilty in a certain measure, we are not perfect in knowledge or in holiness and therefore we are slow to act.

When we face the justice of God, however, we are dealing with One who is absolutely perfect in knowledge, who is absolutely holy, and who is perfect in His justice.

193

JUSTIFICATION

THE HYMNBOOK IN THE HAND

When I was about fifteen years old, I heard a man give a vivid testimony for Christ. I spoke to him about his experience because I was not very settled in mine, and I knew that he had something that I did not have.

He took my left hand and drew it out, palm upward, all the while fixing me with an intense gaze. "This hand represents you," he said. On that hand he placed a large hymnbook. He then said, "This book represents your sin. The weight of it is upon you. God hates sin, and His wrath must bear down against sin. His wrath is bearing down upon you, and you have no peace in your heart and life."

He drew my other hand forward, palm upward, and said, "This hand represents the Lord Jesus Christ, the Saviour. There is no sin upon Him, and the Father must love Him, because He is without spot and blemish. He is the beloved Son in whom the Father is well pleased." I saw my two hands before me: one covered with the large book, the other empty; I realized that I had the sin, and the Lord Jesus Christ had none.

Then this man put his hand under my left hand, the hand that represented me, the hand upon which the Book was lying; with a sweeping gesture he turned my hand over so that the Book came down upon the palm of my right hand—the one that represented Christ. My left hand he put back as it had been; I could see that the burden was gone from it entirely. He then said to me, "This is what happened when the Lord Jesus

Christ took your place upon the cross. He was the lamb of God, who was bearing away the sin of the world.

This is the justification that acts upon our sins to take them away from us and to place them upon the Saviour.

PAYING BILLS

Every one of us at some time or other has walked into an office to pay a bill—for telephone service, electricity, or some other obligation we have incurred. We hand the money to the teller who counts our money, takes the bill we owe, and presses a rubber stamp upon an ink pad, stamps our bill and hands us a receipt. The company could never collect that bill from us again, for if they tried to do so, we could produce the receipt and they would know that the matter had been cleared, and that we were free from the obligation forever.

The Lord Jesus Christ walked up to Calvary, which was God's desk for the payment of the bill of our sins. The account was heavy against us, and the Lord Jesus Christ could settle the account by shedding His blood in dying for us.

THE RENTED FIELD

Suppose that one man rented a field from another and promised to pay a hundred dollars for the rental. The agreement is signed; the day of payment comes. If the harvest has been poor because of drought, pest, unseasonable storms, or poor fertilizing, the man who rented the field may wish that he had not signed the agreement. He may wish that the owner would take half of the harvest instead of demanding cash, but the agreement has been signed; there is nothing to do but abide by it. If, however, the owner should say that he would accept fifty bushels of corn instead of money, there is an end to the argument. If the owner should say that he would accept twenty bushels of grain instead of the money, there is an end to the matter. If the owner should say that he would free the man from his debt provided that the debtor sing for him, then that would be the end to the matter. It is the owner who must be satisfied.

God must be satisfied in the matter of our sin. Justification is expression of the fact that God declares Himself fully satisfied by virtue of what the Lord Jesus Christ has done for us.

THE WRONG CRIMINAL

Bertram Campbell spent three years and four months in Sing Sing prison for a forgery he did not commit. The real criminal finally confessed and cleared him. The innocent man was taken to Albany and the Governor of New York, who had been the prosecuting attorney who convicted him, signed a pardon that was not really a pardon at all. The traditional wording of the pardon had been changed from "fit object of our mercy" to "innocent of the crime for which he was convicted." In other words, Campbell was not pardoned; he was justified.

The Lord Jesus Christ does exactly this for the one who puts his trust in the work of Calvary. The blood cleanses us from all sin so that in the sight of God we are justified. Justification puts new Paul alongside of old Saul, glorification takes old Paul out of the picture, and new Paul is forever absolutely justified in Christ.

LAW

CATHETERIZING THE HEART

Several years ago I learned from an outstanding medical professor, who is a member of my church that a new process had been devised to study the heart. A slender, hollow plastic tube can be introduced into the antecubital vein at the elbow, and skillfully worked up the vein until it passes over the shoulder and down into the heart. A cloudy chemical can be released which shows the fluoroscopist the nature of the flow of blood within the heart; by maneuvering the catheter through the ventricles, a blood sample can be secured from within the lungs. This work preceded the operations which have cured so many "blue babies."

It interested me greatly that the Scripture verses that speak of the Lord as "trying the heart" are rendered in the great French translations as "catheterizing the heart." ". . . by the law is the knowledge of sin" (ROMANS 3:20). Paul is really telling us that the instrument the Lord used for this delicate work was the law He gave through Moses. The law is a probe that enters into the inner recesses to reveal the true nature of Adam's being which is in us.

HYDROGEN BOMB EXPLOSION

Suppose a great hydrogen bomb exploded over Washington, D. C. at a moment when every member of the executive, legislative and judicial branches of our government was present in the capital. Not one high official would escape. Since it would be necessary for some authority to take control, let us further suppose that a strong man arose to lead the nation. He might govern by a benevolent dictatorship, issuing decrees that would establish some sort of working order, but his decrees would also become the working law of the land, and he would not act according to the provisions of the federal constitution. Such a change in government would obviously do away with our constitution.

The coming of the Lord Jesus Christ worked a far greater change than that from a constitutional republic to a one-man dictatorship. The coming of Christ established Him as the Lord God Almighty stepping into his own visible universe to do what He pleased. His coming did away with the law and established the rule of the Holy Spirit. Henceforth, the Holy Spirit is the *only*—it is important to repeat it—the *only* representative, the *only* vicar of Christ on earth. Christ is the end of the law for righteousness, but love is the fulfilling of the law, and believers are to receive each other in love.

THE MIRROR

If a man observes himself in a mirror and sees that his face is dirty, he does not take the mirror down from the wall and start rubbing it upon his face. The mirror shows him that his face is dirty, but the mirror cannot wash his face. The purpose of the mirror is to drive him to water. Any other use of the mirror is plain folly.

Anyone who tries to be saved by keeping the Ten Commandments or by living by the Sermon on the Mount resembles those who would seek to wash with mirrors. It cannot be done. All he will do is to smear himself yet more.

THE NICK IN THE CUP

Many years ago, in London, I bought a set of china at wholesale prices. In the providence of God, we still have it in our home and there has never been a nick in any piece. I bought only demitasses because I did not have enough money to buy cups and saucers. Over the years we enjoyed our plates and other dishes, but we needed larger cups.

Once while I was preaching in Cleveland, Ohio, I came to an antique store that displayed a Wedgewood cup and saucer. I had read enough about china to know they were real Wedgewood—possibly part of a set. I bought them for a modest price, and as I traveled over the years I picked up a cup and saucer here and another there. I always set a price, in advance, for I would not pay more than a certain amount for it.

One day, in Vancouver, British Columbia, I passed an antique store that had a beautiful cup and saucer finished in a green tint that I knew was powdered jade. "How much is this?" I asked. He gave me a price that was beneath my set price. I said, "There is a little nick in it," and he replied, "If that little nick wasn't there, that cup and saucer I am offering you for a few dollars, would be worth a hundred." I bought the cup and saucer because the little nick didn't mean that much to me. It was only about as big as a pinhead, but from his point of view, that nick prevented the cup and saucer from being a perfect one.

God says that the little nick is JAMES 2:10: "For whosoever shall keep the whole law, and yet offend in one point, he is guilty of all." If you had committed only one sin—a little pink-white lie—God says that you are also guilty of murder; you are guilty of adultery; you are guilty of thievery; you are guilty of pride and arrogance. But you say, "Lord, I only did this." God says, "The law is one. You have broken it, and it doesn't make any difference whether you break it here or there. If you've broken it, you've broken it, and that is it."

NO SPEED LAWS

Fifty years ago no road signs set up fifty-mile-an-hour zones. Why not? Because no one had ever gone fifty miles an hour. Then men began to drive recklessly. Cars buzzed through villages and towns, causing chickens to scatter, horses to run away and wagons to be turned over. Men looked darkly after the speeding cars and said, "There ought to be a law." Before long there was a law, and the highway department sent employees out along the roads to put up signs: slow, curve—35 miles; school zone—15 miles; and so on.

Thus it was before the time of Moses. God had called Abraham and had saved him by grace alone. There was nothing but the covenant of grace—promises that were absolutely without condition. Abraham and his descendants transgressed. It was though an angel might have said, "There ought to be a law." And so God called Moses and gave him the law. Moses came along, somewhat like a highway employee, and put up the signs of the commandments: "Thou shalt not. . . ." "Thou shalt not. . . ." "Thou shalt not. . . ."

Probably no automobile driver in this whole country has ever obeyed all of the traffic laws.

Unfortunately there are those who have a similar attitude toward the laws of God. They think that if they go along approximately in the general direction they think the laws indicate, God will not be too hard on them. They think of being brought before the judgment bar of God somewhat in terms of a traffic violation. They do not realize that the slightest infraction of the law of God is spiritual death—with a penalty that can be removed only by the shedding of the blood of the Son of God.

THE PARKING METER

An item in the *New York Times* told about Louis Booth from Poughkeepsie, N. Y. A policeman put a summons on Booth's windshield for failing to put a coin in the parking meter on Church Street. City Judge Charles Corbally dismissed the case when it was brought out that the meter had been set up after Mr. Booth had parked his car. The policeman had not seen the workman who did the job.

If we grant that parking the car in the spot indicated, was in itself harmful to general traffic, this incident becomes a perfect illustration for a spiritual truth. Something was added to the wrong that gave it the character of a transgression. Before the parking meter had been put up, the man could not be fined. After the parking meter was put up, he could be.

In the Epistle to the Galatians the Holy Spirit, after showing us that salvation is by grace, gives the reason why law has added, four hundred and thirty years after God had given the promise of salvation by grace. He asks the question and answers it: "Wherefore then serveth the law? It was added because of transgressions, till the seed should come . . ." (GALATIANS 3:19). Put in modern language it would mean that it was added in order to give to sin the character of transgression. Also, we read, "For until the law sin was in the world: but sin is not imputed when there is no law" (ROMANS 5:13).

RUSSIAN VERSUS BRITISH JURISDICTION

British authorities arrested a man on the German frontier, at a point that lay just between Russian jurisdiction and British jurisdiction. The Reds asked for the man; they claimed he was an escaped murderer; they wished to try him for his crime. The British knew that surrender of the man would be his death warrant, so they refused to give him up. Finally, he was set free; and defected to the West. All the while he was free from the sentence of death that had been passed upon him in the Russian jurisdiction.

Thus we were once under the jurisdiction of the law of sin and death. But when the Lord Jesus Christ was placed on the cross by the Father and put to death in accordance with the divine plan, God so joined us to our Lord in the death and in the resurrection that followed that He could righteously place us under the jurisdiction of the law of the spirit of life in Christ Jesus. It is this which forever frees us from the jurisdiction of the law of sin and death. God himself cannot hold anything against the believer whom He has joined to the Lord Jesus Christ.

THE TEN LINK CHAIN

A small boat in a stream of swiftly rushing water is secured to shore by a chain of only ten links. How many links must be cut to set boat adrift? A lady, wearing white gloves and wielding fine steel shears, may open one link—there goes the boat. Just one little link, but the boat is gone. A man may come down with a blow torch. He burns out all ten links—there goes the boat.

The man who commits one delicate little sin is the same in God's sight as the man who breaks all the commandments. If a man is less perfect than God, he is seen to be a sinner. Whether one link is broken or all the links are broken, the boat is adrift.

LAW AND GRACE

THE TRUCK COLLISION

Driving along a highway, you are stopped by an accident. A truck driver lies in the wreckage. Half a dozen men from passing cars place themselves shoulder to shoulder and try to lift the bumper. They tug and they pull until you see the veins standing out in their necks, but they cannot free the man. Still they keep straining at the impossible task. Finally, a wrecker drives up and is placed in position to hoist the weight of the disabled truck. But the only available spot for the wrecker to attach its hoist is that bumper at which the men are tugging. If the wrecker is to do its work, *the men must get out of the way*. If they persist in monopolizing that place, the wrecker cannot get in to do its work. There is no moral charge against these men; their strength is simply insufficient for the task.

The law must be abolished in order to let grace do the job the law cannot do.

THE UNDERTOW

I was born within a few miles of the Pacific Ocean, near Monterey Bay. The beach near our home had a very swift undertow and we all were aware that fatal accidents had occurred there more than once. The sandy beach that ran out level for a few yards, dropped suddenly and caught the unwary. One day when I was just learning to swin, I walked into the surf and was pretending to swim. One foot was balanced on the sand every other moment, while my arms thrashed the surface of the water; I looked as though I were swimming. I bounced along in this way for some time until—the bottom was not there. I had stepped off the ledge of sand and into deep water. In the Providence of God, I was buffeted by the waves and caught on a strong incoming roller and pitched up into the shallow water. I scrambled to my feet, retching from the water I had swallowed, and fought my way to the dry sand. I can still remember the terrifying panic at being out of my depth—nothing under me, strong currents pulling at me, the waves tossing me. I was at the mercy of the gray-green flood, not knowing in which direction it might take me.

Many Christians are brought to the place where they must step out of the sphere of doing something for themselves and into the place where they are to be borne along on the will of God without any possibility of doing anything about it. The transition from law to grace is so great and overwhelming that a vast number of believers in Christ never reach the place in their Christian experience where they know the freedom from law and the irresistibleness of grace.

THE WIDOWER'S HOUSEKEEPER

A widower is left with two small children so he hires a housekeeper to help him. He gives her instructions as to what she shall cook, how she is to keep the house and how she is to dress and care for the children. He goes about the house from time to time to see that all is in order, and that she is properly obeying his rules. He watches her dominion over the children and corrects her in a manner befitting the relationship of master and servant. After a year or so he marries the housekeeper. Their relationship is now entirely changed. He no longer follows her around the house to oversee her work. He no longer tells her what to cook for dinner. Now she is his in a relationship of love. Now she delights to do his will. Now she seeks to find out his desires and to perform them. Now she asks him what he would like to have for dinner and goes to some trouble to prepare it. She is no longer under law but under grace.

It is necessary for the Christian to understand that the life of true righteousness comes not from law but from the love of Christ under grace.

LEGALISM

NO MAKEUP

A college girl from my congregation met a girl who had almost no religious background. Child of a divided family, who had little concern with religion, she had reached college age with no church affiliation; she had not even attended any church services more than two or three times in her life. The Christian girl got her friend to attend church; the girl was saved during her senior year. Shortly after graduation the two girls went, with several others, on a trip to Europe. The girl from my church was to attend a Christian convention for a few days in Switzerland, while the others went on to Venice. On the morning she was to go to the convention, she appeared with no makeup. The new Christian cried out, "You have forgotten your makeup!" The older girl explained that the people at the convention did not wear makeup and that she was conforming to their practice. The new Christian was scandalized. If *that* was the essence of Christianity, she didn't want it. The girl from my congregation told me later, "I decided that if going without makeup would cause my sister in Christ to be scandalized, I would never go without it again."

More often than not the baby Christian, who has just come out of the world, is more scandalized by the narrow legalism of some believers than by the normal life of the so-called "worldly" believer.

NO STOCKINGS

Around 1928, I led a Bible conference at Montrose, Pennsylvania, for about two hundred young people and a few older people. One day two old ladies complained that some of the girls were not wearing stockings; these ladies wanted me to rebuke them. Looking them straight in the eye, I said, "The Virgin Mary never wore stockings." They gasped and said, "She didn't?" I answered, "In Mary's time stockings were unknown. So far as we know, they were first worn by prostitutes in Italy in the fifteenth century, when the Renaissance began. Later, a lady of the nobility scandalized the people by wearing stockings at a court ball. Before long, everyone in the upper classes was wearing stockings, and by Queen Victoria's time, stockings had become the badge of the prude." These ladies, who were holdovers from the Victorian epoch, had no more to say. I did not rebuke the girls for not wearing stockings. A year or two afterward, most girls in the United States were going without stockings in summer and nobody thought anything about it.

Nor do I believe that this led toward disintegration of moral standards in the United States. Times were changing, and the step away from Victorian legalism was all for the better. We should not be concerned about those who are well established not only in faith but in the rut of non-biblical legalism.

LOOKING AT CHRIST

SEEING NOTHING

An Eastern prince had difficulty with a riotous-living young man of his court. When the young man was given his choice between reformation and death, he complained that life was too hard—he could not reform. The prince ordered the young man to carry a shell full of oil through the city streets; two slaves walked beside him with swords drawn, ready to execute him if one drop of oil fell. When the young man came back, the prince asked him, "What did you see?" "Nothing," said the young man. "Nothing? Why it is the great market day. What did you hear?" Again the answer was "Nothing. For," said the young man, "I had my eyes fixed on the shell of oil. I could not look or listen, fearing my head might roll in the dust."

When we fix our gaze upon the Lord Jesus Christ we will be able to walk through the temptations of this life with safety.

THE UPWARD GAZE

A young man called my hotel and asked for an appointment. I was busy but I told him if he could walk along with me to my next engagement, I'd talk with him. We had gone only a few blocks when the young man caught my elbow; I turned to see him gazing upwards. I supposed he had seen an airplane, or something similar, but just as suddenly he dropped my arm; we continued walking and talking. A few moments later he repeated the same gesture and look; again he said nothing of what concerned him or what guided his gaze. The third time, I asked him what was going on. He was greatly embarrassed, but finally he explained:

"A few days ago, I met a wonderful girl at a Bible conference. I knew at once that she was the girl I have been seeking
for several years. I sat with her in meetings, played tennis
with her, talked with her, told her I loved her. She told me that
she liked me, but we would have to write to each other and get
better acquainted. I have no picture of her, and I have been
trying to remember as I think about her all the time. Well,
yesterday I was walking along the street, and a pretty girl was
coming in the opposite direction. I looked at her, as a fellow
will, and then, a moment after she had passed I tried to think
of the girl I love; to my horror she looked a little bit like the
girl who had just passed me. I went over to the side of the
curb and stood there, almost sick, and I asked the Lord to
erase the memory of the girl who had just passed and let me
see my true love again. I—I'd rather have *her* on the inside of
my eyelids. Well, I got back the image of her so that I can
recall her at will, but I determined not to look at anyone else
who might even for a moment dim the vision of the girl I truly
love. So, as we were walking along I was deeply engrossed in
our conversation, but when I saw someone approaching who
was pretty. I just looked up in the air, guiding myself as I
walked, by touching your elbow. I wasn't aware that I had
done it so strongly that you would notice."

I looked at him, and was filled with great delight, and I saw
at once the spiritual application. The Lord Jesus Christ is the
fairest of ten thousand and our vision of Him must be the
spiritual vision from the Word of God, not the fleshy linea-
ments of some artist's concept, but our Lord, as He reveals
Himself to each longing heart. We will, if we love Him dearly,
be deeply grieved if our thoughts wander from Him, or if some
vision of earthly things shall intrude to make us think of Him
in the guise of some passing impostor.

VISTA VISION

A picture on a small screen shows a mother, father and child
walking along. The mother and the father slap and shake the

child until the child's teeth rattle, and the child begins to whimper. They slap and strike the child; watchers say, "How cruel!" But look at it in wide-angle: it's forty degrees below zero in Dakota in the middle of the winter; the three have had to abandon their car to walk to safety. The child wants to lie down in the snow and go to sleep; the parents are striking the child to keep it from dying. They keep urging the child on.

When you look at God and the world and see the evil that is in the world, all you are seeing is a little eighteen-inch screen. But when you see it in the light of the whole of the Word of God, you see that the purpose is to know that in this universe God's methods are blessing through humility and yieldedness to Him.

LOVE, HUMAN

THE CRIPPLED SISTER

A crippled girl, living in the slums, underwent an operation that might enable her to walk again. When the operation was over, she needed a blood transfusion; her fourteen-year-old brother, a tough boy of the streets, volunteered. He was taken to the hospital, to the bedside of his crippled sister. He stared in tight-lipped silence while the vein in his arm was opened so, that the blood might flow into the body of his unconscious sister. When it was over, the doctor put his hand on the boy's shoulder and told him that he was very brave. The boy did not comprehend; he had not understood the nature of a transfusion. After a moment, he looked up and said, "Doc, how long will it be before I croak?" As far as the boy was concerned he had been dying; slowly and willingly, he had stoically watched the blood flow—drop by drop, expecting his sister's life to mean his own death.

There, indeed, is the highest in human love. If this human love is to be seen in its highest degree, it will be through the words of Christ, who said, "Greater love hath no man than this, that a man lay down his life for his friends" (JOHN 15:13).

MARRIAGE REQUIREMENTS

A young man thinking about marriage had a list of requirements against which he checked every girl whom he met. Finally, he saw a girl who met most of his requirements, and he became engaged to her within five days. While they were driving to her parents' home, he slapped his foot on the brake, pulled over to the side of the road, and said, "Oh, I forgot to ask you if you are healthy." She was and the marriage was successful but the young man's meticulous caution was a standing joke among his friends.

Now, suppose that the man had put his list of requirements in writing: She is to keep the house clean, prepare the meals and wash the dishes. She will do the laundry. She will not allow herself to weigh over 125 pounds, and she will not cut her hair too short. One day the wife finds this list. She has been doing most of these things before she found the list, but it reveals to her some things that she has not been doing. As she reads the list, she ponders how to live up to his requirements; not because she must, but because she loves her husband.

We so sorely need: *love*. It cannot be pumped up, or forced. Love comes from knowing the Lord Jesus Christ. As we know Him thus, we learn to love Him, and as we love Him we love our neighbors. When we love Him thus, we shall delight to obey Him.

THE OFFICE SECRETARY

One day I was visited by a young man in his thirties, who had a personal problem. He told his story somewhat like this: "I work for such-and-such a company, and I have a private office. Several months ago my secretary was absent and I had to use another girl. One day she brought papers for my perusal; she got too close, and when she leaned over the desk, she let her hair trail across my face. I fought it down, but after all, I am a man, and toward the end of the day I put my hand on her and she came right back to be kissed. Even while kissing her, I was visualizing my two children running to meet me and my wife standing in the door. I hated what I was doing, but I kept on. I had the greatest desire to push her from me, but I kept pulling her to me; my body was doing one thing and my mind was doing another.

"When I went home that night, I hugged my children so

hard that one of them cried, and when we got him to laughing, I told them that it was because I loved them so much. I had tears in my eyes and my wife's eyes were shining. We all clung together in one of those moments that are indescribable. My wife was supremely happy, because I walked around the house that evening, touching familiar things that we had scrimped to buy, expressing my love for the home and for her, and before God I was never more true. Next day, the office intrigue began all over again. I was never more miserable in my life.

"Before a month had gone by I realized that my lust and my love were in a terrible battle. When I came home, there was everything that I wanted in life. When I went to the office, the machine of my body seemed geared to something terrible that was purely mechanical, and which I wanted to get out of more than any fly ever wanted to get off fly-paper. I heard my wife tell someone that I was becoming more and more of a home-body, and that all I wanted to do was stay at home. And it is true. I follow her around the house, talk with her in the kitchen where she is working, and watch her as she puts the children to bed.

"This morning, when I left the house, she told me that she thought she was the happiest woman in the world, because I showed so much that I loved her alone. I could hardly talk. In fact tears came to my eyes, and when I lifted a lock of her hair to dry them, I said to her, 'I love you more than life itself.' She cried and I crushed her to me until she screamed and smiled at the same time. Then I ran off to my train. But now what shall I do?"

With the husband's consent, I called the wife to my office and told her the story. Fear leaped to her eyes, but I reassured her. We took a taxi and went to his office. He was expecting us, and I stood by as they embraced and she said, "I know, I know, I understand, it's all right." Then I called the other girl into the office. The scene that followed typified the mortal struggle between the flesh and the spirit, both striving for the mastery of that body. But the wife was not striving; she knew that the mind, soul and heart of her husband had never been away from her. She understood the glandular warfare of his body, and that his lust had sprung to life in response to the lure of strange flesh. She looked at him with complete understanding and love.

The secretary stood there speechless. I said to her, "She knows all about it. She loves him and he loves her completely; he has never had any thought toward you except one of animal lust. You were never wanted except physically, and you are not wanted at all from now on. Do you understand?" I asked her to wait in the hall while I prayed with the couple. As I left, I saw the secretary dabbing at her eyes; I stopped and talked to her about her need of Jesus Christ.

The lust that draws you away from Christ may not be the carnal lust that attracted the man in my story. It may be some matter of the pride of soul, some inherent dishonesty, some ancient pattern of sin in which you indulged so often that it seems to bind you like a strong cord. The Holy Spirit can bring before you the thing that is marring your victory.

LOVE OF GOD

THE BABY SITTER

We went out one evening and left our children under the care of a baby sitter. When we returned about midnight, the girl was greatly concerned that our oldest child had been crying for about four hours. Nothing that the baby sitter could do would comfort her. I went to the child's room and found her flushed and sobbing, her face red with long weeping. When I picked her up, she threw her arms around my neck and sobbed, "Daddy, say it isn't true. You do love me." I replied that of course I loved her, and the child then said, "She said that if I was bad you wouldn't love me, and I know that I've been bad, so maybe you do not love me."

I pressed her to me, and said, "My dear child; I always love you. When you are good I love you with a love that makes me glad; when you are bad I love you with a love that makes me sad. But I love you, good or bad. I am always your daddy." The child was already more calm, and the dawn of a smile came to her face. I began to cover her gently with kisses, and then I told her that a good daddy had to be with her as the Lord was with Him, and with all of us who have become His children. She smiled and was soon asleep.

A man who has been made alive in Christ Jesus, but who has gotten out of the will of God is in Christ but he is not abiding in Christ. He is not cast forth as a son; he is cast forth as a branch. None of his actions please God, but this does not mean that God does not love him. God does love him, and is watching over him in every way, seeking to bring him back to the place of full fellowship.

THE DAYDREAMER

Several years ago a young woman told me that nothing in her life seemed to make sense to her: she had passed her thirtieth birthday and she was still single; her faith was a distant, intellectual affair that did not seem to enter into her daily life at all; she was unhappy. To all questions on spiritual matters she gave answers that were orthodox clichés; I had the feeling that the truth had not entered deeply into her life. I questioned her about her work and about outside interests. She confessed that she spent most of her free time by herself. When I asked her what she did with her time, she was rather hazy. I accused her of spending a great deal of time daydreaming. She admitted that hours of her time were spent in that way. "And what is the pattern of your daydreams?" I asked her. She was obviously embarrassed and did not want to go on with the subject, but when I probed, she sat foward in her chair and answered me. What she said showed a pattern of interest in self and exaltation of self; I tried to bring her to the point of very definite trusting in Christ. I sensed that she needed an about-face in her thinking. I told her she had to face the fact that she might go on as her boss's secretary until they gave her the gold button for forty years of faithful service to the company, and that she might never know human love as she dreamed of it. She was shocked for a moment, as reality often shocks a dreamer, and then she said, "What shall I do?" I told her that she must realize that the most important things of life are the invisible things, and that there is a love from God that fills all the emptiness of life; it can satisfy even when human loves failed. "God is love," and "God is for us." I told her how to change the direction of her thinking from daydreams to meditation. As time went on her whole life was transformed. She began to meditate on what we are in ourselves and on how much God had stooped to love us. Above all she stopped thinking of faith in impersonal terms; instead of thinking of a distant God who loved a conglomerate world, she came to realize a very personal God who loved her, individually.

Thus it may be for every one of us. Life is planned by God to bring us to our sense of need of Him. The difficulties in your life, perhaps, are God's calling you away from things in order that you may understand how much He loves you.

LOVE TAKEN FOR GRANTED

A mother, in one of those delicious moments that make mothers what they are, drew her two-year-old daughter to her and said, "Oh, I love you!" The little girl, very much occupied with the whim of the moment, drew away and said, "Yes, I know." Love was taken for granted.

As early in life as the second year the Word was being illustrated: "Even a child is known by his doings . . ." (PROVERBS 20:11). Tragedy occurs when someone hears the voice of God saying, as He does from Calvary, and as He does from a thousand thousand circumstances of life, "My child, I love you," and is answered with an indifference that shows that His love is not really returned. Most of life's sadness flows from such an attitude. The windows of heaven are opened when we can learn to feel deeply: "We love him, because he first loved us" (I JOHN 4:19).

THE RIGHT GIRL FOR THE SON

A father and a mother love their son and want the very best for him. They hope he will find a girl outstanding in character and attainments, and that this girl will make him a good wife. They watch him pay attention to two cheap hussies, each of whom is seeking to capture the son for herself. The two girls may be jealous of each other in the modern sense of unpleasant fear and resentment, but the parents are jealous of their son in the Bible sense of the word. They are not jealous *of* him, nor are they jealous *of* either of the girls. They have a feeling of great love and desire for their son; they wish to protect him from any unworthy choice; they wish only that he will turn to that which will be best for him.

God has jealousy for us; He loves us so much that He does not wish us to waste our powers and our affections on the trivial and tawdry. God's whole purpose in the processes of life is to undeceive us, to turn us from hope or trust in ourselves and turn us back to all hope and trust in Himself.

LYING

THE GROUP METHOD

General S. L. A. Marshall discovered that men interviewed immediately after battle are in such a state of shock that they can tell only the truth; officially it is called Group Method. General Marshall says that the average man cannot lie in the presence of comrades who would contradict him if he were telling an untruth; haunted by the memory of the recent dead, he will not lie. Whether this is completely accurate may be open to question.

We do know, however, that when the Lord arrays the lost before Him at the judgment of the great white throne there will be no lying. "Every mouth will be stopped and all the world be brought guilty before God," and all of the judgment of God will be according to truth. The way out is to come to Christ who is the truth.

LEARNING TO LIE

A woman who had trouble with her daughter said, "I don't know where that child ever learned to lie." But the child had heard her mother say, "There's that horrible Mrs. Doakes coming; I wish that woman would keep her face out of this house." The mother cleaned up as rapidly as she could—straightening out, putting things in closets, getting everything out of the way. When the bell rang, the mother opened the door and cried out, "Oh, my darling, it's so good to see you, it's so nice to have you." Where did her daughter learn to lie?

Even a gray lie or a white lie is not justified in God's sight. Your little dears are going to learn more from the way you act and talk than they will ever learn from what you tell them.

MARRIAGE

THE BOSS

A woman, interviewed about the secret of her successful marriage, insisted, "My husband is the Boss. I believe in letting him make all the important decisions."

The interviewer asked, "Who made the decision that he was to be the Boss?"

She replied, "Why, naturally, I did."

The TV audience was supposed to laugh, but this woman had hold of a profound biblical truth. God had long since made this decision (EPHESIANS 5:23,24); the woman had merely accepted the place for which she was created. That is why her marriage was a success. However, husbands should be warned that God has said that if a man doesn't have sense enough to know how to assume this great responsibility, God will not answer his prayers (I PETER 3:7).

REPAIRING THE ELECTRIC LIGHT

A wife asked her husband to repair an electric light over the kitchen sink, and he promised to do so. Next day she again asked him to fix the light and again he promised, but this time with some irritation. Two or three days later she asked again; "Stop nagging me," he shouted. The light was very necessary for her work at the sink, but if she called an electrician to do the job, her husband might explode. Having promised to do the work, he should have done it; his failure showed lack of understanding of his wife's problems. To her it revealed a great flaw in the man she loved—he did not have a proper sense of responsibility and integrity.

The way to avoid such difficulties in the adjustment of husband and wife is to have prayer together every day, asking the Lord to keep both in the way of grace. It is also good for each to be willing to face weaknesses in self and to ask the other, "Is there something that I do that annoys you?" When the answer is given in love, it is a small matter for love to remove the annoyance.

MEEKNESS

THE WINNING HORSE

What is meekness? Many people have a totally wrong idea of it, but they can learn the true meaning by listening to jockeys and horse-trainers after a horse race. The horse that wins the race is "the meekest on the track." This is the horse most under control, the horse that responds most quickly to the jockey's guidance. The self-willed horse, the factious horse, is frequently left at the post; when he does get started he may run faster than some of the others, but he does not finish with the leaders who were meek.

In the Word of God, meekness is presented to us as a vertical virtue, not as a horizontal one. Meekness is the way a man stands before God—even as Moses was able to stand before Pharaoh—he is bolder than any man. "The meek shall inherit the earth."

MILLENNIUM

ON THE WRONG FERRY BOAT

About the turn of the century, a man rushed down to make a New York ferry; just as the ferry was pulling out, he jumped and landed on the rail of the boat. He sat there exhausted, breathing heavily. After a few minutes, he stood up and walked toward the center of the boat. A fellow-passenger said, "You almost missed it."

"Yes," he said, "but I'll get there now in time for the third race."

"The third race? Where do you think you're going?"

"Why, over to the race track."

"Well," said the other, "you're on the Methodist Church chartered Sunday-school picnic boat."

The man went over to the captain and said, "Captain, I'll give you $500, if you'll put me back."

The captain said. "Look, buddy, it took us twenty minutes to get out here; it would take us twenty minutes to turn around and go back, and another twenty minutes to get out here—that's an hour. There are 2,000 children on this ferry and that amounts to two thousand hours of their picnic time. You're on this boat till we get back at nine o'clock tonight."

"Oh," said the man, "where's the bar?"

"It's closed for the day," replied the captain.

No bar, nothing but children prattling and singing hymns—all day this man had to live in that atmosphere. When the boat docked at nine o'clock that night, the race-track man was first off—to get to the nearest bar.

MILLENNIUM

This is a picture of what the millennium is going to be for millions of people on this earth. They hate; they do not want righteousness. Their hearts are deceitful above all things and incurably wicked. All men will be as men here on earth; hatred will increase and multiply; curses will rise in their hearts against the Christ whom they see with their own eyes.

MISSIONS

A CHINESE PARISH

A man I met spoke intimately of a certain section of China; he mentioned specific towns and villages, certain missionaries in various stations and the names of Chinese pastors. I asked when he had been in China, and he replied that he never been there. Years before, his college roommate had gone there as a missionary; they had corresponded regularly, writing once a month, and he had spent a great deal of time praying for his friend. He marked on maps the trips his friend described in his letters. He dotted his map with marks identifying churches and chapels; he memorized the names of believers about whom the missionary wrote. He supported the work with his gifts, sent special sums for special needs, helped to educate some of the young men of the region and daily lifted his heart to God in prayer for what had become his parish.

You, too, can travel with your gifts and your prayers; you can win some of that for which Christ died and lay it at His feet as a part of your own heart.

MYSTERY

MY SECRETARY'S ENGAGEMENT

Many years ago, I had a wonderful, young private secretary. I was rather happy that as far as I knew she never dated any young man; selfishly I hoped that she would postpone marriage indefinitely so that I would have the advantage of her services. At the same time a young man, who was studying in one of the theological seminaries, was working in our church. He was in church often, but I had never known him to have a date with my secretary; I never connected them in my mind. One Sunday morning as I parked my car near the church, a young woman of our congregation came to me and said, "Max and Elisabeth are engaged." I was astonished—it could not be true. I walked fifty yards toward the side door of the church, and a young man on the steps said to me, "Max and Elisabeth are engaged." I shook my head in wonder and walked inside the door. Two young people were standing there and they said, "Max and Elisabeth are engaged." "Impossible," I answered, "but everyone is telling me so." I walked into my office and there stood the young lady in question; her smile proclaimed the well-announced subject. "Is it true?" I asked, and she answered, "Last night. We are going to be married and are going to Mexico as missionaries with the Wycliffe Translators."

Here was a true *mysterion* in the New Testament sense. It had been completely hidden, absolutely unknown, totally unsuspected. Suddenly it was whispered to one person, and the news spread like leaves in the wind.

NEW BIRTH

FOUND

At the Commencement Exercises of a Bible Institute in Canada, a young woman gave a testimony that will never be forgotten. She stood before the great audience and said, "I was found on a doorstep in a basket in Leeds, England, when I was six days old. I was found by the Lord Jesus Christ here in Canada ten years ago."

Many people might think it a great disadvantage to be abandoned by parents and left to the mercy of the world. To be found by Christ, however, is life's greatest experience because it is the beginning of eternity. You may have been born in the wealthiest of homes, been surrounded by loving care, but if you have never been found by Christ, you are lost indeed.

THE GREAT NORTH ROAD

Out in India I traveled on the Great North Road that runs up through the Punjab and the United Provinces. One side of the road was soft earth for the camels, the other side was macadam for the motor cars. In the rainy season the camel path was a miry bog. If a man was walking to Calcutta on the muddy side of the road, another might approach him and say that he had an experience to share with him: walking was easier on the paved side of the road. The man in the mud moves over to the paved road and cries out that his life has been changed. But I come along with my biblical desire for truth and ask two questions: Where were you going when you were walking in the mud? The answer is: Calcutta. And where are you going now that you are on the highway? And the answer is still, Calcutta.

You do not need your life changed, but you need it exchanged. You need an absolutely new life; this comes only from the new birth. Only then will you find yourself on a new road and traveling in a new direction.

THE INTRUDER

A man and his wife telephoned from Philadelphia and said they had a great problem—could they come and talk to me? They did not know Christ, and as they began, I told them that here was the heart of their problem. I spoke to them of their need for Christ, and they talked about their good works—they were kind and charitable. I said to them that there was no other way. Then I said, "Where do you live?" and they gave me the number of their house. I continued, "Suppose someone came there at three o'clock in the morning and put a ladder up to the second-floor window and began to climb in, what would you do?" "Well," said the man, "I suppose I'd shoot him." I said, "What right have you to shoot a man. After all, can't a man come into your house in any way that he wants to come?" He said, "No." Then I said, "You are saying that you can get into God's heaven any way, any time—by any back window that you choose. God Almighty has made definite, positive and absolute rules for entering His heaven—rules as definite as our civilization makes—if you go to somebody's house you ring, you knock. As the Pennsylvania Dutch say, 'If the bell don't make—bump.' Make a noise and come up in the way that a house owner decides. If I approach your house and a sign says, 'Please go around to the side door,' I go around to the side door. This is your order. You have a right."

God has done the same thing. He says that anybody may come in, but they must come by the cross of Jesus Christ. "That's all," says God. "That is the one condition." And if man, in the stupid arrogance of his blind pride, says, "But I'll make me a little ladder; I've been working on my ladder for years. I painted a window on the wall; I put my ladder up to the window I painted and I want it to turn into glass so that I can break it and go through in my own time and my own way." God will not tolerate that.

THE LARGE BOWL

Those who have seen training film made by the cartoon method may understand the following. A large bowl stands in the center of the picture; the bowl is broken into a hundred pieces and the pieces can be seen falling down. At the same time, the cartoonist draws a dotted line to show the form of the original bowl as it was before it was broken. A new bowl is then poured into the old outline—a bowl that cannot be broken. None of the old pieces are used in the creation of the new bowl. Finally, the old pieces are swept away and nothing but the new bowl remains.

If we are saved, we are bowls of wrath and have the power to break ourselves, but we do not have the power to put ourselves together again. God is not going to be frustrated by man's willfulness and sin; He pours new life into our molds. In His own time and in His own ways, both unknown to us, He quickens us, makes us alive in Christ.

ONE OF GOD'S FINGERS

Some one asked a Christian if were not afraid of slipping through the Lord's fingers. The reply was simple truth: "That is impossible, for I am one of the fingers."

By the new birth we become a part of the spiritual body of Christ.

THE RECONSTRUCTED HAND

An orthopedic surgeon described how he restored the hand of a man who had lost his thumb and first finger. First, the surgeon took a roll of flesh—about the size of the handle of a valise—from the wall of the abdomen. The stump of the thumb was then attached to the flesh, and after a few months it had grown to the thumb, so that a further cut left a flapping tube of skin and flesh attached to the thumb base. Then a piece of bone from the tibia was placed inside the tube, and in a few months there was a complete thumb. The process was repeated on some of the fingers so that the man had his hand reconstructed, with 75 percent of the functions restored. I asked the surgeon if it would not be possible to use bones and tissues from bodies that had been killed in accidents. He hesitated a moment and then said, "It is very rare that we can get them soon enough." I pressed him for specific knowledge, and he told me that bones and tissues could be used providing they were secured within a few minutes after death. Then he said, "The whole body from head to foot is filled with a host of invaders that are held back by life. These invaders are everywhere and the moment death comes, they sweep out to destroy the body. Like runners that race from the starting point when the gun opens a race, these invaders sweep into the body. Within two hours the pathogenic organisms have carried their work of disintegration so far, there is nothing to do but dispose of the body."

The same law works spiritually. When Adam first sinned, death passed upon the race. In the spiritual realm, life was lost, and all of the spiritual invaders swept over the entire being of man so that his spiritual nature was completely disintegrated. Henceforth, nothing that was in man or from man could ever be used to repair or to regenerate spiritual life. The new life that is placed within us when we are born again is the workmanship of God.

OBEDIENCE

THE CONGO SERPENT

In the Belgian Congo, the weather was hot and dank. No breath of air stirred; leaves hung from the trees as though they were weighted. In the garden not far from the missionary home a small boy played under a tree. Suddenly, the father called to him: "Philip, obey me instantly—get down on your stomach." The boy reacted at once, and his father continued, "Now crawl toward me fast." The boy again obeyed. After he had come about halfway, the father said, "Now stand up and run to me." The boy reached his father and turned to look back—hanging from the branch under which he had been playing was a fifteen-foot serpent.

Are we always as ready to obey? Or do we say: "Tell me why"? "Explain to me"? "I will after awhile"? Let it be, "Speak, Lord, Thy servant hears."

THE DELAYED FERRY BOAT

A middle-aged man, who was a very young Christian, found in the Word of God that Christians are commanded to obey every ordinance of man for the Lord's sake (1 PETER 2:13). Rushing to a business appointment that involved catching a ferry boat, he was tempted to do seventy in a fifty-mile-per-hour zone. He said to himself as he slowed down to the legal limit, "Lord, You wrote the Book; I didn't. I am going to obey, even if it costs my appointment." He thought he would have to wait half an hour, but to his amazement the ferry had been delayed ten minutes; he made it. He had never known it to be late before. He thanked the Lord who wrote the Book, learning that He holds all circumstances in His hand, and he thanked the Lord who had given him the heart to obey.

231

OLD NATURE

BOOTSTRAPS

Years ago, a family lived in California. The father had been born in Virginia, the mother, in New York. The Virginia grandfather had never seen his daughter-in-law or his grandchildren, so he determined to visit the West to see his family. His impending visit caused great joy and great preparation in the household. The house was painted; the curtains were cleaned; everything was pointed toward Grandfather's visit. Grandfather will be here in two months; Grandfather will be here in one month; in two weeks; in a week; in three days; tomorrow. And then he arrived. He was a handsome old gentleman of the South, with a white beard like General Robert E. Lee's, and a twinkle in his blue eyes.

The small grandson took a large share of the old gentleman's interest, and the boy was greatly impressed with his grandfather. The old gentleman's slippers fascinated him. The slippers had soft leather tops and loops in front and in back by which they were pulled on the foot. One day the five-year-old, put his feet, shoes and all, into the strange slippers, and reached down and put his fingers in the loops. The old grandfather said, "Pull hard, my boy, and see if you can lift yourself off the ground." The boy tugged and tugged, and the old man said, "Well, that's too bad. You'll have to eat some more oatmeal, and then we will try again tomorrow."

The little boy had stopped eating in the midst of his breakfast—there were more important things than food! The parents urged him to eat, and then the grandfather took charge. He reminded the boy that the slippers were waiting, and that there would be another trial when breakfast was over. If the movement of the spoon stopped for too long a period, the old man would wink at the boy, make a gesture toward his room where the slippers were, and the boy would speedily go to work on his oatmeal. When the breakfast was concluded, the pair, old and young, would go solemnly into the bedroom where another trial would be made. The little boy would pull and tug, but he could never lift himself off the ground. At a convenient moment the old gentleman would say, "Well, we didn't make it this morning, but we'll try again tomorrow."

This is the case of the sinner. He cannot lift himself, but the Lord Jesus Christ lays hold upon him and lifts him. We read it in one of the Psalms: "He brought me up also out of an horrible pit, out of the miry clay, and set my feet upon a rock, and established my goings. And he hath put a new song in my mouth, even praise unto our God . . ." (PSALM 40:2, 3).

BUBBLE GUM

A small boy, described as a "shy, second-grader, eight years old, a little owlish in spectacles," was guilty of committing a crime in a New Jersey school. It was Valentine's Day. He brought a Valentine and put it on his teacher's desk; then he went down into the basement and set fire to the school by lighting wastepaper in the boiler room. When the Fire Commissioner conducted an inquiry, evidence pointed to the boy. He readily admitted that he had set fire to the school. When he was asked why, he explained, as the news report put it, with childish simplicity, "In class yesterday, they took away my bubble gum."

The child says in effect, "I am on the throne in my life, and I want everybody else to bow down before me. I want to rule. When I want anything, I want it, and that is sufficient reason for my having it. If I want bubble gum, I am to have it. If anybody takes it away from me, I have a right to lash out and destroy anything that stands in the way of my whim and desire."

There is only one way to curb the fierce pride of the Adamic nature that rises even in a child. That is to plant the new life of the Lord Jesus Christ alongside it through the new birth by which we are made "partakers of the divine nature" (II PETER 1:4). Day by day we must submit our lives to the control of the Lord Jesus Christ, in order that He may keep the old nature crucified with Him.

THE COBRA

When I was traveling in southeastern Asia, I reached a certain town early in January. After looking over some of the mission works, I went to the home of missionary friends for lunch. The thermometer registered over a hundred, and since it is customary to sleep for an hour or so during the period of greatest heat, my friends took me into their guest room. They apologized for the presence of a large packing case, filled with paper boxes and Christmas package wrappings. They said that the case had arrived from America full of presents for themselves and their children, and that it had come several days late. They had opened the presents and had put all of the boxes, wrappings and ribbons in the case to sort out later.

I went to sleep, but was awakened by a rustling noise; something was in the packing case. I dozed off and again I was awakened by the rustling of papers. Siesta time was over; I went out into the main room of the house and told them of the noise in the packing case. Instantly the atmosphere became tense. A quick call brought the servants running to the door; they stopped and looked at the box with wary eyes. The talk between missionaries and servants was in the native language which I did not understand, but the air of excitement needed no translation. A rake was hooked over the top of the case; it was pulled into the living room, then to the door and out onto the porch. It was then lowered, still being pulled from a distance, to the ground level of the yard. By this time a dozen servants had come running from neighboring houses. Each one carried a club, an ax, or a hoe. Finally, the case was turned on its side and out slithered a cobra about seven feet long. It was clubbed to death quickly, while the servants prodded the remaining litter carefully to see if the deadly serpent had a mate. The excitement among the natives continued unabated for more than an hour. They rummaged in every part of the room, including the bedclothes of the bed on which I had just been sleeping; they looked for holes through which the snake might have come, and for evidences that it might have been accompanied by a mate. The missionaries served tea, but the conversation revolved around snakes.

The point that I underline from this story is the tense attitude of danger that pervaded every man, woman and child in the group—missionaries and natives. They knew that something alive and very dangerous was there and they did not lower their guard for even a fraction of a second. No politeness toward a guest was allowed to turn their attention from the peril. There was no thought of avoiding the danger that was there; death was in the case—it had to be dealt with immediately.

The clear recognition of the aliveness of the old fleshly nature should cause every fiber of the new being to be alert to face the potential carnality in order that it may be delivered over to the death which is its proper sentence.

FIVE POUNDS LIGHTER

A lady discovered that her bathroom scales registered five pounds lighter if she stood on her left foot instead of on her right. It made no difference to her that outside scales confirmed the right-foot weight. She wanted to be lighter than she was, so she took comfort in standing on the left foot.

Old nature always wants to believe the best of itself. Its pride is that of Satan, and it takes comfort in anything and everything that speaks well of it. Only in the Word of God do we get the true picture of what we are. Here are the scales that have no false springs and no positions that are off balance. Here we find the slaying of pride and the exaltation of the Lord Jesus Christ. Any other balance is false, and therefore, an abomination to the Lord.

MY OWN WAY

One day, one of my children came out of the dining room with me and walked along to my study. There was a question about what was to be done in a certain matter. As I sat down at my desk I gave a clear and detailed answer. My child hesitated, then broke in with a question. I kept on at my work without looking up. "But, Daddy . . ." the child insisted, and phrased the matter in another way. Mother came along to find out what the delay was in fulfilling the command. The child answered, "I am trying to find out what Daddy wants me to do." At this point I broke in: "No. You are not trying to find out what I want you to do. You are trying to see if you can make me relent on the conditions so that you will be able to do what you want to do instead of doing what you know we want you to do. Now go and do it immediately."

How many times the Heavenly Father has to deal with us in this way. Our old nature is incurably addicted to having its own way. This is inherent in the statement that tells of the distance which separates the soul from God. "All we like sheep have gone astray; and we have turned every one to his own way . . ." (ISAIAH 53:6).

HEINZ NORDHOFF

Before the war Heinz Nordhoff was the manager of Opel, the German branch of General Motors. When the war ended he was forced to take a job as a manual laborer and existed on handouts from friends. The British knew his worth and offered

him a job directing Volkswagen, a bombed factory that manufactured very small cars. He didn't want to leave the production of big cars, but had little alternative; under his leadership,
Volkswagen has become one of the strong links in the great
economic revival in Germany. Said Nordhoff: "The future begins when you cut every tie with the lost past."

All of us are born linked with the lost, Adamic past. As long
as we try to salvage anything from it, we are in spiritual pov-
erty and desperation. But when we come to Christ, the Holy
Spirit begets us anew, and we become a new creation (II CORIN-
THIANS 5:17). The future begins when we cut every tie with
the lost past. We can't do it, but Christ can.

THE NAVAL OFFICER'S PROMOTION

A young naval officer kept his promotion to lieutenant com-
mander a secret, until he got his new gold-leaf collar insignia.
He walked proudly into his home and waited for his wife's
surprise and delight. An hour passed and she said nothing; he saw she was on the verge of tears. He put his arms
around her and asked what was wrong. "You didn't even notice my new hairdo!" she sobbed.

The individual is, by nature, interested in himself. Perhaps
this story can explain many a broken home and many a crisis
in business. Only one remedy for such a situation—the love of
Christ in the heart—can make us esteem each other better than
self, and in honor prefer one another. Such a transformation is
an evidence of the new birth.

STOLEN CHECKS

A thief, who stole GI checks from mailboxes and cashed
them, would not ordinarily make the front pages of the national press and be written up in the great news magazines. In
one such case, however, the thief was the twenty-seven-year-
old son of a high official in Harvard University. The judge, in

imposing sentence of two years in prison, said he could not understand how a man of his "background and intelligence could descend to the level of a common thief."

The judge was ignorant because he thought that education, background and breeding could change the old nature. It is possible, of course, for culture and training to iron out certain wrinkles of sin, such as open thievery, but the heart of man cannot be changed by background or education. When the young thief said that he had stolen "because I like a good time," he was illustrating what God has said, that man has turned to "his own way." The cure is not education, but Christ.

SUSPENDED GRAVITY

Tests made in a T-33 Jet trainer have made it possible to suspend gravity for as long as forty seconds. By flying the proper curve at high speed the occupants of the plane become weightless. A ball tossed from the hand does not fall; gravity is suspended. Half of the men tested felt pleasant, elated sensations. One wished he could live forever at gravity zero. There was a feeling of complete relaxation.

God describes the Christian life in terms of a double pull from the flesh and the spirit (GALATIANS 5:17). When we look to Christ and surrender to Him, we may know what it is to walk in the spirit and to have triumph for forty seconds, minutes, hours. . . . At times our old nature will make its downward gravitational pull known, but God has made it possible for us to return and rest in Him.

THE TONSILLECTOMY

A minister friend of mine had trouble with his throat. He went to the doctor, who said to him, "You must have your tonsils removed at once." The minister replied, "But I have a big speaking schedule." The doctor relented and painted the minister's throat to fix him up for a few days. The climax came in Tucson, Arizona; the minister was stricken; he could hardly talk, and again he went to the doctor. The minister said, "You must paint my throat, you must help me get through." But the doctor said, "Look, if you don't take those tonsils out, your ministry is going to be finished entirely." Now when the doctor used that phrase, *if you don't take those tonsils out,* he didn't mean the man was to get a mirror and operate on himself. When he said, "If you don't take those tonsils out," he meant, "If you don't put yourself in the hands of a competent surgeon."

When the Bible says to put the old nature to death, it doesn't mean that you can do it, it means you are to deliver it over to Him for doing.

PERFECTION

A DOLLAR'S WORTH OF SUGAR

When I was a small boy in California, we spent our summers in Mount Hermon. For supplies we went to a little country store in Felton. In those days, there were no electric scales; bread was neither sliced nor wrapped, nor was sugar sold by weight—you bought a dollar's worth. The grocer scooped sugar from a barrel into a bag on one side of the scale while he placed weights on the other. When the magic moment came and the scales balanced, he left his scoop in the sugar barrel. The question is: How many pounds of sugar did we get for our dollar?

Someone may say, "I think there were twelve pounds because I once read in a book that at that time they sold twelve pounds of sugar for a dollar." Someone else says, "No, I think there were thirteen. I used to visit my aunt who had a grocery store in Vermont, and I personally weighed out thirteen pounds." A third person declaims, "Well, my father told me that his father told him that his father told him—and it's a strong family tradition—that there were twelve-and-a-half pounds of sugar for a dollar."

One person may argue on the basis of what he has read; another, on human experience, and the third on family tradition. But I say, "That grocer in the Felton county store put fourteen pounds of weights on the scales—two five-pound weights, one two-pound, and two one-pound weights. So, for a dollar we got fourteen pounds of sugar."

God says that He has a scale; in the Bible He reveals what He has put on His side. What has God set on His side of the scale? Perfection! God cannot admit anyone to Heaven who is not perfect. If God graded you, and 70 percent were passing,

240

then Heaven would be 30 percent dirty; if He let anyone into Heaven with a grade of 99.44 percent, Heaven would still be dirty. So God must demand perfection.

CUTTING UP THE NATIONAL GEOGRAPHIC

One day I was going through a pile of magazines, clipping various items, when my five-year-old daughter came in. She asked me if she could help. I smiled at the earnest look on her face, and wrote a little note which I told her to take to her mother. The note read, "Please deliver to bearer the small pair of unpointed scissors." A few moments later she came back into my study, carrying the scissors. I then turned over to her the pile of papers and magazines I had finished clipping and told her she might cut clippings from them. She was very pleased and set to work with great zest. A long time passed— perhaps half an hour—and no sign of fatigue with what she was doing, no word of interruption. I had become so engrossed in my work I almost forgot she was there.

I turned, and discovered that she was happily engaged in cutting to pieces the latest copy of the *National Geographic* magazine. If I had cried out at her or punished her, she would never have understood, for, in her heart, she undoubtedly felt, that she was "helping Daddy." There was no doubt that at best she was an unprofitable servant, at least so far as editorial help was concerned. Gently I took the magazine from her, told her the equivalent of "Well done, thou good and faithful servant," kissed her and said, "Now you go and help Mother for a while."

. The true child of God is able to accomplish many things for the Lord Jesus Christ, and these things are accepted by the Lord even though they are not perfect in themselves. It is at this point that the operation of grace in our lives maintains us in our activities for God. We are surrendered to Him and we determine to do His will. We act, and the action is not perfect, but the perfect God looks at that action through the Lord Jesus Christ, and we are accepted in the beloved Saviour.

PLAN OF GOD

FROM CLINIC TO ZOO

In New York City, a high-school boy broke his nose. He was excused from school in order to go to a clinic to have it treated. Coming out of the clinic, he walked across the street to the Bronx Zoo, paid his fare and walked through the turnstile. He was immediately surrounded by officials of the zoo and photographers from the New York press. He was the 100,000,000th visitor to the Zoo since its foundation and was presented with a life membership in the New York Zoological Society.

Not only does everything that ever happens turn out for the best for the Christian, but, even more important, we know it in advance. The most significant part of the promise is the "We know," so come what may, the Christian knows the event has been planned by the Father and that it will bring good in the end, even if we may not see how at the moment of the event.

THE DISMANTLED CLOCK

Small boys are always interested in finding out what makes things go. One day a boy took a clock apart to find out what made it tick. When he tried to put it together again, he seemed to have enough wheels and springs to make two clocks; he discovered that all of the parts must move in their proper way—certain wheels must move forward and certain ones backward. There are wheels that move quickly and wheels that move slowly. There is the large mainspring and the tiny hairspring; all of the parts work together to make the clock go.

In the life of a Christian, when events move forward we are very pleased with the progress. If events move backward, we are inclined to be impatient; we want them to move in the direction of our own will, not understanding the purpose that God has in our lives. There are matters that are great and very important to us—mainspring events in our lives—births, marriages, deaths, triumphs and tragedies. There are matters as fine as a hairspring—petty annoyances, trivial happenings, that seem little and unimportant at times—that regulate the course of our lives. There are events in our lives that move smoothly and rapidly, and we rejoice at their action. Some things lag and incite our impatience as we seek to speed them up to the tempo of our own wills. But when all of these events— backward, forward; fast, slow; great, small—are seen in their relationship to each other, we must conclude that to those who love God and who are called according to His plan, everything that happens fits into a pattern for good.

THE MONGOLOID CHILD

Some years ago, a young minister in whose church I was holding a series of weekly meetings, said to me, "I may not be able to attend every meeting because we're expecting a baby soon." About three weeks later he came to the service, just before its close. Afterward I went to his study; his back was to me, as I asked, "Well, which is it, boy or girl?" He turned, and I saw tragedy written on his face. He said, "God has given me a son, and I love that boy, but he is a mongoloid idiot." I said, "At the very outset you must learn that God Almighty has honored you more than He has honored many people. God does not give the privilege of great suffering to every one of His children. He has chosen you for this purpose."

Then I turned to the fourth chapter of Exodus, in which God talks to Moses at the burning bush; I pointed to verse 11. Moses had just said, "I am slow of speech, and of a slow tongue." And God replied, "Who hath made man's mouth? or

243

who maketh the dumb, or deaf, or the seeing, or the blind? Have not I the Lord?" But I read the verse thus: "And the Lord said unto Moses, Who has made man's mouth? or who maketh him dumb, or deaf, or seeing, or blind, or a mongoloid idiot? have not I the Lord?" He snatched the Bible from me and read it for himself. "Oh," he said, "I never saw this before, but it's true, it's true! It must be true! I believe it!"

To receive the Congressional Medal of Honor is not so great a tribute as to be chosen, as one of God's children, to endure great tragedy. This the Bible teaches everywhere. If you do not think that God has planned these things, then you must believe that there is a power greater than God, or that things happen from blind chance. If you have had tragedy in your life; if you have endured a physical defect or deformity, God planned it. If you are a man, God planned that you be a man. If you are a woman, God planned that you be a woman. If you are five-feet-two, or six-feet-five, God planned that height for you. If you are blind, God planned that you should be blind.

SHEARING ONE THOUSAND SHEEP

In driving from Glasgow to Edinburgh, we followed a road on the border between the Highlands and the Lowlands. As we drove down the road we saw a dozen men shearing a thousand or so sheep. We stopped the car, climbed over the fence, and walked about a hundred yards to watch. How fast the men worked! These sheep, had run half-wild on the moors of Scotland, shepherded mostly by dogs; they were not accustomed to men. Now they were deprived of the wide liberty of the moors; they were packed tight in the folds. We could hear them bleating. The man in charge of the gate let the sheep out one at a time; the next man grabbed the sheep and took it over to another man. The minute the third man flipped the sheep over on its back—all four legs in the air—the sheep became quiet. Snip, snip, snip went the shears, and off came the fleece. In the middle of the group of shearers stood a boy, twelve or fourteen years of age. He was hacking away at a sheep learning how to sear. I suppose it took him as long to do one sheep as it did each of the men six or eight, but he was learning, and his sheep was just as quiet as the men's.

"As a sheep before her shearers is dumb." I got a fresh picture of how my Lord submitted himself. I believe that God created sheep that way to illustrate exactly how the Lord Jesus did, because I am a great believer that we existed in the mind of God before the earth. In other words, before God created the heavens and the earth, He planned us; then He planned the sun, and the moon, and the stars; then He planned this globe, and He planned Adam, and all the rest; He planned Christ, and we had been planned in Christ.

THE SPANISH ESCORIAL

Just outside of Madrid I saw that architectural phenomenon, the famed Escorial—ancient monastery of the Augustinians, the order that produced Martin Luther. The kings of Spain have been buried there for centuries, and the church is a magnificent example of stately beauty. The architect who built the building made an arch so flat that it frightened the king. Supported by the power of his might the king ordered the architect to add a column that would uphold the middle of the arch. The architect remonstrated that it was not necessary, but the king insisted. The column was built. Years later the king died, and the architect then revealed that the column was a quarter of an inch short of the arch, and that the arch had never sagged in the slightest. Today guides pass a lath between the arch and the column, as mute proof of the rightness of the architect's knowledge.

The divine plan does not need human support. It may sometimes appear contradictory to human illusions. Men build their little columns, but God has a way of making them fall a bit short, so that in the end it can always be demonstrated that the column, like the arch, rests on its own foundation and needs no other support.

THE TANGLED WEB

An elderly minister marked his Bible with a bookmark made of silk threads woven into a motto. The back was a tangled web of crossed threads that seemed to be without reason or purpose. When he had to call at a home where there was great trouble, sorrow or death, he would show this bookmark, presenting the reverse side with its unintelligible tangle. When the bereaved one had examined it intently, without finding any explanation for the seeming disorder, the minister would ask him to turn the marker over. Against the white silk background there was the phrase, in colored threads, "God is love." That side made sense.

It is thus with all of the tangled patterns of life for the one who has been called according to the divine plan. When we know this fact, we can be at peace with the world around us, because we are at peace within our own souls; and we are at peace within our own souls, because we are at peace with our Heavenly Father.

THE TOY BOAT

A small boy sailed his toy boat on a pond. The boat floated out of his reach, and he appealed to a larger boy to help him. This boy, without saying a word, picked up rocks and began throwing them out near the boat. The small boy pleaded with him not to hit his boat, but the big boy kept on. Soon the small boy noticed that each stone was falling on the far side of the boat, making a wave that pushed it nearer the shore. Then he realized that the big boy was planning the fall of each stone in order to bring the boat nearer to the shore. Soon it was within reach and the owner had his boat again.

We must never forget that God plans the fall of each stone

within our circumstances, and that each storm and wave is calculated by Him in order to bring us nearer to Himself.

THE VIOLINIST

A man who loves violin music has the means to buy himself a very fine violin. He also purchases the very finest radio obtainable and builds up a library of great musical scores. He is able to take any piece that is announced on the radio and put it on his music stand so that he can play along with the orchestra. The announcer says that Mr. Ormandy and the Philadelphia Orchestra are going to play Beethoven's Seventh Symphony. The man in his home puts that symphony on his stand and tunes his violin with what he hears coming from the orchestra. The music that comes from the radio we might call foreordained. Ormandy is going to follow the score just as Beethoven wrote it. The man in his living room starts to scratch away at the first violin part. He misses beats, he loses his place and finds it again, he breaks a string and stops to fix it. The music goes on and on. He finds the place again and plays on, after his fashion, to the end of the symphony. The announcer names the next work that is to be played, and the fiddler puts that score on his rack. Day after week after month after year he finds pleasure in scraping his fiddle along with the violins in the great orchestras. Their music is determined in advance. What he must do is to learn to play in their tempo and in their key; he must follow the score as it was written in advance. If he decides that he wants to play "Yankee Doodle" when the orchestra is in the midst of a Brahms number, there will be dissonance and discord in the man's house, but not in the Academy of Music. After some years of this, the man may turn out to be a creditable violin player; he may have learned to submit himself to the scores that are written and to follow the programs as played. Harmony and joy comes from this submission and this cooperation.

The plan of God is rolling toward us, unfolding day by day,

as He has planned it before the foundation of the world. The score of God's plan is set forth in the Bible. In the measure that I learn it, submit myself to it, and seek to live in accordance with all that is therein set forth I shall find myself in joy and in harmony with God and His plans. Prayer is learning to play the same tune that the eternal plan of God calls for and to do that which is in harmony with the will of the Eternal Composer and the Author of all that is of true harmony in life and living.

PRAYER

THE BANK ACCOUNT

You might see a sign in the window of a bank that reads: "If you present any checks according to our rules, we will cash them." That is a sensible announcement. But suppose I go into the bank, fill out a check for one hundred dollars, sign it, and ask for five twenties in cash. The teller looks at me, at my signature, and says, "Do you have an account in this bank?" I answer, "No—but I want you to know that I sincerely believe in cashing checks." Such folly would speedily land me in the arms of the law. It is not enough to believe in cashing checks; it is necessary to have an account in the bank.

It is not enough to pray in the name of the Lord Jesus; there must be the true deposit of saving faith. You can draw on this deposit of faith, if you are asking in the Holy Spirit. If He is praying within you, with groanings that cannot be uttered, then you may be sure your prayer will be answered. If you are merely asking for something so that you may consume the gift of the answer on your own desires, then you may be sure that God will not answer your prayer.

FATHER AND SON

A father tells his college son what he is to do; the father also tells the boy that his needs will be provided for. The father does not draw a check in September for the school year and abandon the boy to himself. The father instructs the boy to write home and ask for money. The boy knows he is going to get it, the father knows he is going to give it, but both enjoy the fellowship of the letter, the asking and the answer. A

249

yielded son will not spend beyond his budget, and a loving father will provide all that is in his power to meet his son's need.

The main function of prayer is to link us to God in fellowship and to prepare us in growth for further participation in His plan. In John 10, He made a certain and definite promise concerning the safety and keeping of the believer (vss. 27-29). Yet in John 17, He prayed seven times for the believers, that they might all be kept, though He had said that they would be.

IF TWO AGREE

Many years ago, Mr. George T. B. Davis attended one of my Sunday evening services. Mr. Davis was a well-known leader in Christian work who was responsible for circulating several millions of copies of the New Testament in different lands and to different groups. I made a mental note that there was something I wanted to talk over with him, but he slipped out before I had a chance to speak to him. I went home, sat down and wrote him a note saying that I had missed him and I outlined an idea that we might collaborate on. I added a postscript saying that I was going out at midnight to mail the letter so that he would have it in the morning and could telephone me. In the next morning's mail was a letter from Mr. Davis. He wrote that he had not stopped to meet me after the service because so many others were speaking to me, but that the Lord had laid it on his heart to write me about a certain matter in which we might collaborate. It was exactly the same idea about which I had written him. He also added a postscript that he was going out to mail his letter so that I might have it in the morning. A few moments later my telephone rang, and he was on the phone to express his astonishment and joy that our letters had crossed in the mail during the night. I pointed out to him that here was the true meaning of spiritual agreement.

We had been the objects of this special grace of God and

had agreed on earth; we could be sure that it would be done by our Heavenly Father. And it was.

THE MISSING DIGIT

In making a dial telephone call from memory, one number was missed and a wrong connection resulted. The call did not get through to the right person. One little mistake made all the difference.

In approaching God we must come in the way that He has designed. He has promised very definitely not to hear the prayers of those who do not come in accordance with the way He has determined. Christ said, ". . . no man cometh unto the Father, but by me" (JOHN 14:6). It is absolutely necessary that one believe in the deity of Jesus Christ and in salvation by the blood, in order to approach God. Anyone who attempts to climb up by any other way, though the devil may give him counterfeit answers for awhile, has a "wrong number" as far as God is concerned. A Christian cannot get through to God if he has unconfessed sin in his life. "If I regard iniquity in my heart, the Lord will not hear me" (PSALM 66:18). But if we pray for what is a good thing for us, and if we are walking in the will of God, we are sure to get the answer to our prayer. We have the "right number" and the answer is immediately forthcoming (PSALM 84:11).

THE REQUEST FOR MONEY

Every father who has a child away at school knows what it is to receive requests for money. When my younger son was in college, I had two letters, one following the other closely; both asking for fifty dollars. The requests were for different purposes, and the nature of the letters was quite different. The first letter was about three pages long; it was hedged about with explanations attempting to persuade me to grant the request. He recounted that he was on the Dean's list, and therefore near the top of his class and permitted to cut classes at will. A group of his companions, all with the same liberty of movement because of their high marks, wished to leave college for a five-day weekend; they wanted to drive a thousand miles to the home of one of the boys for a series of parties and good times. In short, his share of the expenses would be fifty dollars. He did not use the exact words, but the equivalent of "if it be thy will," appeared a half-dozen times. My answer was "No." My refusal crossed in the mails a second letter from my son, saying that he knew my answer would be "No"; he was making a substitute set of plans for the weekend. About three weeks later came a brief letter, roughly as follows: "Dear Daddy: There was an accident in the chemistry laboratory today, and the boy next to me broke a beaker of acid. I had to stop at the co-op and order a suit. They are making some alterations, but I need fifty dollars by return mail." There was no "if it be thy will" to that letter. A father may not have to give his boy a five-day party weekend, but he does have to keep him in pants. That is one of the obligations of fatherhood.

Some prayers need add no qualifying words. Some things are God's will so definitely that we need not hesitate, but may come with all boldness to the throne of His grace, expecting to find grace to help in time of our need. From such prayers the Lord God has never turned away His ear. Other prayers He will receive with kindness, and in His mercy He will not answer them, because He knows that we pray in ignorance, and that His answer would be far worse for us than we could ever imagine.

PROMISES OF GOD

THE PORTER'S TIP

Several years ago, a porter took me to my room in the Onesto Hotel in Canton, Ohio. He knew me well and we began talking about the promises of God. I had not yet given him his tip, and I asked him how much money he had in his pocket. He counted it, and found that he had $1.19. It was Tuesday; he would not be paid until Friday, and he had to live and support his family until then on tips, slender at best. I placed a fifty-cent piece in his hand, saying, "I give you this half dollar. Now how much do you have?" He answered, "$1.69." After I had discussed this with him, I took the coin and put it back in my pocket, asking him, "Now how much do you have?" He fell into the trap of faithlessness and answered $1.19." "Then am I a liar?" I asked. "No." "Did I give you that half-dollar?" "Yes." "Didn't you tell me it was yours?" "Yes." "Then how much money do you have?" He smiled and said, "I have $1.69, but fifty cents of it is in your pocket." It was in his before he left the room, and he had learned a little more about the certainty of the promises of God.

THE PROMISE BOX

When I lived in France in my student days, I was used of God to lead a girl to Christ. This girl later became the wife of one of the French pastors in the south of France. She often came to our home and saw us taking verses from a "promise box"—a small box that held approximately two hundred promises from the Bible printed on heavy paper curled into cylinders. We used to take one out and read it when we needed a word of special comfort. This girl made a promise box by hand, writing these same promises in French. Throughout the years this box has been used in her home by her children, and they have been taught to trust in the Lord. She told us of an incident that happened to her during the war. No food was available except messes of potato peelings from a restaurant. Her children were emaciated; they cried to her for food. Their clothing was almost in rags, and their shoes were worn through. In one of her most tragic moments she turned to the promise box in desperation. She prayed, "Lord, O Lord, I have such great need. Is there a promise here that is really for me? Show me, O Lord, what promise I can have in this time of famine, nakedness, peril, and the sword." She was blinded by her tears, and in reaching for the box, she knocked it over. The promises showered down around her, on her lap, on the floor; not one was left in the box. She knew a moment of supreme joy in the Lord as the Holy Spirit suffused her with divine power and light; she realized that all of the promises were indeed for her in the very hour of her greatest need.

So it can be for you today. "Man shall not live by bread alone, but by every word that proceedeth out of the mouth of God" (MATTHEW 4:4). "Who shall separate us from the love of Christ?" You who have once known the love of God surely know that there is nothing in this world or in the world to come that can separate you from the love of Christ which passeth knowledge. "Therefore . . . be ye stedfast, unmoveable, always abounding in the work of the Lord, forasmuch as ye know that your labor is not in vain in the Lord" (I CORINTHIANS 15:58).

PROPHECY

CLIMBING MONT BLANC

When we were living in Europe, we went with two young men for an excursion in the high mountains. We set out to climb Mont Blanc. From before dawn until after dark we worked our way up to that point on the shoulder of Europe's highest peak where there was a tiny cabin, half-buried in the midst of the eternal snows. The next morning, before daylight, we started out on the eight-or-nine-hour climb that would bring us to the summit. We knew from our distant view of the peak that the last miles were over great broad beds of snow, and at last we came to a slope that looked like the final slope. We congratulated each other on making such excellent time; we anticipated mounting the summit more than an hour in advance of our original schedule. Then we came out upon the rolling top of the peak and, much to our chagrin saw a slope down, a long flat valley, and another sharp rise that had to be mounted before the topmost height could be reached. We learned that the place that had deceived us was called in French, *Mont Maudit*—"cursed mountain." Undoubtedly many an Alpine sportsman has come to this place, thinking that the weary labor of the climb was nearly over, feeling the joyous sense of dominance and achievement that reaching the peak brings, blotting out the memories of perilous moments when footholds were precarious and when the rope that bound the party together was all that stood between them and death.

This is a perfect illustration of the Old Testament prophecies concerning the coming and work of Israel's Messiah. From a far distant perspective they were allowed to see the unrolling

255

scene. Their minds fixed upon the summit of glory that lay before them and they forgot completely that they were to pass over the cursed mountain before they could reach the final object of their desire. For there could be no final redemption without the basis of the work of the cross where Messiah would be cut off for the sins of His people (DANIEL 9:26).

THE WATCH

Joe and John, were working with their father, one summer. The father said to the older son, "John, you have done an excellent job, and I am proud of the way you handled everything. At Christmas I want to give you a very fine gold wrist watch; I will give you this because you have been a good boy." Time goes on—October, November—the brothers talk about the watch a bit; and then about December 20th, Joe says to his brother, "John, I have seen the watch." That's all. The father had bought it and shown it to the mother and to the younger brother who says, "I have seen the watch." The promise made in August was just a promise, but now someone has seen the watch, and having seen the watch they know that when the time of fulfillment comes, it will come to pass.

In effect, Peter says in his second Epistle (1:16-21), "I've seen the watch. God made a promise in Isaiah, but I know it is going to be true for I've seen it. God lifted the veil and let me look upon it. The word of prophecy of the Old Testament is made more sure by the Transfiguration because we have been eyewitnesses of His majesty, and so we have the word of prophecy that is made more sure, a word whereunto you do well to take heed."

PUBLIC CONFESSION OF CHRIST

THE CHINESE MATRIARCH'S SON

An old Chinese woman living in Java gave me a beautiful antique Chinese ivory. In the islands of the South Seas the Chinese have long been the principal traders, and some of them are immensely wealthy. I was preaching there for a few days and was entertained in the home of a Chinese matriarch, whose husband had left her a great business and a museum-like home. I had been told that although this woman was a fine Christian, her thirty-year-old son lived a life of debauchery. As I sat down to dinner, the young man came in and sat beside me. We began to talk, and before the meal was over he promised to come to the meeting at which I was speaking that afternoon. He came, and between that afternoon meeting and the evening meeting he talked with me seriously about his soul. He attended the evening meeting at which I presented Christ as Saviour; he left afterwards without speaking to me. The next day, however, he had cards printed and sent them out to hundreds of his friends and business acquaintances. I substitute another name, but this is the message the card bore: "Ah Wong, having become a Christian, wishes to announce to his friends and acquaintances that he will no longer be seen in his old haunts or living his old way of life."

The Chinese are not an effusive people and certainly are not given to showing their emotions. But I shall not forget the old mother as she stretched out her hands toward me, bowing low, almost looking away lest I see the tears that she could not keep back. When we left, she gave me *batik* sarongs fit for a

257

princess, and an antique ivory that could grace the wall of the finest art museum.

The world understands a confession of Christ. When anyone has publicly confessed Christ, the world is astonished if the life is not changed.

ENGAGED!

Many years ago I rode the streetcar home from one of the suburbs of Los Angeles late at night. There were only half a dozen passengers in the car—all men—when a young man got on the car at an intermediate stop. The new passenger paid his fare, lifted his hands and cried out, "I'm engaged to be married. My girl just said 'Yes'." Everyone laughed; there was joshing and wisecracks. Love from his heart had found a response and he could not keep still about it.

Is it possible for an interchange of love between the Lord God and His creature without a great desire to acknowledge it?

THE YOUNG MAN'S RETURN HOME

During the first world war, I had the opportunity of witnessing to the young scion of a family prominent for its social standing and wealth. The young man professed to accept Christ as Saviour; he made public testimony to that fact among the soldiers of his company. When the war was over and he was about to go home to one of the wealthy suburbs of a great city, he told me that he was afraid he would slip back into his old habits with his old friends. I told him that he would not have to give these people up—that they would give him up if he made a public confession of his faith in Christ. He agreed to tell the first ten people of his old set that he met, that he had become a living Christian.

He arrived at the suburban station near his home, he told me afterward, and almost immediately saw a girl whom he had known socially. She greeted him effusively and asked how things were going. He replied, "The greatest thing that could happen to a man has happened to me." "Oh," she said, "You are engaged to be married." He said, "Better than that; I have taken Jesus Christ as my Saviour." Her face froze; she mumbled some words of politeness and quickly went her way. A few minutes later a young man of his acquaintance passed by and shouted that now that the soldier was back there would be some good parties. The young Christian told about his new life in Christ. His friend mumbled some polite remarks and went his way. The same circumstances were repeated with a young couple and with two more individuals. But by that time the word had gotten around. A car passed with very close friends. They waved at him distantly, and that was all. They had heard the news: he had become "queer," "religious," who knows?— they may have called him crazy. But his public confession had aligned him with Jesus Christ; it had alienated those who did not want Jesus Christ and had established and strengthened him in his stand for Christ as his Lord.

REDEMPTION

FRUIT

I was born in a country of fruit in a little valley of California. It was a common sight to see tens of thousands of acres of blossoms in the springtime, and to look out on the vast and abundant harvest of the autumn. Without being conscious of the impression that was being made on me, the glory of the harvest became a part of my being. I still have a sense of solid satisfaction when I think of the thousands of square yards of apricots drying in the sun, of the freight-car loads of strawberries going off to market, of the hundreds of trainloads of apples that flowed through the little town. Fruit was the life of our community. I, like many of the boys in my town, spent many summer days cutting pits out of apricots, and I earned a great deal of money—for a boy—making thousands of apple boxes each season. It was thus we spent our autumn Saturdays.

The heavy black soil was clean and well cultivated, and the orchards stretched away for miles. For me, the North Star will always shine over a mountain peak—Loma Prieta—ten or fifteen miles away, with orchards stretching all the way to the foothills. Whether the wind blew from Del Monte by the sea, or from the fruited hills, the air was always redolent with the fragrance of the blossoms, the fruit, or the black earth, resting for its winter moment before springing into fruitfulness again.

This is the atmosphere of the Bible. The winds of God blow thus for the lives of His children. One of the most important purposes of redemption is that we might bring forth fruit unto God. We were transplanted out of death and rooted and grounded in His love so that we might bring forth fruit.

THE MOTHER HEN

In the pioneer days of wood-burning locomotives, sparks from locomotives often set fires on either side of the railroad tracks. When the trains ran across the wheat fields, there was a ten-to-fifteen day period when the wheat was ripe enough to burn, yet not ripe enough to cut. Wheat fires sometimes burned for ten miles, sweeping great fields before them. A farmer saw billowing smoke in the distance; he knew the wind was coming toward him and that his wheat would burn right down to the edge of his barn, and that he might lose the house, the barn and all of his buildings. So he took a torch and ran to the edge of his own field; he lighted a fire, and the fire in his own wheat began to burn away one hundred yards, two hundred yards. It made a circle so that when the great fire came down on the wind and met the place that was burned over, it passed around and went on; with the backfire he saved his buildings, but he lost his crop. In great grief, he walked out in the burnt stubble and saw the charred body of a hen lying there. He thought that the hen had become confused and had been burned to death. Idly, he turned the body of the hen over with his toe, and out ran a dozen little chicks. The mother's body had been over them; she was burned, but they went out free.

In the day of Christ's dying, there was the dam of God's patience, and there was the flood of God's wrath; the day that Jesus Christ was put on a cross, God said that Christ was guilty of all of the law, having become a curse through being crucified. On the third day, God raised Him from the dead, and I ran out free, and you ran out free, for He was between us and the wrath of God. This is the atonement.

PRICES FOR PAINTINGS

The London Times publishes the prices paid for art objects in all of the salesrooms of the world. If a picture is sold in New York or Paris or Rome or London, the Times gives the full details of the sale. Suppose you are standing outside of a great auction room in London, and you hear a clerk say, "He paid $25.00 for a picture, another man paid $600,000.00 for one." You know quite a lot about the two pictures: The twenty-five-dollar picture, may be any one of 10,000 little dogs done by amateur artists who paint sunsets, trees and seascapes, hoping to get paid for them. The six hundred thousand dollar picture —was it a Gainsborough, Rembrandt, Reubens, Franz Hals, Millet, Michelangelo, ar Raffael? You can judge the painting by the price that is paid for it.

We can judge ourselves by the price Christ paid for us, the depths into which He had to reach in order to save us. Christ died for our sins, and when I learn the price that was paid for our redemption, I form conclusions that are justified from other portions of the Scripture—how great was my sinfulness, the depths of my nature and the height of His love.

THE PRISONER'S CONFESSION

Governor Neff, of Texas, spoke to the assembled convicts of a penitentiary of that state. He finished by saying that he would remain to listen if any man wanted to speak with him. He further announced that what he heard would be held in confidence; nothing a man might tell him would be used against the man.

When the meeting was over, a large group of men remained, many of them life-termers. One by one they each told the governor that he was there through a frame-up, an injustice, a judicial blunder; each asked that he be freed. Finally, one man came up and said, "Mr. Governor, I just want to say that I am guilty. I did what they sent me here for, but I believe I have paid for it. If I were granted the right to go out, I would do everything I could to be a good citizen and prove myself worthy of your mercy."

This man the governor pardoned. So must it be with the great God who alone can pardon. The one difference is that we cannot say that we have paid for any of it. We can come and say, "Oh, God, I just want to say that I am guilty. I am a sinner, a rebel against Thy power and Thy justice, but I believe that Jesus Christ paid for my sin. If, in Thy mercy, because of Him, Thou wilt take me out of darkness into light, I will live as one who is alive from the dead." This, of course, is the man whom God pardons.

THE SAFETY PIN

In one of the rescue missions of Philadelphia, a man had been saved. He had come from a good home, but had been reduced to misery through sin. He had sold his overcoat to obtain a drink; one bitter cold night he walked into a mission with his single coat pinned with a safety pin. On the second anniversary of his conversion he went into the mission to give his testimony. Well-dressed and holding a good position, he was able to give the glory to God. From his pocket he pulled out the safety-pin—plated with gold. Whenever Satan tempted him into thinking he was something, he pulled it out and looked at it.

When we remember the pit from which we have been dug, our desires turn toward God and we want to talk more closely to Him. Looking at the condition from which Christ drew us, we can realize the depths of His love in coming to redeem us.

THROUGH THE MIST

The *Saturday Review* published a portfolio of photographs that had won prizes at the Metropolitan Museum as the greatest photographs of the year. One photographer, who happened to be a Methodist minister, had photographed a ship coming through the fog; over the top of that ship he superimposed mists—mists so swirling you could barely see the ship below.

When I read that Christ died for our sins according to the

REDEMPTION

Scriptures, I can peer through a mist and see the heart of God. I can begin to understand what He was and what He did and what motivated Him. It was love that caused Him to pay such a price. Christ died for our sins, and thus we see the inevitable glory of His grace in this simple phrase.

RESPONSIBILITY TO GOD

TWO YOUNG ROBBERS

Two young men were arrested robbing a service station. When the trial came up one of the men had four or five high-powered lawyers—his family was wealthy. The other boy had a court-appointed lawyer; he had been in reform school and had spent two years in Sing Sing. The two boys were obviously guilty; they had been caught in the act. The judge sentenced the boy who had been in Sing Sing to three years; the other boy was sentenced to ten years. The lawyers howled. The judge said, "This boy is a graduate of Choate Preparatory School and of Yale University. His father was an outstanding man in the community; this boy has sinned against his preparatory school and against Yale University. He has sinned against the whole American standard of ethics. Tremendous opportunities were made available to him, yet he turned against all that he knew to be right. He turned against the code of ethics of his family, his school, his university; he deserves a worse punishment." The judge acted in a biblical way, for God says, "To whom much has been committed, much shall be required."

The fact that we name the name of the Lord Jesus Christ increases our responsibility before God. The more education you have, the more you are answerable to God. The more knowledge you have of the Bible, the more you are answerable to God. The better your health, the more answerable you are to God. The minute that God gives you any advantage whatsoever, the more you are answerable to God.

RESURRECTION

THE LOCKED AUTOMOBILE DOOR

Like everyone else who has ever owned an automobile with a self-locking door, once I locked my keys inside the car. The ventilating window in the front was open so I thought I could put my hand through to unlock the door, but I couldn't make it. Three or four people tried and failed; finally someone with a small wrist tried it and he was able to reach through the window, unfasten the door and let me in.

You and I do not have a right to approach the cross of Christ unless we recognize that once there was a tomb that had the body of Jesus Christ in it, and that He was raised from the dead, and that the cross is on the other side. You and I today must reach our hand through the open tomb of Jesus Christ and grasp the cross on the resurrection side.

WELLINGTON DEFEATED

When I was in my late twenties I went to Winchester, England, famous for its college and for its cathedral. The verger of the cathedral used to show people around the cathedral. He had been there for many, many years, and he loved to tell the story how the news of the battle of Waterloo came to England. There were no telegrams in those days, but everyone knew that Wellington was facing Napoleon in a great battle. A sailing ship semaphored news to the signalman on top of Winchester Cathedral. He signaled to another man on a hill and thus news of the battle was relayed, by hand semaphore, from station to station to London and all across England. When the ship came in, the signalman on board semaphored the first

266

word—"Wellington." The next word was "defeated", and then the fog came down and the ship could not be seen. "Wellington defeated" went across England, and there was great gloom all over the countryside. After two or three hours, the fog lifted, and the signal came again: "Wellington defeated the enemy." Then all England rejoiced.

There was that day, when in the eyes of the world they put the body of the Lord Jesus Christ in the tomb. Men might have said, "Everything is ended, all is gone, sin has conquered, man is defeated, wrong has triumphed." But then three days later the fog lifted. Jesus Christ rose from the dead. The truth has come down ever since and Jesus defeated the enemy.

RIGHTEOUSNESS OF GOD

THE JAMMED TURNSTILE

A friend, who does not see well, entered a New York subway station and found that he needed change in order to get through the turnstile. The man in the change booth gave him the necessary coins, but to my friend's fingers one coin did not feel quite right. The changemaker brusquely brushed him on his way, saying that he knew what he had given in change. My friend put the coin into the turnstile slot, and the mechanism jammed. Quite angry by this time, the changemaker opened the turnstile box, and discovered a foreign coin. An American mechanism, geared for American coins, refused to accept the foreign coin which he had given the man who could not see well. Evidently, the foreign coin looked like an American one, but the mechanism rejected it because it was not an American coin.

Our own righteousness may pass for good coin here on earth, but the only currency that is acceptable in heaven is God's perfect righteousness.

LACE AND BLACK VELVET

Along the Avenue Louise in Brussels are several stores that sell nothing but lace. I looked at the exquisite scarves, veils and handkerchiefs in the windows and decided to purchase a handkerchief for my mother. The two old sisters who ran the store showed me some handkerchiefs; I was rather astonished at the price and asked them if they could explain why they were so costly.

It was a few months after World War I, and I still wore my

army uniform. The ladies had no other customers at that time of day and seemed pleased to tell the young American officer about their wares. One of them spread a roll of black velvet on the counter, and then began to show the lace against this contrasting background. I was initiated into the mystery of bobbin lace, and a few knots were tied for me in order to show me the method of making it.

Finally, they went to their safe and took out the marriage veil that had just been completed for the wedding of the Duchess of Brabant. Rather gingerly I took hold of the edge of it—the thing was valued at over ten thousand dollars—and began to look at it more closely. One of the ladies immediately lifted the black velvet that I might use the contrasting background to bring out the intricacies of this Brussels rose-point lace. From that day on I have always been interested in the beauties of lace, beauties which two old ladies taught me to comprehend against the blackness of velvet.

It is unquestionable that the glories of God's love and mercy and righteousness and goodness, and tenderness—all of the attributes of His grace—are known by the fact that God took the black velvet of man's sin and threw the web of His grace against it.

THE ROCK DISPLAY

In the Benjamin Franklin Museum of Philadelphia is a display of rocks, housed in a special room that is entered by a corridor shrouded in darkness. The darkness is necessary to accustom the eyes to a different light diffused in the special exhibit room. The light in the exhibit room is an indirect fluorescent light of rays that are ordinarily invisible to the human eye. In the darkness this light shines upon rocks that ordinarily appear gray and dun-brown; in the new light they glow with a brilliance and beauty that is incredible.

So it is with the righteousness of God as seen through the eyes of the world and as seen through the eyes of the Spirit.

RIGHTEOUSNESS OF GOD

The world looks upon the righteousness of God as a drab thing, even imagining that it robs man of the happiness that the world promises so freely and gives so poorly. Around the shoulders of the poorest sinner shall be draped the robe of the divine righteousness, unto all and upon all who believe.

SAINTS

WHAT IS A SAINT?

A little boy was accustomed to attending a church which had beautiful stained-glass windows. He saw that the windows contained pictures: "St. Matthew, St. Mark, St. Luke, St. John, St. Paul," and others. One day he was asked, "What is a saint?" He replied, "A saint is a person the light shines through."

Does God's light shine through you? Christ commands, "Let your light so shine before men, that they may see your good works, and glorify your Father which is in heaven" (MATTHEW 5:16).

271

SALVATION

DROP IT

When I landed at Makassar in the Celebes a few years ago, I was met by a little Malay boy who carried a bamboo cage containing tiny monkeys about six inches high—perfect little creatures, and very cute. The boy trailed me, saying, "Buy a monkey, Mister? One dollar; buy a monkey, Mister?" I looked at the monkeys and walked along; the boy followed, lowering his price as he pleaded, "Buy a monkey, Mister? Seventy-five cents!" and finally, "Fifty cents!" The missionary who had met me at the ship explained that we couldn't take the monkey; I gave the boy a tip and he went away happy. The missionary then told me how those monkeys are caught.

There is a gourd that grows long like a string bean and, upon reaching its full length, begins to swell. When the gourd is in the string-bean state, a boy ties a cord around half of it so that half stops growing; the other half continues to swell, and thus a narrownecked bottle is formed. Then the boy cuts off the gourd, hollows it out, drops in a couple of handfuls of rice, and ties the gourd to a tree. The monkey smells the rice, thrusts in his paw to grab it, but cannot pull his paw out. If he would drop the rice, he could get away, but so long as he holds on to the food his paw acts like a cork in reverse; he is a prisoner of his own greed. Although the animal chatters, pulls and tugs, he still holds onto the rice, and the boy slips a bamboo cage around him, then breaks the gourd. The monkey eats the rice and is sold down the river.

That is the picture of many people who have their hands full of sin, full of themselves. God says, "I will give you salvation to take you into heaven if you will admit that you have your paw full of something and if you will drop it. Admit that you are less than perfect, that you are the sinner that I say you are. Unless you open your hand and drop what you are clutching, I cannot give you my righteousness in Jesus Christ."

THE ONLY WAY

Many European towns still bear the marks of walls that surrounded them in the Middle Ages. Streets near these old walls are curved and sometimes wind up in a dead end. A man asked a stranger how to reach a certain address. When the stranger directed him, the inquirer was still a little dubious. "Is that the best way?" he asked. The stranger answered, "It is the only way. If you follow the other turning it will bring you back here."

That is a great illustration of the way to God. Go through Jesus Christ and His death on the cross. "Is that the best way?" someone might ask. The only answer to that is the truth: "It is the only way." Any other turning will take you—not back to where you are, but off into outer darkness of separation from God.

A ROCKET TRIP TO THE MOON

Let's suppose that we have reached the day that a rocket ship is ready for a trip to the moon. It has been built on the desert sands of southern California, about a hundred feet below sea level. It has not been built on top of the nearby Sierras, nor on top of Mt. Everest. A certain Colonel Eager Beaver, immensely wealthy and very egotistical, wants to go to the moon, but he declares that it is not becoming to him to go all the way down into the desert, below sea level. He is going to do the thing in a grandiose way. He is going to finance an expedition to Asia and get a party to climb to the top of Mt. Everest and take off from there. So Colonel Eager Beaver creates a great stir. Many men are willing to accept the high salary he pays to go to Asia on the expedition. Plenty of sales-men are willing to sell him all the equipment he wants; they pocket their profits with a smile. Finally the Colonel reaches Asia, and he and a small company of guides even reach the summit of Mt. Everest; they build a small shelter so that they can stay there month after month.

Then Colonel Eager Beaver hears that some skeptics criti-cize his plan. They know the reality of earth's altitude and the principles of rocket ships. But the Colonel is very proud and describes in great detail all that he has done. He argues that we must admit that he is closer to the moon than anyone else on earth. He is more than five miles above the level of the sea, and therefore five miles nearer to the moon than those poor creatures who have gone down to the rocket station to take off for the moon.

There is only one way to reply to him. In terse words, he must be told that he is a fool. There is no place for pride in an attempt to reach the moon. If any man is going to go to the moon, he must stop talking about mountain climbing expedi-tions, and go to the one place where there is a craft capable of crossing the reaches of space. Furthermore, when he gets to the launching area he must be willing to go through one small door into the rocket. Only then can he hope to achieve his purpose. By climbing high on the surface of the earth he is, in reality, farther from the moon than he would be by going low.

Some may think that my illustration is slightly fantastic, and I readily admit it, but the efforts of men to get to heaven are even more fantastic than those of the Colonel. There is only one way to get to heaven. That way was opened at one geo-graphical spot on the earth—Calvary, outside the city wall of Jerusalem—where the cross of Jesus Christ was set up and where Christ, the Son of God, God the Son, died that He might become the Saviour of men. All over the world there are those who outfit their private mountain climbing expeditions of good works, and imagine that they can be nearer heaven because they have done this good deed or performed that philanthropic act. But in reality the farther they are from Jerusalem the farther they are from God.

THE RUBBER RAFT

An aviator, forced down in the middle of the ocean and drifting on a piece of flotsam, would not be concerned about the identification of the workingmen who had made a rubber raft that was being dropped to him from a rescuing plane. He would not stop to argue with nearby sharks as to whether the raft was made in Chicago or Detroit. With a last gasp he would wiggle on and be tremendously glad he was there.

So a soul in need will not be primarily concerned about who wrote the Epistle to the Hebrews or whether a Hebrew copyist made a false brush stroke in transcribing one of the letter figures which tell how many men fell in one day in a given battle. The soul in need sees in the Word of God: SALVATION. It is the Word of Life that is held forth to him (PHILIPPIANS 2:15,16). The believer knows that it came from God, that when it left God it was absolutely perfect, and that it will take him from death to life.

THE SALVATION ARMY WOMAN

The late Handley Moule, Bishop of Durham in the Church of England, was a very godly man. One day as he was walking along Princess Street in Edinburgh he approached a corner where a group of Salvation Army workers were conducting an open air meeting. He paused for a moment to listen and one of the young women of the group spoke to him saying, "Sir, are you saved?" The venerable Bishop looked at her with a kindly smile and twinkling eyes and asked her, "Do you mean . . . ?" Here he used three Greek words which were utterly incomprehensible to her. She showed her ignorance by her stupefaction, and the Bishop continued in English, "Do you mean 'I have been saved,' 'I am being saved,' or 'I shall be saved'?"

True salvation is in all three of these tenses. In the past, the believer has been saved from the penalty of sin; in the present, he is being saved from the power of sin; and in the future, he will be saved from the very presence of sin. If any one of the three were left out, there would be no reality of salvation.

THE WAY TO ICELAND

During World War II, the late President Roosevelt used this particular expression in one of his great speeches. Poland, with some of the other countries of Western Europe, had been conquered by the German hordes and Great Britain was hard pressed. The battle of the Atlantic was about to begin. Addressing his remarks to England, the President said, "As for Iceland, we are determined at all costs *to keep the way* to Iceland." What did he mean? Iceland, situated strategically in the North Atlantic, was in the hands of the American government. Thus the sea lanes were assured of the safe transit of ships as long as Iceland remained in friendly hands. Roosevelt said in so many words that no matter what the cost, we would keep the way to Iceland open in order for shipping to make its course across the ocean unimpeded. The way was to be kept open.

God has not only provided a way, but He has seen to it that it shall be kept open in order that men might come to Him.

SANCTIFICATION

CLEANSING

The difference between special cleansing and regular cleansing is the same as that between special and regular washing of the hands. A woman may work around the kitchen and go to the sink a score of times to rinse her hands because there has come some special need for cleansing. Or a student may get ink on his fingers and need special cleansing. But in the evening as we come to the time of retiring, we go through our regular cleansing even though there may not be any special dirt upon us.

Thus it is with the life that is brought to the Lord day by day. There may come special outbreak of sin, some rising surprise of the old Adamic nature, and for this we will need to rush back to God for special cleansing and restoration to full fellowship. But at the end of a day when nothing of special evil has touched our lives, we still need to return to Him and ask for forgiveness for the faults which He can see and which we may not recognize.

` SANCTIFIED PEACHES

In August the streets of China used to be filled with fruit sellers, in village as well as in city. A huge assortment is on display—half a dozen kinds of melons, varieties of peaches, apples, grapes, and other fruits. To one accustomed to eating fruit freely, it was a distinct disappointment to see this wealth and be unable to eat any. In those days the methods under which the fruit was grown and the filth involved in the handling made it impractical for a foreigner to spend a few coppers, rinse or peel the fruit, and enjoy it. Before the fruit can be

277

eaten, it must be sanctified. Strawberries and peaches had to be washed in a solution of potassium permanganate, then dipped in boiling water and carefully pared. If the skin was broken the pieces had to be cut out meticulously and discarded. If the skins of tomatoes had been broken, they could be eaten only after they had been cooked. Travelers in the Orient learned to take sanitary precautions they never dreamed of at home. All of these preparations correspond to sanctification.

We live with a terrible source of infection. Radical treatment is necessary. The cause of infection has to be delivered over to death. As peaches and fruit must be prepared with chemicals, and open spots cut away with a knife, so the old nature must be delivered over to the Lord Jesus Christ for crucifixion death. This is the meaning of the "I die daily" of the apostle. It is the moment by moment disinfection of sanctification.

SATAN

THE BLACK EYE

Suppose a man has angered a group of men who are standing with the world's champion heavyweight boxer. One man says, "You are going to get a black eye!" The offender says, "Well, if I am to receive a black eye, please let the world's champion give it to me. I can at least boast about that!" But they reply, "No, you will get it from the water boy, who is the weakest one here."

So Jesus Christ, made lower than the angels, was to inflict ignominious defeat upon the most powerful of all created beings. How did He do it? In Deuteronomy, Christ answered Satan, "It is written, 'Man shall not live by bread alone, but by every word that proceeds from the mouth of God.'" No wonder Satan hates the books of Moses and does all he can to bring them into disrepute! Christ wielded the Sword of the Spirit, and the flashing power of the Word of God inflicted the first wound on Satan.

INFLATED DECOYS

The Army has revealed that it misled the foe by the use of pneumatic decoys. In the middle of the night soldiers inflated rubberized tubes and painted fabric so that enemy aircraft, flying over our positions on reconnaissance, would think they saw fleets of tanks and masses of artillery when, in reality, they were looking upon inflated decoys.

There is nothing new under the sun. The devil has been using this device for ages. How many Christians have been afraid of what they thought they saw and felt, when, in reality, they were faced with the ruse of a foe who was defeated at Calvary. There the Lord Jesus "spoiled principalities and powers, he made a shew of them openly, triumphing over them in it" (COLOSSIANS 2:15). From the moment Christ died, Satan was left with inflated decoys instead of power. True victory is available for those who lay hold, by faith, on the spiritual weapons of our warfare, which are mighty, through God, to the pulling down of strongholds (II CORINTHIANS 10:4).

THE OVERBLOWN BALLOON

I once saw a small child playing with a toy balloon. When it had no air in it, it was a small thing that could be hidden in the palm of the hand. When it was blown up it was a frightening thing; it had a devilish face painted on its side. The child had blown and blown until the face was quite large. The child did not know the technique too well, so a great deal of spittle had gone into the balloon. Suddenly it exploded; all the child held in his hand was a messy little bit of rubber, with the distorted face reduced to little or nothing. The child attempted to stretch this out but the face had lost its power to frighten.

When I thought of this in retrospect, it reminded me of what happened to Satan when Christ died. The devil and his principalities had been filled with pretentions, but Christ had disarmed them and made a show of them—a public example. We can thank God that Satan was effectively put to an open shame, exposed publicly. His overblown balloon burst, leaving him nothing but the messy remains of his grinning pretentions.

STEAMING THE OCEAN

Duveen, the famous English art connoisseur, took his little daughter to the beach one day, but she would not go into the chilly water. After persuasion failed, Duveen borrowed a tea-kettle, built a fire, heated a little water until it steamed beautifully; then, with a great flourish, he poured it into the ocean. His greatly impressed daughter went in without a murmur.

Where can we find a better example of one of Satan's tricks? He dilutes an ocean of unbelief with a steaming teakettle of Christian ethics and people go wading in, self-satisfied but unaware that they are bathing in unbelief.

SECOND COMING

BLACK SAND

When I was a little boy, I sometimes went down to the beach, five miles from our home in California, and played on the sands of Monterey Bay. Some little distance up the beach there is a great stretch of black sand; it is black because it contains a great deal of iron. I can remember taking a box of sand and drawing a magnet through it. Fine black grains clung to the magnet—particles of iron. I put these grains in another box, and drew my magnet through the sand again. Each time I got some more grains, I removed the particles of iron until nothing was left in the box but sand. Though I could not tell the difference between the sand and the iron on the beach, the magnet could tell the difference immediately. Had I been able to use a stronger magnet, I could have taken all of the iron out of a large box of sand in a moment.

The day is going to come when the Lord Jesus Christ will rise from the throne of God where He is now answering the attacks of Satan upon us, by telling the Father that we belong to Him because of His work on the cross. When He rises from that throne, it is time for judgment to begin. But God tells us that before judgment comes, He is going to do a wonderful thing—like the work of the magnet picking the grains of iron out of the grains of sand. He is going to remove from the earth all who are trusting Christ, and take them to be with Himself.

THE COMING FRIEND

Did you ever get a letter from some friend or relative announcing that they were coming to your home for a visit? You don't know when they will arrive. You keep looking for them at any moment. Suddenly the doorbell rings; you go to the door and find the baggage man with the trunk and valises of your coming guest. The door closes. You stand looking at the baggage in the hall. Surely it will not be long until you see your loved one in person.

So the Christian waits for Christ. The events of current history are but the baggage that mark the nearness of His coming. Our Lord is at the door.

OUR CLUBHOUSE

When I was a boy, I lived on a street that came to a dead end a block from my home; beyond a fence across the street lay an undeveloped tract of land. One day the fence was taken down, and the street was extended. Soon a contractor built many houses there and families moved in. One house remained unfinished. Workmen came for two days and then absented themselves for a week or two; they returned again for several days, then were absent for another long period. My father explained that the contractor was using that house to occupy his men when they were not needed on some other house in the tract. That house became the headquarters for a group of us boys. We retrieved every discarded scrap of board, every short end, every fallen nail. Before the floor was laid, we had enough pieces to cover several square feet of bare joists; a good length of two-by-four served as the upright to which we nailed other pieces. Finally, we had a clubhouse big enough for a couple of Newfoundland dogs, or four or five boys. It was our delight for many days. One day after school we heard hammering and sawing and knew that the job was going forward. At five o'clock when the mill whistle blew the men left the job. We swarmed in and discovered that they had knocked our clubhouse apart and thrown the whole thing through a window opening. It lay, disjointed and wrecked, on the ground outside. The work proceeded with some steadiness for many days. The floor was laid and on top of the first, rough pine flooring, quartered oak boards for the finished floor were laid. One piece, cut and ready to put in place, had been left lying there, and the idea came to us that we could nail it into place. Carefully, we examined the other pieces to see how they had been nailed in: We wrapped a rag around the nails and tapped lightly with the hammer lest we leave some scar. It took us almost an hour to secure one piece of board. We wondered if it would be allowed to remain; we marked the board and the wainscot so that we could tell whether "our" board had stood the test. The next evening we entered the house and were thrilled to find "our" board in the center of the finished floor.

Three or four years later, passing that house at night when the shades were up and one could see the warmth of that room with its lights and curtains, I stood outside for several minutes, recalling with pride that I had helped place a quartered oak board in that floor.

When the Lord Jesus Christ comes again we shall account for the materials we have used. Some buildings—some lives—are like a patchwork doghouse built on open joists, destined to be destroyed. But some will endure as part of God's eternal structure. Let us bow before God and ask Him to wreck everything in our lives that results from our own efforts apart from Him. Ask Him to confirm everything that is being built according to the plans and specifications of His Word.

THE FISHING FLEET

In a city near Edinburgh, a large fishing fleet goes forth each year on a long expedition to the Newfoundland banks. When the fleet returns, the whole town is notified, and as the boats come over the horizon, everyone is at the dock waiting for loved ones who have been away for two, or three long months. On one such return, as the fleet approached the shore, the captain stood on the deck of one of the ships with his field glasses, reporting to the sailors. Naturally, they were all wondering about their loved ones. The captain said, "Jock, I see your Mamie and the two bairns there; Bill, there is your Freda; John, I see. . . ." As he told each man of his family and wife, each was relieved to know that all was well—there had been no sickness, no death. One man came to the captain and asked, "Do you see my wife there?" The captain turned and said, "I'm sorry Angus, I don't see her; she's not there." Angus began to worry because his wife was not in the crowd on the wharf. When the ship docked, the men greeted their loved ones, but Angus moved through the crowd looking everywhere for his wife; he could not find her. He passed quickly through the village to his house on a hill. With hurried step he opened the door—there was his wife. She said, "Oh, Angus, I've been waiting for you." He replied, "The wives of the other men were watching for them."

Believers in the Lord Jesus Christ should not be only waiting but also watching for the Lord to come.

JOHN'S HOMECOMING

The atmosphere of the believing church should be that of the mother and father who have been told that their son at the war front has received his rotation papers—he will be home any day. In this day of airplanes they know it is possible for him to get on an airplane and be in Philadelphia and at the front door perhaps quicker than a cablegram and telegram could be delivered. So the house is gotten ready. John is coming home; he may be there any moment. You may be sure his fiancee is thinking with great joy of the imminence of his return. Every step on the stair, every ring of the bell, every ring of the telephone, may be news from John, he may be there in a moment.

Now that is undoubtedly the psychological atmosphere in which the early church lived. The thought of His coming should be before us like the returning of the son and the loved one. He has said he will come back.

THE PLANE RIDE

Some years ago I had to go out to Los Angeles on a plane from New York. The hostess seated a girl twenty or twenty-one years of age beside me. Obviously the girl had never flown before. Over the loudspeaker, the hostess said, "Fasten your seatbelts"; the girl did not know what a seatbelt was. I helped her and asked, "You've never flown before?" And she said, "No, this is my first time." As I spoke to her, she opened her pocketbook, and there was a picture of a GI, a fine, rock-ribbed New England face. I said, "You're going out to see him?" "Yes," she said, "he's coming home. I'm going to see him." I talked to her. They had gotten married a year and a half before, had a honeymoon of just a few days, then he had gone to the coast and left for Korea. Now he was coming back home; she was going to see him, and that meant more to her than anything else. Nothing else counted for her; her whole soul was in her eyes. As I told her how to fix the seatbelt, I said, "Now don't be worried, the engines are going to whirl and you'll think that something is going to happen, but it isn't. They're just testing the engines and when they quiet down, then there will be the moment of pull and you'll feel the takeoff." She was interested in everything she was doing, but most of all in the young man in the cellophane-bordered picture in her pocketbook. He was her bridegroom; she was his bride; she was going to see him.

You wonder sometimes why Christians live as they do and make the choices they make. They are on their way to see their bridegroom, yet they go right out and live in the world as though it made no effect in their life at all. Why do people live the way they live in the light of the fact that Jesus is coming again? This is the blessed hope. We are going to see Him.

SEPARATION

DIVIDED ALLEGIANCE

Louis Adamic, a Yugoslavian boy, came to the United States at the age of fourteen. He became absorbed in writing and eventually mastered a vivid prose style in his adopted language. His first book, *Dynamite,* was a history of the American labor conflict in its more violent phases. *The Native's Return* made him famous; he wrote this book after a visit to the land of his birth. From that time on the author's allegiance was divided. He wanted to do something for Yugoslavia; thinking that Stalin was Yugoslavia's best friend, he abandoned our democratic ways, fought against granting Trotsky asylum in America, and little by little became more interested in Balkan politics than in American democracy. When Tito broke with Stalin, Adamic followed Tito. Louis Adamic was found dead at his New Jersey farm below Easton. It was widely suspected that he had been murdered by a member of an anti-Tito Slavic party. One commentator said, "The moral seems to be plain: divided citizenship, divided national loyalties, can mean terrible tragedy in the modern world."

The spiritual analogy is just as plain. God will never accept a compromise. The world and the flesh seek to draw the allegiance of a believer in a thousand subtle ways, but God demands separation. The separation is in the heart, while the activity is in the midst of the market place, the church organization or the social whirl.

287

SEPARATION

DOUBTFUL AND DIRTY

A newspaper comic once showed a man dressing in a hurry for an evening engagement. He called out to his wife, "Mary, come and see if this collar is clean enough to wear." The answer he received was, "If it's doubtful, it's dirty."

God says, ". . . come out from among them, and be ye separate . . . and touch not the unclean thing . . ." (II CORINTHIANS 6:17).

Many Christians are worried as to whether or not they should partake in this or that form of the world's work or play. A very good rule for the Christian who is really seeking to follow the Lord closely, is that the doubtful thing is generally unclean. The doubt in our mind probably comes from the presence of the Holy Spirit who is warning us. The closer we come to yieldedness, the more quickly doubt will turn to certainty.

THE GREAT ALBATROSS

Ornithologists now know that the great albatross flies around the world several times in the course of its life. These birds can stand buffeting by ocean gales for days, but they become seasick if they stand on the deck of a moving ship.

The true Christian can go across the face of life, buffeted by all the winds of time and space, as long as he remembers that he is in the world but not of it. When he comes down and becomes a part of the movement of this world he loses his Christian joy and power, because he is entirely out of the element for which God created him.

TOPS AND MARBLES

A boy does not give up playing with tops and marbles. Tops and marbles give him up. He may be playing marbles one day when the older boys come by; if they are short a man for a ball game, they may ask him to play. He covers his field as if his life depended upon it; when he is at bat, he swings hard enough to break himself in two. When the game is over, he walks—struts—with the older boys; he sees the "little fellows" with whom he had played so recently, playing marbles. His lip curls contemptuously as he says, "Kid stuff." He has not given up marbles, marbles have given him up.

The believer in the life of Christ does not have to give up "things." The new life of Christ will push off the old, dead habits and these "things" will give him up.

SIN

A SPLASH UNDER THE LIGHT

A person, walking on a dark night, gets splashed by a taxi going by. Oh, he says, "I got some mud on me." In the reflection of a light about fifty yards away, he says, "I don't think it is too bad." As he gets nearer the light, he says, "It's worse than I thought." Right under the light, he says, "I'm going to have to go back to the apartment and change."

The nearer you get to the Lord, the more you are going to see what sin is in your life. The nearer we get to God, the more we will see what we really are.

AUTOMOBILE LAWS

Back in the early days of automobiles there were no laws against speed. A man who had learned the joys of fast driving bought one of the fastest cars available and took it out on the roads, driving as fast as road conditions allowed. He crossed the border into another state, and was confronted by a large road sign stating that the state speed limit was 35 miles per hour. Every mile or so he found another announcement of the speed limit. The law infuriated him, so he broke it at every opportunity. As he sped he passed still another sign reaffirming the speed limit; it further announced that the road was patrolled and that the law would be strictly enforced. The law had not created his desire for speed—that had existed long before the law was enacted—but the law made him conscious of his fierce desire to speed, and it also made him conscious of his rebellion against the restraining demand of the law. Each succeeding sign brought the same swift rebellion. His foot

290

moved from accelerator to brake, from brake to accelerator as his mind veered from desire for speed to fear of arrest. The coming of the law brought out both the desire to have his own way and conflict with authority that sought to restrain him.

Before the law, sinful desire had occasionally cropped up; but with the law, rebellion became open, and the sinner determined to satisfy his desire at all costs. If we are to live in triumph, with righteousness reigning through Christ, we must pass through the experience that is set forth here in order to be brought to God's own method for victory over sin's thrust from within us.

THE BLACKBOARD MARKS

A little girl, coming home from her first day at school, asked her mother where the marks on the blackboard went when they were rubbed out. The mother answered that they disappear. "But where do they disappear to?" the little girl questioned. "They vanish," her mother told her. "But where do they vanish to?" the child insisted. The mother used all the words she knew to explain but she could not make it clear to the child.

This story illustrates what God has done with our sins. He goes so far as to say that He, who is all knowledge, will remember our sins against us no more.

BROKE

A young man in college was so engrossed in preparations for final examinations and in extra-curricular activities, that he neglected to write home for five weeks. Then his parents received a letter, which said, "The inevitable consequence of not writing for five weeks is that I am now broke."

The inevitable consequence of not keeping in close communication with the heavenly Father is that the child becomes spiritually bankrupt. It doesn't take five weeks, either. A day will destroy fellowship. It is sin which cuts the communication lines and anything which cuts them is sin.

EXTINCT FLOWERS

During World War II, great bombs fell right in the center of London, and buildings were completely leveled. When the debris was cleared away, there was earth in the center of London, and flowers sprang up in the bomb craters. Botanists had thought these flowers died a hundred years ago, but their seeds had lain dormant under the city, and now flowers came back that men had thought extinct.

When men face tragedy or complex crises in their lives, seeds of sin rise up from their dormancy and strike out. Occasionally you hear of men of exemplary character becoming murderers or thieves because the seeds are there. Unhappy is the man who does not know that every seed of sin lies in him. Only by the grace of God in Christ and by the building of the edifice of faith over the top of it, can the light of day keep the explosions of life from bringing the subsoil out with all the horrors that are there ready to spring into growth, if they are not curbed moment by moment.

THE GI'S LOAN

An ex-GI went into the Chase Manhattan Bank in New York to get a loan from their small loans department. The Chase Manhattan is one of the largest banks in the world and negotiates loans of millions of dollars with great industries. But they also have a small loans department that lends a few hundred dollars to a working girl or a laboring man. The former soldier had to fill out a lot of forms because the government was guaranteeing the loan; it was necessary for him to come back a second day.

When the GI returned he was kept waiting for quite a while. Finally, the president of the bank came up to the GI, introduced himself, and asked him if he'd mind being photographed.

The day before, the bank records had shown that some-time on the following day the total monies loaned by the small loans department would reach the sum of one billion dollars. The bank authorities decided to publicize that fact by granting a "free" loan to the customer who appeared at the right moment. The soldier was the fortunate man—the depart-ment had just reached the billion-mark. He had signed all the papers and had obligated himself to repay the sum of six hun-dred dollars in installments, but now, before the news cameras, he was *given* the sum of six hundred dollars; his note and other papers were returned to him. The bank, of course, got much more than six hundred dollars' worth of publicity on the trans-action, but we might well say, "O the blessedness of the GI to whom the Chase Manhattan Bank will not impute or charge his loan." The bank had effectively said, "This one is to be placed to our account. You will never have anything to pay."

God has declared that it is His sovereign plan to charge to the account of Jesus Christ the sins of all who will admit that they are personally bankrupt spiritually, and who will throw themselves upon His grace to save them.

THE GOSSIP

A woman received a juicy bit of scandal on the telephone one Sunday morning. She was eager to communicate the news to another close friend and tried to reach her by telephone. The line was busy and she could not get the call through. Again and again she tried, but without success. Her impatient husband was waiting to take her to the communion service. The woman reluctantly went to church, but she hoped that no one would tell her friend the morsel of gossip before she got home to relay the news.

The woman reached for the bread and the cup with the definite knowledge that she was planning sin as soon as the church service was over. She thus eats and drinks unworthily, and is eating and drinking condemnation to herself, not discerning the Lord's body.

THE HUNTER AND THE BEAR

As the hunter raised his rifle, the bear called out, "Can't we talk this over like two sober human beings?" The hunter lowered his gun. "What's to talk over?" he asked. "Well, for instance," said the bear, coming closer, "what do you want to shoot me for?" "Simple," grunted the hunter, "I want a fur coat." "All I want is a good breakfast," smiled the bear. "I'm sure we can get together sensibly on this." So they sat down to work out an agreement. After awhile the bear got up—all alone. They had reached a compromise. The bear had secured his breakfast, and the hunter had on his fur coat.

There has never been any other result in the warfare between the flesh and the spirit when the spirit permits any compromise with the flesh. Sin is deceitful and will always destroy even while putting forth a pretense of fair words. The Word of God gives us only one possible course of action, "FLEE."

THE INCOME TAX

A man working on his income tax forms, does not get the job accomplished on Saturday evening; he plans to continue on Sunday afternoon, following the communion service. He knows that he is juggling figures and claiming invalid deductions to cheat the government.

When he takes the bread and the cup he is announcing to the world that there is no course of action in his life that is wrong and that is not surrendered to the Lord. It is a public lie. The proper state of mind must be that *as far as a man knows,* Christ is Lord of every area of his life. He must be living after the Spirit, and surrendering the deeds of his mortal body for mortification—putting to death—by the work of Christ. God will continue throughout life to reveal new areas for the growing Lordship of Christ, but at the moment of taking communion properly, the man has surrendered every area of which he has an awareness of conflict.

IRON OUT OF ORE

In Venezuela there are great iron mines, from which ore is shipped to the largest iron works in the world, near Philadelphia. If a man were to try to get iron out of ore with a hammer, he could not do it, because iron is not a mechanical agglutination; it is a chemical union. The ore must go into a great furnace; as the temperature rises, the iron within the ore turns to liquid, and the pure metal runs out.

This is exactly how God works in your life and mine. This is why we must be salted with fire. You and I cannot hammer sin out of our lives. Rather, we must recognize that God loves us and that He will salt us with fire until the slag is burned away and only pure metal remains. So, if you and I desire to be delivered from sin, we must be willing to go into the flame. There is no other way.

KICKING HIS SHINS

A little girl was very mean to her younger brother; she treated him so badly, he went crying to his mother. When the mother learned what had happened, she said to the little girl, "Mary, why have you let Satan put it into your heart to pull your brother's hair and kick his shins?" The little girl thought it over for a moment, and then answered, "Well, Mother, maybe Satan did put it into my heart to pull brother's hair, but kicking his shins was my own idea."

The evil in the earth does not all come from Satan; much of it comes from the heart of man. To be sure, Satan tempts man to sin, but a great deal of sin is man's own idea.

MEERSCHAUM PIPES

When we were in Holland, we wanted to spend Sunday at Marken, a beautiful little island northeast of Amsterdam. Since there was no hotel there, we stayed in a town four miles away in order to take the ferry over in the morning. The women of the town wear turned-up caps, and the men wear big, baggy trousers and wooden shoes, and smoke meerschaum pipes— great big pipes about as big as a saxaphone. In the morning, while we waited for the ferry we noticed several hundred villagers gathering for the Catholic church service across the street. The bell began to ring, and little girls began to scurry into the church. Then followed the teen-age girls, the young matrons, and finally the older women. None of the men moved; they went right on talking and jesting, as stolidly as though there had been no motion at all. When the last old woman had gone in, there were two seconds of breaks; then the little boys went toward the door, and successively the teen-agers and the older men. As the smokers approached the church, we noticed something we had not seen before. In front of the church were large wooden racks with number holes. The men came up, hung their pipes in those niches in the racks and went on into the church. When the last man had gone inside, we saw 75 or 100 meerschaum pipes. Not a man was in sight. Of course, when the Mass was over, they would come out, each man would reach for his pipe and light up.

I said to myself, "I wonder what we would see if out in front of our churches, we had a rack for our little packages of sin— something we were doing, a nice neat little box, Christmas-wrapped. As you entered you hung your package on number 18, went inside and took communion, said, 'I surrender all,' and hurried back to that box."

NEVER GOT CAUGHT

A man filling out a job application blank came to the question, "Have you ever been arrested?" His answer was "No." The next question, asking "Why?", was meant for those who had answered the first part in the affirmative. Nevertheless, the applicant answered it with, "Never got caught." That was the truth.

He had sin in him, but he did not have it on him simply because a policeman hadn't been there at the opportune moment. But the sin that is in us in the sight of God is also on us, as we are answerable to God. That is, the sin is on us unless it is on the Saviour, and then it can never be on us again, since He bore it for those who put their trust in Him. There are not three places in the universe where sin can be. Your sin is either on yourself or on the Saviour.

RADIOACTIVITY

One of the most terrible aspects of atomic energy is the terrific lingering radioactivity imparted to anything nearby. Human beings go near the place where an atomic explosion has taken place at their own peril.

What an illustration of the effects of sin! Someone may think that their loss of temper or their crisis of passion lasted for only a moment, but corroding effects may continue for months in the life of a Christian and the wages are death in the life of a non-Christian. The death that proceeded from Adam's sin is still causing casualties.

THE TESTIMONY EXHIBITION

During my late teens I observed the corruption of sin in a rescue mission in Los Angeles. I listened to the testimonies of men with criminal records: The first said that he had been in prison three times, and had lived a life of sin; the next had been in prison four times, and had sinned even more; the third man had had six imprisonments, and added dope to the alcohol of the first two. I was uneasy; these men seemed to be exhibitionists, though I did not know the meaning of the word at that time. If the man who had testified first had waited till last he might have remembered a few more convictions, and have found a deeper black for his portrait. Finally, I could not contain myself any longer. I rose to say that I had a greater testimony than any man who had spoken. There was an intense silence as these men, eroded with cancerous sin, turned to look at the beardless youth who was seemingly raising their bid to take the game. And then I cried out that the reason I had a testimony greater than any that had been given was that I was able to say that Jesus Christ had saved me from all these horrors, and He had kept me from them. I can remember a very dirty old man bursting into tears. Perhaps looking upon me conjured up the memory of his youth and what he might have been.

But although I had such a testimony, and still have it, I am able to look down through the electronic microscope of the Word of God and see the corruption of the nature which is mine by inheritance, and to acknowledge that all of the seeds that brought forth such corruption in these men were and are within my being, as they are within yours. It is in the light of this truth that the true Christian will be very humble, and will desire to grow in compassion toward those who are out of the way.

THE TREACHEROUS CREEK

Just outside the town in California where I was born is a creek that winds across the country, eventually flowing into the Pajaro River. Many a spot along this creek would make a magnificent swimming hole, but no boys are ever seen there. It is not even necessary for parents to tell their boys not to go near these waters. Were any new boy to suggest a swim, others would quickly tell him that the name of the creek is *Salsipuedes;* Spanish for "Get out if you can." There are quicksands in the creek. Legend has it that a man attempted to cross and was caught in the terrible grip of the sand; a Spaniard, coming by, called out to him, *"Sal si puedes,"* and that is how the creek got its name.

Nothing could be more terrible than the locking of that

invisible power that catches a man and pulls him down steadily to suffocation and death. This is the picture that God Himself has given us of the force of sin that holds every man and woman in this world until the redemption provided by Christ Jesus has been made effective in their lives.

THE WHINE OF THE SHELLS

During the first world war the soldiers near the front line trenches learned to know the whine of the different types of shells as they screamed their way over to bring death. When a shell was heard, men flung themselves into the nearest hole without any worry as to what kind of filth or death might be in the hole. Nothing in the hole could be as bad as the exploding steel.

So it is that men run away from life when God speaks to them. He uncovers their sin and tells them of their need and immediately they run for cover. There is no honesty behind the evasions, and this Christ will not tolerate, but where there is an honest doubt, He will meet it.

SONS OF GOD

THE DIRTY BEGGAR CHILD

If you were walking down some important street in the midst of great crowds, and should see a dirty beggar child holding out his hand toward you, your heart would be moved to pity. But if that child kept running after you and called out to you "Mother," or "Father," when you have never seen the child before, you would be stirred to righteous indignation. What right would that child have to attract attention to you and turn the gaze of all the passersby from the child's filth to you? Desire on the part of a child cannot create a parental relationship. If you go to the child in the street and lead him to your home, give him new cleanliness and new clothing, and adopt him into your family, then he has the right to call you father, and the law will recognize that right. But the right and authority must be given by you.

In the divine relationship God has made full provision for sonship. If we are to become sons of God, the first step is that we must realize that we are not sons of God, and cannot be except through the channel which He himself has opened up to us through Christ.

SPIRITUAL LIFE

THE CHRISTIAN STUDENT

A Christian student must understand that it is sin for him to be lazy, for mental laziness is a sin. If a student has a brain capable of earning a grade of A, it is a sin for him to get only a B. If he is capable of earning a B, it is a sin for him to get only a C. If this be true in our mental life, it is also true in our spiritual life.

We are not to be lazy in our spiritual life. Man is a soul; he has a body and a spirit. We must spend much time on the body, keeping it fed and clothed, and letting it sleep in order to recuperate. But we are not to be lazy. Spiritual laziness is the cause of spiritual defeat.

COROT'S POND

While Jean François Raffaeli, the French art critic was walking near the village of Barbizon he saw the renowned Jean Baptiste Corot painting a meadow, with woods in the background. Raffaeli saw that Corot had put in a small lake, although actually there was no lake in the field before him. "But, Monsieur Corot!" he exclaimed, "is it permissible to paint a pond where there is no pond?" Corot retorted, "Young man, it is eleven o'clock. I have been here in the field since six this morning. I became very thirsty, so I put water in the picture to refresh myself."

Therein we recognize our own thirsts and hungers, our need for refreshment; so Paul expresses his need of refreshment and gives the clue as to how we are refreshed.

THE SUBMERGED BOTTLE

If you submerge a bottle in water, what happens? Some will say, "The air bubbles out and the water flows in." But I have seen a bottle submerged in water and no air came out nor did any water flow in. There was a cork in the bottle, which must be pulled out if the bottle is to submerge.

God is like that with us. He has the purpose and the power, but He will not ravish our beings. Love can never be commanded, and He wants us to love Him, so He woos us by creating all the qualities which go with emptiness and frustration. But when we tell Him to go ahead and do His work, out come the obstacles which keep Him from filling our beings, and in comes the power of the Holy Spirit, so that life at once takes on abounding quality. There is no abounding without the pressure of His power behind it. Nothing can overflow from us until we have first been filled. And we cannot be filled until His power comes in with the enabling.

TIME AND PATIENCE

Fabre, the greatest naturalist who ever lived, began the main part of his work at sixty; he was able to give all his time to it when he was seventy; and he was discovered by fame at the age of ninety. He had done all of his work without a laboratory; all of his insects had been raised in old flower pots and sardine cans. He always referred to his two best instruments as *"time"* and *"patience."*

God tells us that He uses these two things in developing our spiritual lives. How many times we are told to wait upon the Lord! The flesh does not want to take time, but God does, for He is dealing with eternity. And, too, patience is to have her perfect work.

STANDARDS

GENERAL PERSHING'S PARADE

In a certain mountain village about a hundred miles from Paris, a group of American soldiers, consisting of a lieutenant and about forty men, guarded an ammunition dump. The lieutenant received permission to go on leave for two weeks, and he left the group in charge of the master sergeant.

A few days afterwards a motorcycle messenger rode in from General Pershing's headquarters stating that 2,700 men were to be chosen to march in the peace parades of London, Paris, Brussels and Rome. But as they read the order, they discovered that there were two conditions imposed as standards for selection. The first brought them no difficulty, for it stated that every candidate had to have a clean record—no man would be chosen who had been court martialed. But the second condition gave them pause. The order stated that every man applying had to be at least one meter and eighty-six centimeters tall.

The corporal looked at the sergeant and the sergeant looked at the corporal and then one of them asked how much one meter and eighty-six centimeters was. There was no answer. Then the corporal said, "At any rate, Sarge, I am taller than you."

When mess time came and the news spread around the group, it was the same thing over again. No one knew the metric system. The men got into an argument as to their relative heights, and soon they were standing up, back to back, to see who was the tallest man in the company. Finally, they knew their comparative heights, all the way from Slim down to Shorty.

The officer returned, heard the news, and asked if there were any candidates. The sergeant replied, "The trouble is, Sir, that we do not know what one meter and eighty-six centimeters is." The lieutenant knew enough French to go out into the village and bring back a meter measure. Soon a mark of the required height was made on the wall. Now the men no longer measured themselves against themselves. They measured against a mark on the wall that was unchanged and unchangeable according to the orders from headquarters. One or two men backed up to the mark, and their companions told them that they were an inch or so short of the requirement. Some men merely looked at the mark and knew that there was no hope. Finally a call was made for Slim and he came to be measured. He puffed himself up to his greatest possible height and stood there, rigid and swollen as they measured him. When the ordeal was ended, it was discovered that he, too, was short, even though he was short by no more than a quarter of an inch.

Of course, General Pershing got his 2,700 men. I saw them that day when they came under the Arch of Triumph on Bastille Day, the fourteenth of July, in what must have been one of the greatest parades of all history. These men, all in new uniforms, with American Beauty roses tied to their bayonets, made a proud sight as they marched down the Champs Elysees, each one of them 186 centimeters tall at least—more than 6 feet one-and-a-fifth inches.

The rule God has made for entry into heaven is that men shall measure up to His glory and be as perfect as He. This rigorous standard is to be found expressed throughout the Bible, and it is to be found exemplified in the man, Christ Jesus. The Old Testament was built around the command of God: ". . . ye shall be holy; for I am holy . . ."(LEVITICUS 11:44).

NINE FEET HIGH

A little boy came to his mother, saying, "Mama, I am as tall as Goliath, I am nine feet high." "What makes you say that?" asked the surprised mother. "Well, I made a little ruler of my own and measured myself with it, and I am just nine feet high!" said the boy.

There are many people who follow the little boy's method, measuring themselves by some rule of their own. God tells us of those who, "measuring themselves by themselves, and comparing themselves among themselves, are not wise" (II CORINTHIANS 10:12).

God has the standard measurement and He tells us: ". . . all have sinned, and come short of the glory of God" (ROMANS 3:23).

OUT OF TUNE

Several years ago, musicians noted that errand boys in a certain part of London all whistled out of tune as they went about their work. It was talked about and someone suggested that it was because the bells of Westminster were slightly out of tune. Something had gone wrong with the chimes and they were discordant. The boys did not know there was anything wrong with the peals, and quite unconsciously they had copied them.

So you will tend to copy the people you are most with; you will borrow your thoughts from the books you read and the programs you listen to, almost without knowing it. God has given us His Word, never out of tune, to set the standard for our song. Here is the absolute pitch of life and living. If we learn to sing by it, we shall easily detect the false in all of the music of the world.

STANDING AND STATE

THE ENGLISH HEIR

The younger son in a certain family in England disgraced his name and family by outrageous conduct. The family told him that if he would leave the country, he would receive a check each quarter that would permit him to live in some comfort, but that he would be refused all income if he remained in England. He emigrated to Canada and received his check every three months. He spent it within a few days, and the rest of the time he lived the precarious existence of a semi-bum. He drifted down into the United States, after making arrangements for the Canadian bank to send him his money at a certain time and place. In the meantime his father died suddenly, and his older brother was killed in an automobile accident, all within a matter of hours. By British law, he became heir to the title and estates. But he had dropped from sight in the United States and could not be traced. His wife left England, arrived in New York, and undertook the search for her husband. He had just drawn a remittance and supposedly would not be heard from for another three months. The best detectives were employed to locate him and within a few days he was traced to a small town not far from Chicago where he was eking out a precarious existence as an elevator operator in a cheap hotel. His *position* was that of a noble earl of England with access to the House of Lords. His *condition* was that of an underpaid starveling in a cheap job in a midwestern town. His wife flew to meet him and flew him back to New York. It was then that the newspapers discovered the story and printed the details. The man was in New York, in the process of acquiring a new wardrobe; he was awaiting passage on the steamship that was to take him back to his ancestral castle, his estate and his new life.

OLD JOHN

Years ago in Scotland a simple fisherman was bound by strong drink; on too frequent occasions he took the money from his catch and spent it on liquor while his wife and children suffered miserably. They lived in a little hovel off at the end of the fishing village, out of sight of most of the villagers. But one day there came a great change. Old John, as he was called, came to the knowledge of the Lord Jesus Christ as his own personal Saviour. There was an immediate transformation. He brought his full money home and gave it to his astonished wife. He worked more steadily, and soon they had more money than they had had in years. The wife bought new clothes and new shoes for the children, and new dresses for herself. There was food on the table, coal for the fire and all was going very well. After a few weeks of this, his wife said to him one day, "John, if you are going to keep on like this we should begin to think of moving out of this miserable place and taking a better place."

"Right," said John, "I shall go and see the landlord about a new house at once." He made his way through the town to the landlord and asked to rent a good house which was available. The landlord said, "I would never rent a good house to you."

"Why do you say that?" asked John. "You don't know me at all, and I am quite sure that I am able to pay the rent and that I would be a model tenant for you."

"Of course I know you," said the landlord. "You are old drunken John, the fisherman."

"I know you are quite mistaken," said John quietly. "You have never seen me before. Old John is dead and I am new John, a new creature in Christ Jesus." He opened his purse and poured out a good handful of gold coins on the table before the eyes of the astonished landlord. I do not know whether the man was convinced by the testimony of the new John, but he was convinced by the sight of the gold coins. Soon new John was living in a new house.

From our perfect standing under justification, the past life of every born-again man has ceased to exist so far as God is concerned. I suppose that there were people who lived in that village who still remembered, even after years and years of calm sobriety, that new John had once been old John. The world has a tenacious memory for past sins.

THE RICH BEGGAR

A lawyer in New York received papers from a Texas lawyer, asking him to look up the next of kin of a wealthy client who had died in the southwest. Evidence showed that a rough but strong character had emigrated to the west at the close of the war between the states. He settled on land that later brought in great gushers of oil; he died leaving a tremendous estate, and no will. His movements were traced back to Philadelphia, and it was discovered that a sister had lived in that city. She had died leaving no heir except a grandchild who turned out to be a beggar. That beggar, we will say, is attempting to wheedle a few coins out of passersby. The lawyer begins to investigate; after considerable checking, doublechecking and triplechecking, he becomes convinced that the beggar is the rightful owner of the estate in Texas. He communicates this knowledge to the attorneys in Texas, and they arrange that a considerable sum of money shall be arranged for the immediate use of the heir. You walk downtown with the lawyer until you locate the beggar. "That man," says the lawyer, "is worth approximately thirty million dollars, and I have just deposited one million of it in the bank for his drawing account." The observer might say with some justice that the man certainly did not look like a man who was worth millions. And not only was it certain that he did not look like a millionaire, he was not acting like a millionaire. His condition was that of a beggar; his position was that of a millionaire. The lawyer informs the man of his new position and estate. The man, who has some memory of his grandmother and has heard tales of a great-uncle who went out to the new frontiers and struck it rich, acknowledges his identity with great joy. He is overwhelmed by the prospect of his riches.

Let us face the fact that there are many Christians who live a life that is not far from such a condition. They have been given all things in Christ, but they do not joyfully avail themselves of the riches and go on to live in the power and possession of the wealth which has become theirs in title.

THE SCOTCH LADY

A young minister came to visit a woman who was dying. Just out of theological seminary, he had more theology than Bible in his head; he had not experienced much of the experimental joys of long and close living with the Saviour in the knowledge and power of the divine love. Appalled at the apparent joy and certainty of the patient, he began to counsel her to give diligence to make her calling and election sure. But the dear old saint had been walking with the Lord for many a year and was long past the stage of learning the ABC's of the gospel. She gave a testimony so clear that the young man was frightened; he pressed her to go back and be less presumptuous with God. She answered, "Young man, if I should nae be in Heaven the guid Lord would lose more than I could ever lose." This amazed him more than her first attitude and he asked for an explanation. The old lady answered, "If I should nae be in Heaven all that I could lose would be my own soul, for that is all I have to lose. But if I should nae be in Heaven the guid Lord would lose His name and honor, for He has promised to save them to the uttermost that come to Him by Christ, and that is the way which I have come."

If we come to that place where we are aware of our position in Christ, we will be like this Scotch lady whose answer to her young minister showed such clear faith and realization of the truth of her position in Christ.

STEWARDSHIP OF TIME

TIME

A city employee or a former city employee, mailed Frank J. O'Brien, city treasurer of Albany, New York, a $100 bill marked "money for stolen time."

We are stewards of our time as much as we are stewards of our money. We are going to give an account of our moments as well as of our words. One of the most terrible thoughts ever devised by man is that which is inherent in the common phrase that this or that occupation is engaged in as a "pastime." Usage may have dropped the second "s" from the spelling, but the idea is that we must find something to pass the time away. May God help us to change our thinking that the idea of "pass time" is to "steal time." That is more true, and in stealing it, we rob both ourselves and God.

SUFFERING

A POLISHED SHAFT

In the British Museum in London, Mrs. Barnhouse and I visited one of the Egyptian rooms containing a magnificent collection of flints. Instruments of all sorts had been chipped from the hard rock. Certain arrowheads, even under the microscope, defied detection of the manner of manufacture. Yet we knew that somewhere, sometime, a workman had patiently chipped particles from the rough rock until a polished shaft was ready for the quiver of the huntsman or warrior. Read the text from Isaiah: ". . . he hath . . . made me a polished shaft; in his quiver hath he hid me" (ISAIAH 49:2).

When Isaiah tells us that God had turned him into such a shaft, he is telling us that he had undergone the cutting of the chisel. It was a process that was filled with pain, but when it was completed Isaiah tells us that he was a polished shaft. What is more, the Lord had made of him a useful instrument; he was hidden in the Lord's quiver, under the shadow of His hand, so that when an instrument was needed, he was available for the Lord's purposes.

LANGUAGE STUDY

Our school systems include the study of languages because of the effect of a second language on the mind. If one knows but one language one is tempted to think that everything is understood; in reality the sound and pattern of words and syntax go through the mind, bringing forth reactions, ofttimes without bringing forth thought. If it is necessary to translate an idea from one language to another, it is no longer possible

312

to fool oneself. The translator is forced to think the thing through. He is forced to understand.

In this may be found some of the reasons why God permits His people to suffer. Long ago we read, "To have suffered much is like knowing several languages; it gives one access to so many more people." Many of God's children have found, in the midst of suffering, that things which they had allowed to flow normally in life, without giving serious consideration to their meaning, must be thought through in suffering. Those who have not lived with suffering cannot understand the crystal-clear thought of the sufferers. To them God has revealed Himself in a way that they would not give up for anything.

PRAYING FOR PATIENCE

A young man came to George Goodman of England one day and said, "Mr. Goodman, I wish you would pray for me that I might have patience." Mr. Goodman answered, "Yes, I will pray for you that you have tribulation." "Oh, no, sir," the young man replied, "it is patience that I want." "I understand," said the Bible teacher, "and I will pray for you that you may have tribulation."

The astonished and disturbed young man was shown a passage in the Bible: "And not only so, but we glory in tribulations also: knowing that tribulation worketh patience" (RO-MANS 5:3).

Some of the people of God have patience—a resigned patience that cannot honor Him very much. But there are instances, and they constitute a real testimony to the faithfulness and goodness of the Lord, where the joy of the Lord is the strength of His suffering child. Life is lived, one breath at a time, in a patience so mixed with the joyfulness that only can be seen in the midst of suffering. That life is seen as the life of God.

SUPPLYING MAN'S NEED

INLAY PROCEDURE

When a dentist fills a cavity with an inlay, he first grinds out all of the decayed matter, then he takes an impression in wax or some other substance into which the inlay is cast. If the work has been properly done, the inlay will fit the cavity perfectly; it will fit no other cavity in the world. Its contours, exact to less than a thousandth of an inch, fit the contours of the cavity.

It is thus that God's supply is able to meet man's need. Your particular need is as individual to you as your tooth cavity. God alone can meet every contour of that need. The perfection of His ability is seen in the amazing completeness of His perfect supply. All He asks is that you let Him cut away the dead matter of your sin, then He will meet your need completely.

RAISINS

A small boy in a grocery store was told to take a handful of raisins from a large box. He shook his head and refused. Finally the grocer took a handful and filled both the upturned hands of the little boy, who received twice as much as he could have taken for himself.

If you are missing the best in the Christian life, why not try turning your hands over so that God may fill them? He reserves the best for those who leave the choice with Him.

TACTLESSNESS

"ARE YOU SAVED?"

On Sunday evenings our young people's services are attended by many college students. One evening some years ago, during a social time before the meeting, I was greeted by a young woman who made it her business to approach every stranger and ask, "Are you saved?" She so greeted a brilliant young woman—a teacher of mathematics in a Philadelphia high school. In answer to her question the newcomer replied, "I do not believe in the divinity of Christ." The tactless Christian proceeded to introduce the young teacher to one and all with the words, "I want you to meet Miss Blank; she does not believe in the divinity of Christ." When Miss Blank was introduced to me in this manner, I shook hands and merely remarked, "Oh, she will some day." Then I brought other people into the conversation in order to relieve her embarrassment. After the meeting I stood near the door while the young people were leaving. I smiled at Miss Blank and said, "I should like to talk with you sometime." We made an appointment, and when she came to my office she remarked, "When that girl introduced me to you, I was about to leave. I just could not take any more. When you waved her aside and got me out of her clutches, I decided to stay."

As a result of our conference that day, Miss Blank trusted Christ as Saviour and Lord, and within a year she enrolled in a Bible training school. Three years later, she was teaching on a foreign mission field, where she led many students to know Jesus Christ as Lord and Saviour.

An attitude of love on our part is quickly detected by those

315

who do not think as we do; they also detect any lack of love! We must be careful not to alienate people who express unbelief they really do not mean. I suppose that "doctrine detectives" would have flailed this young woman with arguments; they would have given her a hard time with apologetics trying to convince her of the deity of Christ. Beyond question, that doctrine is central to the Christian faith; but there are many on the fringes of belief who are unsure, but who can be won to our Lord when they see Him in us, holding out His hand to them in love.

TEMPTATION

TEMPTATION

THE KNOCK AT THE DOOR

A little girl was asked what she did when she was tempted.
She replied, "Well, when I hear Satan come knocking at the
door of my heart, I just say to the Lord Jesus, who lives within
my heart, 'Lord Jesus, will You please go to the door?' And
then, when the Lord Jesus opens the door, Satan draws away
and says, 'Oh! Excuse me, I have made a mistake.'"

God has given us Himself to dwell within our hearts. The
Living Word is there with a full command of the Written
Word. When we let Him meet the temptation in our behalf we
shall know the joy of positive victory. We are fortunate that
one victory does not help us to win another, for our hearts are
kept from feasting upon an experience so that we may gaze
upon the living Lord Jesus Christ.

PASSING A TRUCK

We had been following a big truck for several miles up a
narrow mountain road. It seemed that every time there was a
place to pass, a car was coming in the opposite direction. Finally the moment seemed propitious. We were almost ahead of
the truck when an oncoming car appeared. We tramped the
accelerator to the floorboard, and the rush of reserved power
practically pushed the car to safety.

It is precisely this rush of reserve power that God has promised the Christian with every spiritual emergency. With every
test there is a way of escape (I CORINTHIANS 10:13). The accident (the spiritual defeat) takes place only when you are

passing on a blind curve (out of the will of God). No defeat was ever caused by any lack in Him.

THE PIANO MOVER

A newly-arrived pastor of a large church in Arizona did not know that many people live in that desert climate for their health, until he called upon a stalwart passerby for help in moving a piano. Without a word, the man disappeared. Friends told the pastor, "You must never ask that man to do any work; he is here for his lungs. If he had pushed that piano, he would have used so much strength that he would have had to go to bed for a week." The pastor said, "I have to be careful whom I ask to do certain tasks."

God sees the heart and knows our strength. He will never permit us to be tempted above what we are able, but will with the temptation make a way of escape, that we may be able to bear it. We can praise God that "he knoweth our frame; he remembereth that we are dust" (PSALM 103:14). Therefore, He provides for all our need and makes His strength perfect in our weakness.

TONGUE

WHALES JUMPING THE ROPE

At the trainer's signal a 16-foot whale, weighing 34,000 pounds, leaped straight out of the water until his tail was a foot above the surface; he opened his mouth to receive the handful of fish and fell back into the pool with a splash. A second whale took one end of a rope from another trainer and carried it 100 feet down the pool to the first trainer. When the two trainers pulled the rope so that it was six feet above the surface, the second whale broke the water and jumped the rope. For an hour, whales, porpoises, sea lions and seals went through their paces at Marineland, near Pacific Palisades.

Here before our eyes was a striking illustration of James 3:7: "For every kind of beasts, and of birds, and of serpents, and of things in the sea, is tamed, and hath been tamed of mankind." When I saw this truth, I was forced to admit the truth of the next line: "But the tongue can no man tame. . . ." I asked the Lord to keep mine cleansed that it might praise the Lord in holiness.

TOTAL DEPRAVITY

THE AMNESIA VICTIM

A young man, suffering from amnesia, lived a new life amid old surroundings; he could remember nothing that had happened before he fell off of a haywagon. As he fell he had cried out, "Hand me that pitchfork and I will. . . ." He was eighteen when the accident occurred; ten years of his new life passed. One day he got into a fight, and received a sharp blow that knocked him to the ground. His head struck a stone and he cried out—finishing the sentence he had started ten years before—". . . spread the hay." He arose, thinking that he was still eighteen years old, still on the haywagon.

The blow that struck the race in Adam made all his sons unconscious of the true nature and being of God. In that unconsciousness we were born; and in that unconsciousness we live until the moment we are saved. Immediately we are made aware of the holiness of God. We go back to a comprehension of our own creaturehood and of our total dependence upon the Saviour.

THE CANOE

Human goodness may be likened to a canoe. A canoe is a lovely little boat for its purpose—to be used on rivers and lakes in calm waters. It is admirably suited for young people on a beautiful day or evening in June. But the canoe is not suitable at a seaport or to cross the ocean. It is a totally unfit boat for such a purpose. The trip from New York to France cannot be made by a canoe, even in the month of June when the ocean is generally calm.

So the human character is admirably suited to take an individual around the daily course of life in the midst of a sinful world, but it is a totally depraved thing for the passage from earth to heaven. If a canoe be adjudged by all canoeists to be the best canoe that was ever made, it is still insufficient for the ocean passage. If a human character be adjudged by all men to be the best human character that ever developed, it is still insufficient for the passage from death to life, from earth to heaven.

THE GRAND CANYON

Several years ago, I motored across the continent with my family. One summer day we saw some of the beauties of the national parks in southern Utah; we drove on to the north rim of the Grand Canyon of the Colorado, arriving there after sunset. We found our rooms for the night and ate our dinner; then we walked down the path to the wall that guards the edge of this mighty chasm. There was no moon and we looked out into pitch darkness. I told my children what lay before them, but it was impossible to see anything whatsoever in the inky blackness. Far to the south we could see the lights of the hotel on the south rim of the canyon. I told the children that between us and those lights was a distance of many miles, and that separating us from the lights was the greatest canyon in the world, going down a mile to the great river which lay hidden beneath us. I suppose that the children accepted what I said on faith, and that they formed some sort of mental picture of what I described to them, but if we had left the place and driven on, they would never have really understood what the canyon really was.

In the morning we arose early, before sunrise, in order that to see the coming of the dawn. The canyon was still invisible beneath us, but far to the southeast we could see the great range of the San Francisco peaks. At first, they were but a faint shadow; then they became etched in outline, and soon the first rays of the invisible sun touched them. The canyon remained invisible beneath us. The line of things that we could see descended from those peaks to the rim of the canyon near us, and then to the distant rim to the south, but the depths of the canyon were still not visible. After the brilliance of the new day broke, our sight began to pick up the walls of the canyon, and little by little we were able to see farther and farther—to the very depths of the canyon.

My own awareness of the total depravity of my being and the incapacity of my fleshly nature is a close parallel to the experience we had on the rim of the Grand Canyon. At first I was aware of the biblical statement concerning my nature just as a man might be aware of a geographer's description of the Grand Canyon. Then as time passed I stood on the brink of my own sinfulness without knowing it was there in reality. At last, I saw, not the canyon of my depravity, but the distant mountain peaks of the cross of Jesus Christ, brought to my vision by the illumination of the Holy Spirit. Only then did I begin to see the edges of the abyss that is in the human heart, and as the years have passed my sight has gone deeper and deeper into that sinful depth. I discover from the Word of God the statistics of my depravity without having known at close range the depths of its capacity. Every Christian must come to this knowledge for himself.

"I'M A CAPTAIN"

A young man who had been brought up in one of the worst slums of New York, rose to fame and fortune in the theatrical field through his literary talents. He bought a yacht, and although he hired a man to run it for him, he himself assumed the title of "Captain." He got himself a resplendent uniform—complete with gold braid and brass buttons—and invited his old mother to go for a cruise. His mother had come to the United States from eastern Europe, and she had retained the native common sense that many such immigrants have. The boat stood out from the harbor, and the young man went below to change into his uniform. A few moments later he came out on the deck to parade before his mother. "Look, Momma," he said, "I'm a captain." The old lady surveyed him calmly and then, as one accustomed to deflating the ego of a bumptious child, she answered, "Sammy, by you, you is a captain, by me you is a captain, but by captains you is no captain."

Many people need to realize the importance of this illustration. By you, you're a good man; by your neighbors, you're a good man; but by God, you have no goodness. ". . . all our righteousnesses are as filthy rags . . ." (ISAIAH 64:6).

THE STREAM

A spring comes forth from the side of a hill—clear, cold, limpid, and containing a certain metal content from the earth. As the stream flows down through the countryside it becomes polluted. Each time man builds on its shores the stream becomes more foul. If it passes through a village or town it becomes undrinkable; if it passes through a city, it bears the germs of death for anyone who drinks of it. Yet there are traces of its original state for the chemical analysis still shows the presence of the original values. Even in its depraved state the stream still has its uses—its flow can carry away the sewage that would mean pollution if left in the city, although it becomes more polluted itself in performing this task.

So is the goodness of mankind. Adam came fresh from the hand of God, and there was no sin within him. When he chose to follow his own will instead of remaining in creature submission to the will of God, death entered into the human stream, which, under the analysis of the great chemist is seen in all its component parts in Romans 3:10-18. This is God's analysis of sin.

THE TRINITY

HEAT, LIGHT AND AIR

Any one of you may hold your hand before you and look at it. Between your eye and your hand are three things which are one, and which are also three. Each may be studied separately, but it is impossible to have one without the others. Between your hand and your eye at this moment are light and heat and air. Your eye can see your hand because of the light waves that are in the visible spectrum. Even when there is no visible light, there are invisible rays below the red and beyond the violet—infrared and ultraviolet. Darkness is only a matter of human eyes—that which stimulates the rods and cones of our retina we call visible light; the rest, no less real, is invisible light.

Before you in the light that you see there is also air. If you blow on your hand you can feel the air. You breathe it in; you breathe it out. You live by it. And there is heat between you and your hand; take a thermometer and measure it—see its variations as you go from a warm room to the winter snow without. You cannot have heat, or light, without having them in some relationship to our atmosphere. And you cannot have heat or air without having them in some relationship to our atmosphere. Science can use any one of them apart from the others, but can never separate them totally. To all intents and purposes they are three, and they are one.

We Christians do not believe that there are three Gods, but that there is one true God who is in three persons.

TRUST

THE FARMER AND THE NEST

A farmer watched a bird building her nest in a heap of branches pruned from the apple tree beside the farmhouse. All day long the bird toiled; in the evening the farmer destroyed the work she had done—scattering the tiny twigs about and trampling them beneath his feet. The next day the bird, undaunted, began her building once again. Again at evening time her work was destroyed. Judged by the feeble standards of the bird, ignorant of all beyond the cycle of her instincts, the man was cruel and not to be called good. The third day she began her nest once more, but this time in the rose bush beside the kitchen door. In the evening the farmer smiled upon the bird and her work remained. Day after day she continued her cyclic round; the nest was completed; the eggs were laid and warmed beneath her bosom. But long before the time for hatching, the pile of branches from which she had been driven had been removed. Had the farseeing farmer allowed the bird to have her way, all of her nest, her little ones, and her hopes for the season would have been destroyed. She did not see beyond one summer; he saw the end from the beginning.

So our God knows the end from the beginning, and the true believer who has submitted himself to God in Christ has received a new set of senses by which he learns to trust God in all things, even those which he cannot understand. The Lord Jesus said to His disciples, ". . . What I do thou knowest not now; but thou shalt know hereafter" (JOHN 13:7). The simple child of God has learned this lesson well and goes on in confident trust in Him who worketh all things after the council of His own will.

TRUSTING THE UNKNOWN

A college girl once said to me, "I have never trusted anyone in my life. How can I trust the Lord Jesus with all the problems of my daily life?"

Since it was Easter vacation, I asked her how she was going back to college. She said, "I am going to fly."

"Do you have your ticket?" I asked.

"No," she said, "I have to find out what time I can get a plane."

"How are you going to do that?" I inquired.

"Well," she replied, "I am going to telephone the airline and find out what time the plane leaves and reserve a seat on that plane. Then I shall take a taxi out to the airport and board the plane."

I said, "Do you know the reservation clerk at the airline?"

She replied, "No, I don't."

I asked, "Are you going to taxi to the airport, trusting the information of this unknown clerk?"

"Yes, I am."

"Do you know the pilot of this plane?"

"No, I don't."

Then I said to her, "You trust the word of an unknown clerk at the airline office, and put your life into the hands of a pilot whom you do not know and probably will not even see. But you will know what real trust is when you take the word of the Lord Jesus Christ who died for you and rose again, and allow Him to pilot your life by His resurrection power."

TRUTH, SEARCHING AND OWNING

THE ORNITHOLOGIST'S DISCOVERY

An ornithologist discovered a new plant in Scotland which had never before been found in the British Isles, and botanists immediately traveled to see the plant in its natural habitat. The plants were growing on two little rocky crests, composed of a slightly richer rock; they were surrounded on all sides by miles of nothing but wilderness. An ornithologist discovered the plant because any normal botanist would have despaired of the whole mountain long before he came in sight of its one rewarding acre.

Many men go their way in the search for truth. There are few who find it. Wandering in the wilderness of their human reason they will not go to the Word of God which appears from the distance to be but a barren outcropping. The Lord Jesus Himself said: ". . . I thank Thee, O Father, Lord of heaven and earth, because thou hast hid these things from the wise and prudent, and hast revealed them unto babes" (MAT-THEW 11:25).

UMBRELLAS

Many of us own more umbrellas than we possess. We have bought them, but they have a habit of disappearing. They are ours, but they cannot keep us dry when it rains. They are as though we did not own them.

This simple illustration should be sufficient to remind us that we own truth which we do not always possess. The title has been put in our name, but we do not enter into its possession.

327

UNBELIEVERS

BARGAINS

The world is always looking for a bargain. Many a store-keeper has made money by taking an 89-cent article that no one would buy, marking it up to 98 cents, and saying it is something very special. Once we were attracted to a pile of advertising folders on the counter of a railroad ticket office. There in large letters was the interesting offer, "$5,000 for 25 cents." This looked worth investigating. But like many of the world's offers, and like all of Satan's offers, there was a hitch to it. If the whole truth had been printed, it would have read, "$5,000 for 25 cents and your life." Or else, "$5,000 for 25 cents and two eyes." Or again, "$5,000 for 25 cents and both hands." The money part of the offer was less attractive by the time the details were known.

The devil comes with the word, "The whole world for just a bit of worship of me." It sounds attractive, but the omitted words should be added: ". . . and the loss of your soul." This is what Christ indicated when He said: ". . . what shall it profit a man, if he shall gain the whole world, and lose his own soul?" (MARK 8:36). Yet there are many at Satan's bargain counters, willing to pay the present price, but unmindful of the second payment.

THE BAYONET

If you were out on Guadalcanal with a rifle and a bayonet, and an enemy soldier approached you and said, "Oh, how well you are equipped, what wonderful shoes, what a magnificent gun, but that bayonet I really believe is soft rubber and a

Hollywood prop." "Well," you might say, "If you really believe that it is soft rubber and a Hollywood prop, I guess I had better put it over here against the tree. I can't use it, if you don't believe that it is real steel." "Now," says the enemy soldier, "we are ready to fight with judo," and over his shoulder you go and land in the jungle.

The devil wants to get you off guard and to abandon the weapon that God has given to you. If a man comes and says, "I don't believe that your bayonet is steel," the best way to convince him is to cut the button off his shirt and perhaps nick him slightly. He will be convinced immediately that it is not soft rubber. The Lord Jesus cut deeper than the button on the man's shirt—He penetrated right through to the heart. What are you going to do with somebody who says, "I don't believe that the Bible is the Word of God"? I answer that the only way to deal with him is exactly what the Lord Jesus Christ did, He deflated Satan with the sword of the Spirit.

THE BLACKOUT

At the beginning of the second world war, I was holding a union meeting in the city of Belfast in Ireland. The great hall in which the meetings were held was roofed with a skylight, had it been lighted by night, it would have shot a beam like a searchlight over the darkened city. Each evening the chairman of the meeting announced that at the blackout hour the lights would be put out. One night in the midst of the sermon, someone pulled a switch that lighted the great hall. I immediately stopped speaking. There was great consternation; ushers ran to rectify the error. One man clawed at his companion, crying out in fear, "What's the matter? What's the matter? Why did he stop?" The companion replied that the lights had been turned on. Need I say that the reason this man had to be told that the lights were on was because he was blind? The coming of the light meant nothing to him.

That was why it was necessary to send John the Baptist to

tell the world that the light had been turned on. God sent His light, lighting every man that cometh into the world. But the effect of that light was not to bring sight to blind men, but to bring condemnation to men who thought that they could see, and who were therefore doubly blind.

THE FERRYBOAT RIDE

Michael Patrick O'Brien, got on a ferryboat in Macao, without a passport; he could not get off in Hong Kong, nor could he get off in Macao when the ship returned. For weeks he went back and forth between the two cities while his case was shuttled between various embassies; some called him a Hungarian, others an Irishman or an American.

How many people are there in this world who shuttle back and forth between one opinion and another—spiritually stateless—because they refuse to abandon all earthly citizenships and build their hope in the Lord Jesus Christ. Ever learning and never arriving at the knowledge of the truth—this is the ferryboat upon which men go back and forth in their futile lives because they have refused to own the Lord Jesus.

THE FOUNDERING SHIP

If a ship were foundering at sea, and if the crew had taken to the water, we would recognize their peril at once. If rescue boats came near and ropes were thrown to the struggling survivors, we would hold our breath in the hope that they might be rescued. How would we feel if we saw one swimming man catch hold of the rope with a free hand and fling it from him with a gesture of defiance? We would find the sight incredible, and we would wonder if the man's reason had tottered, and if he were unaware of the consequences of his act.

There might be some rational explanation for a swimmer refusing to come into a rescue boat, but there can be no such explanation from the divine point of view for men refusing to heed the Word of God and come to salvation through Christ.

HAMMERING A SHELL

At Fremicourt, near Baupaume, France, two farm workers found a World War I artillery shell in a field. One of them began hammering on it with the hope of salvaging the copper. Suddenly it exploded, killing one man and injuring the other. How terrible to think of a man hammering away on something that will destroy him.

Yet how many people in daily life keep clinging to that which will destroy them for eternity, thinking that they can gain a little pleasure, a little self-satisfaction. "Then desire when it has conceived gives birth to sin; and sin when it is full-grown brings forth death" (JAMES 1:15, RSV).

THE INDIAN AND FEAR

If we had no more knowledge of God than as Creator, we should be possessed by terrible fear, like the savages in the heart of Africa and along the banks of the Amazon. Their whole existence is one of great fear. An Indian told a missionary that his people never know a moment without fear. "We are afraid when we rise in the morning, and when we go to sleep at night," he said. "We are afraid when we sit down to eat and when we rise to work. We are afraid of the jungle, and when we are in our dugouts, of the river. We are always within an arm's length of death, and we see an evil spirit in every tree and plant, in every snake and animal; yes, in every other man, woman and child."

That would be the condition of us all, were it not for the Lord Jesus Christ. But when we read His assurance, "He who has seen me has seen the Father," we enter into His rest. For the Lord Jesus Christ revealed not only that the God of Heaven is His Father, but also that He wants to be our Father and invites us to come to Him through His Son, Jesus Christ.

331

UNBELIEVERS

THE LOST HUNTER

The newspapers carried the story of a hunter who got lost simply because he was stubborn. The man had a compass with him, but he was so confident that he was woodsman enough to find his way without consulting it, that he neglected to look at it until it was too dark to see. He had no matches and was forced to bed down in some leaves in the shelter of a rock. In the morning he decided again to trust his own gift of woodsmanship. The day wore on and he made little progress. He decided he had played the fool long enough, so he pulled the compass from his pocket and was soon on the right road home. This man was lost until he admitted that he was lost and only then was he able to find his way

If a man will come to the place where he admits to God and himself that he can do nothing for himself, the Lord will immediately reveal to him the way of salvation and will plant new life within, making the man a partaker of the divine nature (II PETER 1:4).

THE LOST SHIP

Legend has it that Prince William, son of Henry I of England was aboard a ship that was lost at sea; only one or two survived the catastrophe. The story says that the nobleman in charge of the young prince was a very proud man. He went into the captain's room and discussed the course with him. The captain said he was sailing his ship in a certain direction because, on his last voyage, he had discovered a rock at a certain point. The nobleman pointed to the chart and insisted that there was no rock because it was not charted and ordered the captain to go straight on, under pain of death. The captain was forced to obey, but the ship went aground on the rock and was lost.

This legend shows the tragic position of those who blindly reject the truth that is revealed in Christ Jesus. Unbelievers may say that the rocks of judgment do not lie in the path of the future, but the wreck will prove the truth of God.

MONTGOMERY STREET

Signor Guiseppe Bartolo flew in to the New York airport and took the bus into Manhattan. He loaded his baggage into a taxi and said, "Montgomery Street." The taximan took him to such a street and Bartolo pulled out a picture of a house and tried to find it—it wasn't there. He left the cab and started to walk. An hour later the cabby took the baggage to the police. That evening the police brought Bartolo in, still insisting that the house was gone. There was the picture of his son's house—on Montgomery Street, San Francisco! The father wouldn't believe the "New York" on the policemen's badges, until they got his son on the telephone. Only then was he convinced, only then did he consent to start on his way west.

How many people there are who think they are in a place of spiritual safety when in reality they are lost souls! They have some vague trust in religion of some sort and are far, far from Christ. The only way to be sure is to have the definite assurance of the Bible—the Word of God—a full commitment to the Christ of the Bible, backed up by the Holy Spirit's witness with our spirit that we are the children of God, and a definite knowledge of spiritual growth in likeness to Christ.

NOW

A great hotel publishes a little booklet of chatter for its guests. Whoever prepared it needed a line to fill up space and inserted this sentence: "On the great clock of time there is but one word—NOW." The hotel probably thought the phrase was a good one for salesmen who need to be about their business, and a good maxim for others who are likely to let important matters slip.

Every sinner should realize that this time is going by most rapidly. ". . . behold, now is the accepted time; behold, now is the day of salvation" (II CORINTHIANS 6:2). The sinner must realize that NOW is not only the single word on the clock of time; it is also the word on the door of eternity. Fail to enter in while you have NOW to do it, and you will find that the door is closed to you forever.

TESTING THE NEW AUTOMOBILE

Glenn Leonard, a bulldozer operator driving to his home in the country, decided to test the acceleration of his new automobile. He passed the side road to his farm, made a sharp U turn at the next road, sped back and turned in the far road. Meanwhile, the driver of a station wagon observed the rapid turn and burst of speed; he mistook the light-blue machine for an unmarked police car, and turned into the road to Leonard's farm to escape detection. The station wagon driver was closely followed by Leonard, who was only interested in getting home. The alarmed driver continued at high speed to the dead end of the road, where he abandoned the station wagon, which was loaded with stolen coffee, cigarettes, and shotgun shells.

The Bible says, "The wicked flee when no man pursueth . . ." (PROVERBS 28:1). How often it is that men run away from nothing more than their own conscience, carrying it with them all the time.

UNION WITH CHRIST

BACKSTAGE AT THE MET

I once had the privilege of going backstage just before a performance at the Metropolitan Opera House in New York. Before the curtain went up, dozens of individuals walked about in the wings, doing vocal exercises. Completely oblivious of others, each singer concentrated on his own voice; the result was piercing discord. We are all familiar with a similar effect in the tuning-up of orchestra instruments before a concert.

Too often the bystander in the world looks upon the church as a group of frivolous amateurs, each concerned only with his little part. But the Lord Jesus Christ prayed, "That they all may be one; as thou, Father, art in me, and I in thee, that they also may be one in us: that the world may believe that thou hast sent me" (JOHN 17:21). Some may "view with alarm" a movement to join believers in divine oneness; nevertheless, the Lord intended such a union.

THE FOREST OF REDWOODS

On the coast of California are great forests of redwoods—*sequoia sempervirens*. The manner in which these trees grow is unlike that of any other tree. Two trees of this species may grow up year after year, a few feet from each other. Finally, sometimes after fifty or a hundred years, the trees touch, and the bark begins to overlap and fill out, so that the two trees ultimately become one. There have been cases where a dozen trees, springing up from the outer roots of a tree that has fallen, have formed a perfect circle. After a century or two, all have grown together so that one may walk between two trees into the empty heart of a great tree, and the ultimate outward appearance will be that of a single giant tree. Near Santa Cruz are two trees: one grows at an angle to the other, yet contact has been made a hundred feet in the air, and from that point upward two trees become one—a single top growing from two totally different trunks.

God looking down into time from His eternal vantage point, saw us in Christ—grown into Him, one plant with Him. We had been of the root of Adam, and Christ, in becoming sin for us grew into us so that our death became His death, and His death became the death of our death.

MEETING AT THE CORNER

Several years ago a fad among teen-agers was a series of jokes—a play upon words or lines spoken by one inanimate object to another. One day one of my children came to me with this one: "Do you know what one wall said to the other?" As a good father should, I did not attempt to guess the answer, but replied dutifully, "No. You tell me what one wall said to the other." The answer came crisply, "I'll meet you at the corner."

I can say to every man in Christ, "I'll meet you at the Lord Jesus Christ." If we can come to an agreement as to who He is and as to what He has done for us, we should meet there with Him.

UNIVERSAL BROTHERHOOD

THE CARPENTER'S CHILDREN

A missionary in Central America once preached on the subject of universal brotherhood. At the close of his address, two professors from a local school said that they thought they had found a flaw in his reasoning. Were not all individuals of the human race descended from Adam and Eve? And did not God create Adam and Eve? And therefore, were not all individuals thereby the children of God? The missionary pointed to the benches in the room and asked, "Who made these benches?"

The man replied that they had been made by the local carpenter.

"And do you, therefore, call these benches the carpenter's children?" he asked.

"Of course not," they answered. "They are not the carpenter's children because they do not have in them the life of the carpenter."

"And do you have the life of God in you?" was the searching question that revealed the reality of man's departure from God. No one can be called a child of God, if he does not have within him the life of God.

WILL OF GOD

THE BIRD AND THE BUTTERFLY

A large home had fine plate-glass windows that looked out on a beautiful garden. A bird outside tried to catch a butterfly that was inside; the bird flew against the window while the butterfly flew up and down trying to get away. The butterfly could not see the glass and expected at every moment to be caught; the bird did not see the glass and expected at every moment to catch its prey; yet the butterfly was as safe as though a wall of stone were between them.

We who are Christians must not forget that the invisible presence of Christ is between us and every difficulty of life. There is nothing that can touch us unless it passes through the will of God in Christ. Our Lord has shown us that we are between His hand and the Father's. ". . . neither shall any man pluck them out of my hand. . . . no man is able to pluck them out of my Father's hand" (JOHN 10:28,29). This is why the believer is so sure.

FORMULAS NOT UNDERSTOOD

Revelation of the production methods of the atomic bomb is bringing to light some remarkable stories. Time and again companies were asked to design a machine according to a "mathematical formula which they did not fully understand." Out of this amazing gadgetry have come scores of new products and processes that have nothing to do with atomic power, such as new ways to dehydrate foodstuffs. Factories that followed the uncomprehended will of the atom staff

338

learned that they had been working smoothly in an overall plan that was for the honor of their nation.

God's will is not comprehensible to many; therefore they refuse it. But those who take it, even as "a formula they do not understand," and work conscientiously to its fulfillment, find the results above and beyond all they could ask or think. Christians who will to do the Lord's will, who definitely make up their minds to do the Lord's will, learn to know the inner meaning of the truth that is of God and not of man.

GOTHIC OR ROMAN MISSALS

One of the oldest Spanish proverbs is: "*Alla van leyes do quieren reyes,*" or "Laws go the ways that kings desire." It arose when Alfonso VI, at the beginning of the twelfth century, had to decide whether his country should use Gothic or Roman missals. The king resolved to leave the matter to chance; he threw both into the flames, saying that the one that came out unburnt should be chosen. But when the Gothic missal survived the ordeal, he threw it back into the flames and decided in favor of the Roman. From this act the proverb became popular throughout Spain.

Many people treat the will of God in just this way. They will put a choice up to God and will keep on trying until the matter turns out to suit them. Unless a person is a surrendered Christian, it is correct to say that actions follow the will of the flesh. The only way to have the will of God is to be willing to do it, and 90 percent of knowing that will consists in being willing to do it before you know it.

NO FOG ON THE BRIDGE

Terrified passengers lined the railing of a Mississippi River steamer, as it sped through a dense fog. A committee, sent to remonstrate with the captain, for going too fast, discovered that it was clear on the bridge. The fog was dense for about twenty feet above the water so that the passengers, on their level, could see nothing, but the captain could see everything.

The next time you are in a fog remember that God is not and never has been in a fog. He knows all things and is in complete command. Nothing can ever touch you until it has passed through His will.

THE PIN CUSHION

A little girl acknowledged a gift from her aunt: "Thank you for your present. I have always wanted a pin cushion, but not very much."

Many Christians act this way about the will of the Lord. They are so filled with their own desires that they do not want what He sends. The whole Word teaches us that He reserves His best gifts or those who delight to do His will.

SCIENTIFIC INSTRUMENTS

Every science has its own instrument. The geologist uses a hammer to take his samples from the rock. A biologist uses a microscope. An astronomer uses a telescope. You would laugh if a geologist left his work with rocks, and hammer in hand, and said: "I am tired of studying rocks. I am going to study astronomy." Not with a hammer! You cannot learn astronomy with a hammer! You would laugh at the astronomer who sought to turn his great telescope down into a meadow to look at a daisy. You cannot learn anything about a daisy from a great telescope! No, the telescope is made to look at the stars; the microscope for the small daisy; the hammer for the rock.

In the science of God, theology, there is an instrument that belongs to Christianity and it is the surrender of the will to the will of God before you know it.

THE TEXAS COW

I often think of a certain cow I saw along the road in Texas. As we were driving by one of those ranches where they have 500,000 acres and very fine fences, a cow came through a hole in the fence. The cow wandered into the road; when it heard the engine of our car, it started to run. By the time we caught up to the cow, she was some 400 yards away from the hole in the fence, and still going. Finally we passed her. If that cow was ever going to get back into the field with those strong fences, she was going to have to go back to the place where she got out.

That is exactly how you are going to get back into the will of God. If you keep running down the road, you won't find it. You go back and get in the will of God at the place where you got out of the will of God. This is God's method.

THREE SIGNS IN LINE

During the war, I was invited to the Panama Canal Zone where tens of thousands of troops were guarding that most important link in our communications. Our meetings were held in the baseball park, and thousands of people received blessing from God. A general in the United States Army came to me after one of the meetings and asked if there was anything that I would like to see or do while I was in the Zone. I told him that I wanted to see the working operation of the canal from the bridge of a ship. He whistled and made a gesture of doubt, telling me that only one civilian had gone through the canal since the beginning of the war and that he had been a brother of a cabinet member. But the general said he would try.

The next day he came back with permission from the commanding general, and the following day I spent several hours on the bridge of a ship, with the chief pilot of the canal. When we had gone through the first locks, moving from the Pacific towards the Atlantic, we came out on the great inland lake which had been created by a series of dams. The pilot pointed out the locks by which we were to leave the lake. I asked the natural question: Why did we not steam directly toward that point? He told me that in the beginning of canal navigation the channel had been dug in a direct line, but as time went on the inflow of jungle rivers brought so much silt that the channel was being filled in. A survey of the bottom of the lake showed that a zigzag course across the lake would follow the lines of least silting. But how can a ship find its bearing for a zigzag course? Ahead of us was a series of markers. The first, just above the surface of the water, was a large sign, several times larger than an outdoor advertising billboard. Across it was a black line, while a vertical line split it in the middle. A hundred yards behind this sign there was another, exactly like it, but considerably higher. A third sign stood another hundred yards away—again much higher above the water. As we moved toward these signs the vertical marks on the three signs appeared to be exactly in line with one another. Far away to the right we saw a similar set of signs. The vertical marks, of course, were not in line with each other; but as we approached the first set, there was a moment when the vertical marks on the second set came in line, one with another. At this point the order was given and the ship turned directly toward this new indicator. The same process was repeated again and again until we finally came in line with the exit locks, and moved on into the canal.

I told the pilot that the lining up of the markers was a good illustration of the way in which a Christian must live his life. There are three things which must be in line if we are to know the will of God and remain in it. First, to be in the will of God any step of faith must be in accordance with the Word of God. Second, we must be surrendered to the Lord so that we are willing to do His will before we know what it is. Finally, the Holy Spirit working in our lives shows us through circumstances, exactly what the Lord wants us to do.

THE YOUNG WHEELMAN

A confident young man walked into the captain's cabin of a Mississippi riverboat, and asked for a job as a wheelman.

"What experience have you had on the river?" asked the captain.

"Five years, sir."

"Do you know the location of all the shoals and snags?"

"No, sir, but I know where there ain't any, and that's where I calculate to steer." He got the job.

In the Christian life the path of safety in Christian living is not in knowing all the nature of sin, or the path of wickedness, but in knowing the will of the Lord and in being willing to stay in it. The obedience of the saints in Rome at the time Paul wrote to them had become famed throughout the Christian world. Paul complimented them: ". . . I am glad therefore on your behalf: but yet I would have you wise unto that which is good, and simple concerning evil" (ROMANS 16:19). We must steer where sin is not.

WITNESSING

CARLISLE CASTLE PRISONERS

Carlisle Castle has slits in its walls that used to serve as windows; an iron bar stretches from top to bottom. In the sill you can see and feel grooves worn into the stone by the fingers of men who were imprisoned in the castle. When the Scotch border was a place of feud and skirmish, the prisoners looked out toward the hills of Scotland. They so longed to get back to their homes that they literally pulled at the stones with their fingers. Perhaps in their spirits, this made them feel that they were escaping from prison, and away to Scotland.

I wonder if Christ in your heart is straining to get out in love and mercy to those around you. Perhaps He cannot get out to live His life through you. Christ liveth in me to indwell and to possess to the full, in order to shine out, to live out, to flow out. That is the normal experience of the Christian when he is right with God.

THE ELEPHANTIASIS CONVERT

A disease known as elephantiasis is a terrible scourge in tropical countries. The skin of the diseased becomes very thick, very hard, and fissured like an elephant's hide; the part affected is enormously enlarged. I have seen unfortunate people whose lower legs—running from above the knee down to the foot—were from twelve to fifteen inches in diameter. One poor sufferer from this disease heard the gospel of Jesus Christ and was transformed. He became a radiant Christian and did nothing but tell people of the grace of God, which He had showed in sending His Son, Jesus Christ, to die for them.

This man lived in an African village; he was determined that every soul in the village should hear the good news of salvation. Although it was extremely difficult for him to walk on his monstrous legs, he thought nothing of the pain and toiled from hut to hut telling those who dwelt there about the Saviour who had come into his life. Each evening he returned to his own hut, where he was maintained in life by the kindness of his relatives. At the end of several months he was able to tell the missionary that he had visited every hut in the village; now he was starting to take the gospel message to a village about two miles away. Each morning he started out painfully, walked the two miles to that village, went from hut to hut spreading the gospel, and returned the two miles to his own hut before sundown. Having visited every hut in the neighboring village, he remained at home, but after some weeks, he began to be more and more restless.

He asked the pastor and the missionary medical doctor if the gospel were being taken to a village that lay ten or twelve miles through the jungle. As a boy, before he had become afflicted, he had traveled the jungle path to that village; he remembered that there were many people there, and he knew that they needed the good tidings of the Saviour. He was advised not to go to the village, but day after day the burden grew upon him. One day the man's family told the missionary that the man had disappeared from the hut. He had slipped out just before dawn; they had heard him go, but supposed it was just for a moment. He did not return, and the family was concerned about him.

Afterwards, the full story became known. Step after weary step the afflicted man dragged his leathery legs and gigantic feet along the path that led to his goal. The distant villagers said that he had arrived after noon; his feet were swollen, bruised, and bleeding. He was offered food, but before he would eat, he began to tell the people about Jesus. Up and down the village he went, to the very last hut, telling them that the God of all creation was Love and that He had sent His only Son to die that their sins might be removed. He told how the Lord Jesus had been raised from the dead and had come into his heart, bringing such joy and peace.

There was no shelter for him in that village, so though the sun was low, he started on his way down the jungle path toward home. The darkness of Africa is a terrible darkness, and the night can bring forth many jungle creatures. The sun went down and the poor man dragged himself along the dark path, guided by some insight which kept him from going astray. He told the pastor later that his fear of the night and the animals was more than balanced by the joy he felt in his heart, as he realized that he had told a whole village about the Lord Jesus Christ.

About midnight the doctor was awakened by a noise on his front porch. He went to the door with a light and there was the elephantiasis victim, his legstumps wounded and bleeding. The doctor and his helpers lifted the almost unconscious man into one of the hospital beds. Seldom had any of them seen such a frightful sight as those bleeding feet that had come back from such an errand of love and mercy. Unashamedly, the doctor told how he had ministered to those feet—cleaning and dressing them—and how his own tears had fallen into the ointment he put upon the stumps. The doctor ended by saying, "In all my life I do not know when my heart was more drawn out to another Christian believer. All I could think of was the verse in the Word of God, 'How beautiful are the feet of them that bring glad tidings, that publish peace.'"

Here was a man who had been sent by God to tell the story of what Christ had done for him. Although he did it at the cost of much personal agony, he had not flinched; he had gone through to the end to tell needy men the good news of salvation for their souls.

HASTE, POST, HASTE!

Not many people who use the word "posthaste" realize that the word goes back to the time of Henry VIII. During the reign of "bluff King Hal," postmasters and relays of horses for carrying messages were established at the principal towns in England. The postmasters endorsed each letter with the exact time each missive was delivered to them. The messengers were sometimes rather irresponsible people who delayed to play games with acquaintances in inns or to waste time in some other way. On this account a very drastic law was put into effect—every dispatch carrier should "ride for his life"; this had a literal meaning, for the penalty for delaying *en route* was hanging. Letters of the sixteenth century were often ornamented with a drawing of a dispatch carrier suspended from the gallows; beneath the figure was the admonition, "Haste, post, haste! Haste for thy life."

This law held good for many years, and there were numerous hangings. Gradually opinion changed, and the penalty for delay was lessened; hanging was only for those messengers who were bribed or coerced into allowing someone else to read a dispatch. Later, a still lesser punishment was adopted: imprisonment for a short time, or a period of confinement in the stocks or pillory. Not until the nineteenth century was simple dismissal applied in such cases; but the old expression "posthaste" still lingers with us.

So our King has given us a message that must be delivered to all men. The King's business requires haste (I SAMUEL 21:8). Let us be out with it. "Go ye into all the world . . ." He has said, and to those who go, He has added, ". . . and lo! I am with you . . ." (MATTHEW 28:20). There is no death penalty, but there is a reward for obedient servants and for those who do not obey, even though they be saved, there is "the terror of the Lord . . ." (II CORINTHIANS 5:11).

WITNESSING

INDIRECT ADVERTISING

Near the Kingsport Press in Tennessee a southbound bus makes a scheduled midday stop of twenty minutes so that passengers may freshen up and get a bite to eat. One driver said, as he brought his bus to a stop: "Folks, we'll be stopping here for twenty minutes. This line makes it a strict policy never to recommend an eating place by name, but if anybody wants me while we're here, I'll be eating a wonderful T-bone steak with french fries at Tony's first-class, spotlessly clean diner directly across the street."

Indirect advertising is indeed important and often more effective than the direct pitch. So is the indirect witness for Christ. The believer who reveals Christ by the way he lives, moves, walks, talks, eats, reads, pays his bills, keeps his garden free of weeds and a thousand other details of life, will probably do more than the fanatic with the sandwich board that reads, "Prepare to meet thy God."

THE LOST RACE

To the participants in one of the Olympic games, loss of the four-hundred-meter relay race for women was a tragic incident. The Germans were far in the lead when the next-to-the-last girl came to pass the baton to the last runner. With a clear five-yard lead and the race as good as won, the baton was dropped. Pictures showed the despair on the face of the last runner as she realized what had happened. We sat one evening in Berlin looking at an illustrated magazine that showed pictures of the Olympics. The magazine had texts under the pictures in several languages. The English read: "They muffed the baton"; the French read: *"le temoin,"* the French word for "witness." The idea was that the runner who reached the tape had to have the baton as a "witness" that the full distance had been covered by each of the runners.

If the witness is lost, the race is lost, provides a great spiritual lesson. These girls had made the Olympic team and had the honors attendant upon their prowess. They were eligible to run the race. They lost the prize, however, by losing the witness. They were castaways from the medals.

So it is in the Christian life. All who are born again are eligible to run the race. No one can run the race until he is made eligible through saving faith. All who are received into salvation in Christ will be in Heaven, but not all will receive the prize in addition to salvation.

TOADSTOOLS VERSUS MUSHROOMS

A woman risked her life and that of her family on a page from the *National Geographic Magazine*, when her husband brought some strange-looking things in from the fields. The family was undecided whether they were mushrooms or toadstools, until someone dug up a *Geographic* that showed plates of edible varieties. Their harvest was pictured, under the name of "Shaggy-mane," definitely "edible." With this as the basis of their faith, they prepared and ate the mushrooms. Nobody suffered.

Here is a perfect illustration of "receiving the witness of men." But God has said that "If we receive the witness of men, the witness of God is greater . . ." (I JOHN 5:9). You can risk your life ten thousand million times more securely on the Word of God than on the pages of the *Geographic*. You can even risk your eternal life on the Word of God. In fact, if you do not risk your eternal life on the Word of God, you will have eternal death. ". . . these are written, that ye might believe that Jesus is the Christ, the Son of God; and that believing ye might have life through his name" (JOHN 20:31).

WITNESS OF THE SPIRIT

GOING TO PRINCETON

A young man from the west, got off an express train at Trenton, New Jersey. He wanted to go to Princeton, and he had been told that at that hour of the day, his best connection would be to walk a block or two from the railroad station and take a streetcar. It was his first time in a city of any size, and he was proud enough to wish to get along without asking for information. He walked to the car tracks where he saw a car marked "Princeton." He boarded it, and paid his fare. After fifteen or twenty minutes the conductor came through the car, collecting another fare for the next zone of travel. The young man paid this fare also, and another at the next zone change. He realized they were nearing the end of the line, when the conductor began turning the seat backs to face the opposite direction. As the young man picked up his valise he finally asked, "Which way is the campus of Princeton University?" The conductor looked at him, dumbfounded, and asked, "Did you want to go to Princeton? You should have taken this car going in the other direction. You are in Hamilton Square."

The important point in this story is that the young man *felt* as if he were going to Princeton. He had traveled for ten miles in quiet confidence that he was going where he thought he was going; suddenly, he was miles away in another direction.

I am quite sure that there are many men and women in this world who are on their way to the lake of fire, without hope and without God, but who *feel* as if they are going to heaven. The witness of the Spirit is always based on the Word of God and is in tune with the sacrificial death of the Lord Jesus

350

Christ. It, therefore, follows that the witness of the Spirit is not a mere feeling, in the sense of some spine-tingling emotion, or vague, sense movement. It is definitely an intelligent, controlled and related work of God in our hearts.

HANDSPRINGS

Several years ago I was preaching for a few days in Portland, Oregon. At the close of one of the evening meetings a young minister invited me to drive with him the next day, to view the noble grandeur of the Columbia River Valley. I never like to go to the Northwest without seeing this, for I believe it to be the most beautiful river valley in the world. The next morning he and his wife picked me up at my hotel. The wife remarked on the blessing of the service the evening before when I had preached on the joys of being joined to the Lord Jesus Christ. Her exact words were, "Oh! Doctor! That message last night was such a blessing to me. All the way home my heart was just turning handsprings at the thought of all that we have in Christ." I replied, speaking rather slowly, "Turning handsprings? Cartwheels? Somersaults? Well, that is a very interesting way of describing it; but the Bible gives it in different terms. There we read, 'The Spirit himself beareth witness with our spirit that we are the children of God.' "

SITTIN' PRETTY

One Sunday I was preaching in Philadelphia. My subject was a rehearsal of the verses in the Scripture in which God treats His work concerning our sin. As I preached this great message of deliverance, I noted a boy about twelve years old. He was sitting in the gallery, and he leaned forward, holding the rail, listening with great intentness. When I came to my summing up I put all of the promises into a single sentence. Our sins are forgiven, forgotten, cleansed, pardoned, atoned for, remitted, covered; they have been cast into the depths of the sea, blotted out as a thick cloud, removed as far as the east is from the west, remembered against us no more forever, cast behind God's back.

After the closing hymn, I went to the back of the church to greet the people as they were leaving. In a few moments the people from the galleries began to come down, and the boy came toward me. He caught my sleeve and said, "Good sermon, Doc!" I smiled and he continued, "Gee, we're sure sittin' pretty, aren't we?" And then he went on his way.

I looked after him for a moment and a great joy came in my heart, because I knew there had been in his heart the witness of the Holy Spirit.

WORK OF GOD IN US

THE ARTIST AND THE BRUSH

An artist who plans to exhibit a painting inspects every brush stroke, adding a slight touch here, deftly changing a shade there, until the very day of exhibition.

The Lord God is working that way with us now. The differences between Him and human artists is that when He finishes we shall be like the Lord Jesus Christ. There is no doubt about that.

BINDING GUY ROPES

A balloon cannot ascend as long as a single rope binds it to its moorings. If every cord but one is cut, it may struggle, but it cannot rise. Not until the knife severs the final stay will it arise. Nor does it ascend of itself. It would remain as heavy and inert as the earth beneath it were it not for the gas within it.

Have we gladly taken the knife and with one decisive stroke forever severed the last guy rope that binds us to the sensuous things of earth and time? Or have we at least said, "Lord, I am willing that Thou shouldst cut that rope for me. I find it impossible to do it myself." That is enough for the Lord. He has lifted many a soul into the heights, by the breath of His Spirit, who was unable to say more than that at first. A mind, willing to be made willing by Him is all He asks.

THE FLAW IN THE MARBLE

The great Italian sculptor, Benvenuto Cellini, told of receiving a vast block of marble with one flaw. Because of this flaw, no artist would submit a design—except one.

353

In the public square of Florence a fence was built around that piece of marble, and a little shack was erected for the artist. For two years the sculptor labored; then the fence was torn down, and the shack was taken away. All of Florence beheld the result and marveled. Since then, Italy and all the world has marveled at Michelangelo's "David."

In that block of marble was a statue; others did not see it, but Michelangelo did.

In the lump of clay which is you, God sees an image too—the image of Jesus Christ. And God wants to form the image of His Son in you.

THE GRAND LAMA

In Tibet, the government used to be a theocracy and the ruler was the Grand Lama. When he died, it was believed that his spirit entered into a boy baby who was born at the very instant of the lama's death. The high priests of the religion cast horoscopes, wandered over the land and pounced upon a child whom they declare to be the Grand Lama. The choice might be a boy living in filth, in a herdsman's tent, far removed from any culture or education. In an instant this child, with matted hair and filthy body, was declared the Grand Lama of Tibet. In that instant he is as much the Grand Lama as he is, years later—enthroned in his palace in Lhassa, in undisputed control of the entire forces of the country. Between the moment of his choice, which was totally apart from him or his people, and his rule, has been a long period of training; but from the first moment the priests who surrounded him have bowed before him and accepted him for what he was declared to be.

There is a great similarity here to the work of God. For us He stooped from Heaven and found us in our sin. It was He who declared us to be His sons. It was He who declared us to be justified. He said that He saw us righteous, the reign of death broken. He said that in that instant we were the possessors of eternal life and that we were His heirs and joint heirs

354

with Jesus Christ. All of this occurred simultaneously and instantaneously, apart from any merit in us. It was on the basis of sheer grace. The process of training us for the throne life began at once. He will keep on perfecting us until the day of Jesus Christ.

MY VASE

Years ago in France, as I watched a potter at work, he asked me if I would like to try my hand at making something. So I took a lump of clay, wet my hands, shaped the clay and threw it against the wheel. As it began to turn, I pressed my hand against the clay and it rose up into a pillar. Then I put my finger into the middle and made an opening.

I had formed a lovely vase with a flange at the bottom. Then it bellied out and narrowed to a neck.

Thinking that it should be just a little narrower above the flange, I put my fingers there. Suddenly the vase broke.

Looking at it, I asked, "What can be done with that?"

Smiling, the potter took the same bit of clay and made a beautiful vase. Then he put it in his kiln to bake. When it came out, it was beautiful.

God works like that in our lives. We mar them but He makes them beautiful. When God takes a life deformed by sin and molds it into the image of Jesus Christ, all heaven rejoices. We are to the glory of His grace.

WORKS

A COPPER PENNY

In 1947, a rumor spread that the Ford Motor Company would give a Ford in exchange for every copper penny dated 1943. The rumor spread so fast that Ford offices throughout the country were jammed with requests for information, and in spite of a telephone strike, thousands of inquiries came in by telephone as well as by telegram and mail. Washington also reported that a large volume of queries had been received at the offices of the mint. It all turned out to be a joke. The statistics of the mint show that in 1943 there was no copper available for coinage and that 1,093,838,670 pennies were minted of steel-zinc, but that the number made of copper was exactly zero.

There has been a rumor abroad in the human race for centuries that entrance into heaven could be obtained by presentation of works. The fact is that there are no works made on earth which are acceptable in heaven. They all show the counterfeit of having come from the mold of the human heart. God has declared that He will accept only the work that bears the image of the Lord Jesus Christ performed on Calvary in dying for sinners. There is no hope apart from this. "Not by works of righteousness which we have done . . ." (TITUS 3:5). "Not of works, lest any man should boast" (EPHESIANS 2:9).

A DRINK

If I ask if you would be willing to take a drink of the finest spring water—the purest water that could be obtained by any chemical standards of analysis—you might answer that you

356

would certainly be willing to drink such water. Then suppose I tell you that I have not said a word about the glass into which the water is to be poured. That should give you pause, for the glass in which that pure spring water is conveyed to you has just been emptied of diphtheria culture from a medical laboratory, and multitudes of deadly germs are spread through the water. Now will you take a drink? You refuse, of course.

It is even so with God. You may argue or boast about the works which you have produced; you may even think that by your standards of analysis your works should be acceptable to God. But the Word of God comes bluntly to tell you that your good works are contained in a glass of your sinful Adamic heart, and that they have infected every part of your being so that they are an offense to God because they have touched you.

THE HALF-BAKED PANCAKE

I have a venerable friend who has a sweet spirit that reflects long living with the Saviour. While he was staying in a large hotel in the South, he spoke to his waitress about her soul and she began to justify herself before him. She told him about her character, how hard she worked, and how she took care of an aged mother. Day after day as she waited on him, three meals a day, she would tell him more about her good deeds. After about two weeks of this, my friend said to her one morning, when the rush was over and few people were left in the dining room, "Mildred, will you bring me something special from the kitchen?" "Why, certainly, I'll get you anything you want." The old saint of God then carefully described his order. He wanted a pancake that was cooked on one side and not touched on the other. She expostulated that it would be terrible, and that he wouldn't want to eat it. He insisted, and she went out to the kitchen. My friend heard the chef talking in loud tones, and it took a definite repeating of the order to get what had been asked for. Finally, the waitress came into the dining room bearing the pancake cooked only one one side; the chef followed her to the door to watch what happened. My friend looked at her in great kindness and said, "Mildred, for the past two weeks you have been telling me how good you are; how you take care of your mother; what a fine character you have. I will admit that humanly speaking you are well-done like the under side of this pancake. But as God sees you, you are this uncooked mess of runny dough, unpalatable and nauseous. What you need is Christ and Christ alone." The woman looked at the plate and saw herself as God declared her to be; she was broken down by the force of the illustration. It was the means of bringing her to the knowledge of her own sinfulness in the sight of God, and to trust in the Lord Jesus Christ as her Saviour.

Perhaps you need to see yourself thus today, as a half-baked pancake. For, as J. B. Phillips puts it, "This, then, is what has happened. Sin made its entry into the world through one man, and through sin, death. The entail of sin and death passed on to the whole human race, and no one could break it for no one was himself free from sin" (ROMANS 5:12). Multitudes of believers praise God that the Lord Jesus broke the power of canceled sin, and set them free forever.

THE PHARMACIST'S MATE

Aboard a United States submarine in enemy waters of the Pacific, a sailor was stricken with acute appendicitis. The nearest surgeon was thousands of miles away. Pharmacist Mate Wheller Lipes watched the seaman's temperature rise to 106 degrees. His only hope was an operation. Said Lipes: "I have watched doctors do it. I think I could. What do you say?" The sailor consented. In the wardroom, about the size of a pullman drawing room, the patient was stretched out on a table beneath a floodlight. The mate and assisting officers, dressed in reversed pajama tops, masked their faces with gauze. The crew stood by the diving planes to keep the ship steady; the cook boiled water for sterilizing. A tea strainer served as an antiseptic cone. A broken-handled scalpel was the operating instrument. Alcohol drained from the torpedoes was the antiseptic. Bent tablespoons served to keep the muscles open. After cutting through the layers of muscle, the mate took twenty minutes to find the appendix. Two hours and a half later, the last catgut stitch was sewed, just as the last drop of ether gave out. Thirteen days later the patient was back at work.

Admittedly this was a much more magnificent feat than if it had been performed by trained surgeons in a fully equipped operating room of a modern hospital. Study this analogy and you will know the real meaning of Christ's words: "Greater works than these shall he do; because I go unto my Father" (JOHN 14:12). For Christ, perfect God, to work directly on a lost soul to quicken and bring out of death and into life is great, but for Him to do the same thing through us is a greater work.

TOO WIDE FOR THE DOOR

In his mission field, a certain missionary had to do many things for himself and his family. When the baby grew too big for the carriage he started to build a bed for the child. After he prepared the wood, he glued the mortised pieces and was ready to complete the bed. His wife thought it too cold to work in the shed so he brought the materials into the kitchen and started to work. When the bed was finished, the baby was brought to the kitchen and placed in it while his parents gazed admiringly. Suddenly the father had a disquieting thought. Suppose the bed would not go through the door! Quickly he measured bed and door and found the bed one inch too wide to pass through.

There are many people who spend their time building their lives according to the plan of this world. They take great pride in their work, but they make it broader than Christ. The day will come when they suddenly realize the measurements will not allow it to pass Heaven's door. ". . . strait is the gate, and narrow is the way . . ." (MATTHEW 7:14), and no human works can take us through. Christ alone can bring us to God, and when we get there we will find that He has been gracious enough to bring some of our works along, not as the price of our entry into heaven, but as a part of His love for which He will reward us.

THE VISIT WITH THE WARD PATIENT

A Christian visited a hospital and paused at each bed to say a word of prayer and give out a gospel or devotional tract. At the close of the visiting hour he came to the last bed in the ward and spoke to the patient very briefly: "Dear man, when you come to the end of this life, will you go to heaven?"

In a tone of defiance the man replied, "Oh, I think I shall get to heaven all right."

"What do you think they do in heaven?" asked the visitor.

Taken aback, the man hesitated, then said, "Well, I hadn't thought about it, but I imagine they sing a great deal."

"That is right," the visitor said, "and we have the words of the song in the Bible." He opened the New Testament to the book of Revelation and read:

> and they sang a new song, saying,
>> "Worthy art thou to take the scroll
>>> and to open its seals,
>> for thou wast slain and by thy blood
>>> didst ransom men for God
>> from every tribe and tongue and
>>> people and nation,
>> and hast made them a kingdom and
>>> priests to our God,
>> and they shall reign on earth" (5:9, 10 RSV).

The visitor said, "I must go now, but I leave this New Testament with you, and ask you to consider this question: If you were taken to heaven tonight, could you sing heaven's song?"

Next day the Christian returned and went straight to the bed of this man, who greeted him with the words, "I read those verses fifty times, and I shall never talk about my good works again. In heaven they sing praises to Christ for redeeming them by His blood. I have been trying to get to heaven without a Saviour; but now I know heaven's song, and I have trusted in His blood so that I can sing that song now!"

How many people are like this man! They rush through life without a thought of what will certainly follow, hoping against hope that somehow they will reach heaven. They advance reasons for being received on the basis of their good works, fulfillment of religious rites or ceremonies, or their superiority of character over others. But none of these can avail. The refrain of heaven's song is, "Thou wast slain and by thy blood didst ransom men for God." If you do not learn to sing that song on earth, you will never sing it in heaven.

WORSHIP

WORSHIP GOD

As we were leaving Beaumont, Texas, we saw a large sign along the highway calling upon people to acknowledge God. "Go and worship God in the church of your own choice," we read. We pulled to a stop in front of a red light. Another car drew alongside us. A child's voice read the sign and said, "Daddy, what does worship mean?" The father replied, "It means to go to church and listen to the preacher preach." Could there be a more horrible definition? Worship—three or four hundred years ago it was pronounced worth-ship—means the acknowledgment of the worth that is in our God.

Worship in heaven is described in terms of God's angels and sons falling before Him, saying, "Blessing, and glory, and wisdom, and thanksgiving, and honour, and power, and might, be unto our God for ever and ever" (REVELATION 7:12).

YIELDING THE BODY TO CHRIST

YIELDING THE BODY TO CHRIST

THE ACCELERATOR FOOT

I was riding with my wife whom I consider a very good driver. She is a better driver than most men, and her life is so ordered that she drives many thousands of miles each year. We came to a small town, and she slowed down to 35 miles an hour, then to 25 miles as the signs indicated. I believe that most drivers go 30 in a 25-mile zone, 40 in a 35-mile zone and 55 in a 50-mile zone. This Christian woman was going exactly 15 in a school zone and I commented on her driving. I knew that her overall time from one city to another was approximately the same as my own, and I had not been as careful as she to obey the letter of the law. Her answer was something like this:

"I can think of three reasons why a Christian should obey the law. The first is because the law has a penalty. The second reason is that our own personal safety is involved, and we should take care of ourselves. The third reason," and this was the reason which concerned my wife, "is the fact that the Bible commands the Christian to keep even the petty ordinances of the municipality. We read in Peter's first epistle, 'Submit yourselves to every ordinance of man for the Lord's sake. . . .'" She then continued, "I prayed about this a great deal when I came to this verse in the Bible, and I concluded that since I delight to worship God, since He has told me that we are to obey him, and since He tells us to submit ourselves to every ordinance of man *for His sake,* I would consider that I was worshiping the Lord with my accelerator foot." I had to admit in my heart that I could find no way to excuse improper driving when the

363

matter was considered as an act of worship of our Lord. The whole of the passage reads: "Submit yourselves to every ordinance of man for the Lord's sake; whether it be to the king, as supreme"—that would correspond to our federal laws—"Or unto governors"—that would correspond to our state laws—"as unto them that are sent by him for the punishment of evildoers, and for the praise of them that do well. For so is the will of God, that with well doing you may put to silence the ignorance of foolish men: as free, and not using your liberty for a cloke of maliciousness, but as the servants of God" (I PETER 2:13-16).

There is one other detail of this same story that merits recording. I lamely explained that if I sometimes speeded it was because my mind was on other things, and my foot grew heavy on the accelerator; that when the road was clear I drove by road conditions, and I did not mean to break the law. My companion answered: "That's like the story of the little girl who was reproved by her mother for something she had done. The little girl said, 'Mother, I didn't mean to do it.' And then after a moment she said, 'But mother, I didn't mean *not* to do it either.'" It is the meaning *not* to do it that really counts.

The next time I was driving was on an eighty-mile trip into New York. I started down the road and found myself consciously keeping the car at exactly 50 miles an hour—not 51. In my heart I was saying, "Lord, I have a good car and am a good driver; I could do 58 here without difficulty, but I am submitting myself to the 50 ordinance for Thy sake." And I found myself feeling good about it. Then came a 35-mile zone to test me and a 15-mile-school zone. I poked along, doggedly determined that I was going to worship the Lord with my right foot on the accelerator. I soon found that I was getting a great joy out of this; beyond any question the Lord was answering me within my heart. But the thing that amazed me most was that I found myself making very good time. It seemed also as though there was an opening in the traffic at every turn. When I finally swept into the Lincoln Tunnel and out into Manhattan, I found I had almost tied my best record for the distance—a record I had made without thought of anything except the car I might see in my rearview mirror.

Thus it may be that we, as true believers in the Lord Jesus Christ, may help solve the terrible problem of traffic deaths by taking this text in the epistle to the Romans and listening to it as though it read, "I beseech you therefore by the mercies of God that you present your accelerator foot as a living sacrifice, holy, acceptable unto God, which is your reasonable service."

SELLING THE HOUSE

A friend of mine bought a house for $11,000, and lived in it for about five years. Then he had to move to another city. Knowing that prices had gone up, he hoped to get $13,000 or $14,000 for it. He advertised the place for sale, and almost immediately a prospective buyer came to see him. When he was asked the price, the owner said, "Make me an offer." Without batting an eye the visitor replied, "$17,000." Hiding his amazement, my friend replied, "Well, I would like to get $20,000 for it." The buyer pulled out a checkbook and said, "Let's split the difference, I'll pay you $5,000 on account. I've got to catch a plane and get back home to get ready to move." So the deal was concluded on that basis. $13,000 or $14,000 would have been acceptable; $17,000 was agreeable; the final price of $18,500 was very well-pleasing!

The Lord God planned our redemption, and Jesus Christ accomplished it by giving Himself for us. When we understand this and present our bodies to the Lord as living sacrifices it is not only acceptable to Him, it is agreeable, it is well-pleasing to Him. In return He shows us His will for our lives, and then we learn by experience that His will is good, well-pleasing and perfect.

THE YOUNG MAN

A man was going with a girl who, some of us thought, was not at all worthy of him. Some breathed a sigh of relief when he went into the army and was gone for two or three years. The girl drifted around with other fellows, and the worthy young man met a worthy girl in a distant city, fell in love with her, and married her. When the war was over, he returned to his home with his bride; one evening the first girl drove by the house and dropped in to see her old flame and to meet his wife. But the wife was not there. The first girl made no attempt to hide her affection; the man realized that he had but to reach out his hand and she would be his. He told me about it afterwards. There was within him all that goes with male desire, but there was something more within him also, and he began to talk about the wonderful girl he had married. He showed pictures of his wife to the first girl and praised his wife to the skies, acting as though he did not understand the obvious advances of the girl. It was not long before she left, saying as she went, "Yes, she must be quite a girl if she can keep you from reaching." The young man was never more joyful in his life. He said that in that moment all of the love between him and his wife was greater and more wonderful than ever; he could think of his wife in a clean, noble way. A philanderer might have scoffed at him, derided him for "sacrificing" his pleasure. But there was not the slightest hint of sacrifice in the generally accepted sense of the word.

There was, however, every sacrifice in the sense of Romans 12:1, "I beseech you therefore, brethren, by the mercies of God, that ye present your bodies a living sacrifice, holy, acceptable unto God which is your reasonable service." The turning of his heart and mind and soul, yes, and body, to the love of his true wife was the living sacrifice which praised her and made him all the more noble because of it. It is in this sense that the believer in Christ presents his body as a living sacrifice to the Lord.

INDEX

INDEX

INDEX

INDEX

INDEX

INDEX

INDEX

INDEX

INDEX